He was the bulwark of the Montreal Canadiens' defence for more than fifteen seasons – a 6'4", 220-pound package of puck-handling savvy and body-crunching authority.

Now Larry Robinson is providing these skills to Wayne Gretzky and the Los Angeles Kings. Having sipped champagne from the Stanley Cup six times with the Canadiens, Robinson — a two-time Norris Trophy winner and perennial NHL All-Star — hopes to drink again from the cup of victory, this time under sunny California skies.

Robinson for the Defence is the first-person chronicle of the defenceman's amazing career, from childhood days spent skating on frozen ponds and creeks in the Ottawa Valley to heady nights of hockey grandeur at the Montreal Forum.

"Candid . . . provides interesting insight into Robinson and the people around him."

– Montreal Gazette

"A good piece of hockey history by a man who saw it firsthand."

– Vancouver Sun

LARRY ROBINSON began his National Hockey League career with the Montreal Canadiens in 1971 and won the first of his six Stanley Cup rings with them in 1973. Since then he's been regarded as one of the finest defencemen in professional hockey history.

CHRYS GOYENS is a Montreal-based writer and broadcaster. He is the co-author of *The Lions in Winter*, a history of the Montreal Canadiens.

LARRY ROBINSON
WITH CHRYS GOYENS

ROBINSON
FOR THE DEFENCE

M&S

An M&S Paperback from
McClelland & Stewart Inc.
The Canadian Publishers

An M&S Paperback from McClelland & Stewart Inc.

First Printing October 1989

Canadian Cataloguing in Publication Data

Robinson, Larry, 1951–
Robinson for the defence

(M&S paperback)
Rev. ed.
ISBN 0-7710-7551-0

1. Robinson, Larry, 1951– . 2. Hockey players –
Canada – Biography. 3. Hockey – Defense.
I. Goyens, Chrys. II. Title.

GV848.5.R6A3 1989   796.96′2′0924   C89-094327-3

Cover design by Tad Aronowicz
Cover photo by Shaney Komulainen (Canapress Photo Service)
Back cover photo courtesy Los Angeles Kings

Typesetting by Vellum Print & Graphic Services Inc.
Printed and Bound in Canada

Published by arrangement with McGraw-Hill Ryerson Ltd.
330 Progress Avenue
Scarborough, Ontario
M1P 2Z5

McClelland & Stewart Inc.
The Canadian Publishers
481 University Avenue
Toronto, Ontario
M5G 2E9

I dedicate this book to my wife, Jeannette,
without whom I would have never succeeded.
Also, to my children, Rachelle and Jeffery, whom we
both love and live for. To my brothers and sisters,
Carol, Linda, Brian, and Moe, and to our great
friends, Donny and Heather, Julien and Celia,
Gilbert and Arlene, and the many more that I'm
unable to mention. To all the hockey players that I
played with and against throughout my career,
with special thanks to the Flower, Serge, and Pointu.
They say to leave the best for last; well in this case it
also applies. The two people that influenced my life
the most: Mom and Dad. "This book's for You!"
Love Ya.

ACKNOWLEDGEMENTS

Pages 16–17 and 195–96 from *The Montreal Star*. Pages 27–28, 117, 162–63, and 163–64 from *The Game* by Ken Dryden. Published by Macmillan of Canada, 1983. Page 33 from *Tretiak: The Legend* by Vladislav Tretiak, Sam Budman, and Maria Budman. Published by Plains Publishing, 1987. Page 44 used with permission of *The Kitchener-Waterloo Record*. Pages 61, 62, and 79 used with permission of Eddie MacCabe. Pages 140–41, and 229–30 from *Grapes* by Don Cherry. Published by Prentice-Hall, 1982.

Contents

1   Down on Cripple Creek   1
2   The Canada Cup   12
3   Training Camp   42
4   Where Is This Place, Anyway?   61
5   Jeannette   80
6   Fare Thee Well in Nova Scotia   92
7   Transition   107
8   Boston Then and Now   125
9   A Gathering of Solitary Men   150
10   Doing It   175
11   The Flickering Torch   209
12   The Darkness   234
13   On The Way Back   263
14   Stanley Revisited   286
15   A Hard Act to Follow   306
16   A Young Man Goes West   322

ONE

Down on Cripple Creek

THE FORUM. November 18, 1987. It's about 7:40 P.M., and Mike Noeth thinks he's doing me a favour.

Noeth, the referee for tonight's game with the Islanders, has given linesman Ron Finn the high sign to hold onto the puck so the fans can notice me and welcome me back.

The game's about 90 seconds old and maybe because it's early on a Wednesday night, the Montreal fans are slow to notice me and react. This isn't unusual; weeknight crowds are notoriously slow to find their seats. We've been playing 7:30 weeknight games for at least five years now and I'll bet half of the season ticket-holders still think our games start at 8:05.

So Finn is holding onto the puck even longer than he would under such circumstances.

I'm lined up just inside our blue line, near the boards on the right side. The applause starts slowly at first, then builds and starts to go round the Forum like a wave. People are pointing and I know all the cameras are on me. I can hear the play-by-play announcers saying: "Can you believe it? They said this gritty veteran would be out until January, maybe February. And here's Robinson, after only one practice with his teammates. Will the long layoff show?" If you've been in this league long enough you can write the script for the hockey broadcasts.

While they're talking, Larry Clark Robinson, age 36, veteran of 1250 regular season and playoff NHL contests, is on the ice hunched over his stick like a nervous rookie, his mind racing: "Drop the puck . . . drop the puck . . Will ya *DROP THE DAMN PUCK!*"

Still the applause builds and now the other players are getting antsy. They rise up from their faceoff crouches, skate in tight little nervous circles. Our guys know how I feel . . . I've never liked being singled out for ovations, even when they were earned with some play or milestone. We are not talking big play or milestone this time.

No. This time I'm being applauded for the dubious distinction of having broken my leg.

On horseback.

In the summertime.

Far away from a hockey rink.

Frankly, I'm embarrassed by it all.

The Forum fades, the image dissolves. The red-white-and-glacial blue of hockey's most famous ice rink bleeds into the Kodachrome greens, yellows, and whites of a polo field in Hudson, Quebec, on a sunny August afternoon.

I've always thought of myself as a natural athlete. Growing up I played baseball, basketball, fastball, football, and I competed in track and field, as well as hockey, of course. I was good at all of them and fortunate enough to make a very good living for many more years than most hockey players.

Being a natural athlete meant that these sports always came easily. I always had the hand-to-eye co-ordination, the strength, the quickness, and the stamina to excel at the games I played. Although I enjoyed the company of my teammates in summertime baseball or fastball, I was looking for something special to stir my competitive juices in the offseason.

I found it. Polo.

That's right. Me, Larry Robinson, 6'4", 220 pounds, tearing after a ball on horseback and trying to whack it in the direction I want it to go with a bloody big mallet while, at the same time, trying to avoid a group of similarly minded ladies and gentlemen on their own horses. (My wife Jeannette says that while the image of me on horseback partaking of The Sport of Royalty might conjure up a pretty gruesome picture for the uninitiated, it's not really as bad as you might imagine. Really.)

A number of things attracted me to polo, a sport which has a small but very loyal following around the world. On the athletic side, I finally had found the physical challenge I was after. About the only things athletically "natural" about polo are the hand-to-eye co-ordination involved in trying to strike ball with mallet, and the game situations, which are a lot like those in any other contest where two teams each try to defend their goal and score in the other's.

The noble horse, of course, is the whole difference and the true challenge. Riding a horse can be difficult enough for a novice. Controlling a horse in a polo match is the challenge of a lifetime. For the first time in my life, I could say that I was faced with a task that would take a true measure of me because, for the first time, I was up against something I couldn't easily master. It takes years and years of hard work and practice to be able to ride a horse skilfully and I look forward to a challenge that will last well beyond my playing days in professional hockey.

Another reason for taking up polo was social. I grew up on a farm and had pretty much abandoned that lifestyle when I started to play hockey for a living. Stops in Brockville and Kitchener, Ontario; Halifax, Nova Scotia; and, finally, Montreal, had transformed me into a suburbanite. One day when my son, Jeff, was about ten and his sister, Rachelle, was three, my wife, Jeannette, and I did our own version of *Roots*. "Let's look for something a little less citified and a little more like what we grew up with."

I wanted my children to experience more than just the suburbs and television. I grew up on a dairy farm and was proud of my heritage. I wanted Jeff and Rachelle to be able to experience the responsibility and freedom of being around animals.

Steve Shutt, a city boy all of his life, was thinking along the same lines. He was scouting around for properties in the Hudson-St. Lazare area, just this side of the border with eastern Ontario, beside the Montreal-Ottawa highway. He was the first to find a farm. Actually both of us had started bidding on it, unaware of the other's interest.

When I discovered my "competition" was Steve, I told the owner I was dropping out. So Steve was the first to leave the suburbs. One day a short time later, when he was well on his way to becoming the Country Squire, Steve and a visiting Yvan Cournoyer were introduced to the gentleman who now is our veterinarian, Dr. Gilbert Halle. A group of riders was playing polo at Halle's that afternoon and Steve and Yvan each were offered a mount. They had a great time; Steve was hooked.

"You should try this, you'll love it," he told me in his high-pitched squeak the next time we met. His voice had a habit of climbing an octave or two, and he spoke a mile-a-minute whenever he got excited. And he got excited a lot.

"You can't explain the charge you get out of trying to manoeuvre a horse in polo. I've never experienced anything like it."

I'd loved horses ever since I was a kid. But I put myself in the horses's shoes, so to speak, on this one. What would a horse think when 6′4″ and 220 pounds of rider approached with the "I'm your next rider" look? The poor animal would probably inch toward the stable door, check out its escape route, and do an equine Rodney Dangerfield: "No sir. Uh Uh. You ever wonder why jockeys are so small? Because that's the way horses like them. I don't do anybody over 5′6″. I'll do the short business manager (my best friend and manager Donny Cape) but Godzilla the Hockey Player need not apply."

We larger types can be a touch sensitive about these things. But Shuttie wasn't going to take no for an answer.

"Not to worry. They got horses that'll carry anything. Come on, you'll love it." Thanks for the reassurance, kid.

So we went riding. And he was absolutely right, I loved it. Then he stuck a polo mallet in my hand and said "Hit that ball."

It was my turn to be hooked.

Polo is a very social game and it was not long before Jeannette and I were caught up in the polo whirl and had met and befriended a neighbouring couple, Julien and Celia Allard.

The Allards loaned me my first horse to play and practice on. In short, that's how a lumbering NHL defenceman became involved in a very different game. Today I've got five horses of my own. The Allard's daughter Linda is our groom; she comes over and looks after my horses when I'm on the road.

I'm looking forward to polo and raising horses after hockey is over. I see it as a serious endeavour, not just a hobby or a distraction.

That's the very abridged history of Larry Robinson, polo player. By the summer of 1987, I'd played polo for three years and never really come close to getting hurt. I'd received the usual bumps and bruises, but nothing more than I'd get in a hockey game.

This preamble serves to enlighten those who might have thought polo was my version of thrill-seeking or living dangerously, right up there with motorcycle racing, cliff diving, and bowling for dollars.

All of this leads up to the events of Sunday, August 9, 1987 and the Montreal Polo Club (actually in Hudson, about 30 miles west of Montreal) where we play every Tuesday, Thursday, and Sunday.

In August, our Sunday matches are what we call Sponsor Games; anybody who donates $1,000 to the polo club to buy an ad in our program can be our sponsor and bring as many friends as they want to our game, have a picnic, and set up in our gazebo. Very civilized. We play four chukkers, a chukker being a seven-and-a-half minute quarter. The sponsor is responsible for trophies and prizes at the end of the match.

On this particular Sunday, we were playing against a team made up of two of our own members, Randy Greer and Michael Sinclair-Smith and two Saratoga, N.Y. riders, Paul Kant and his son Wayne. It was a close match in the third chukker when someone lost the ball in front of the opposition goal. Paul Kant and I both took off after it, approaching it from opposite directions.

Going at a good gallop, I had just enough time to swerve around a third rider, who fouled me and knocked me into the path of the oncoming Kant. He was intent on his pursuit of the ball. His head was down. There was no way he saw me.

"Look out!" I don't even know if he heard me above the sounds of the horses.

I got off one more "look out!" because it seemed we were about to collide head-on. I put my hands in front of the saddle and tried to lift my leg out of the stirrup so it wouldn't get caught there if we crashed. Too late; we both swerved a little but his horse's shoulder hit me square in the leg.

The next thing I knew I was rolling around on the ground screaming and grabbing onto my leg. There was pain, but I didn't think I'd hurt myself badly. The pain ebbed; I taped up my leg and the game continued.

But in the fourth chukker, I began to sense something was wrong. The leg just didn't feel right and when I got off the horse, I had trouble walking. We wear "whites" when we play, actually white jeans, and when I took mine off to change into shorts after the match, I discovered a knee that was about three times its normal size.

"I think this means hospital," I said to Jeannette. She nodded.

While she drove me into Montreal, I called Dr. Doug Kinnear, the Canadiens team physician for a quarter century, on the car phone and explained the predicament.

"Go to the Montreal General for X-rays. I'll call ahead and tell them to expect you," he said. A couple of hours later, the X-rays taken, I was sitting in the reception area waiting for the results. My knee was a balloon.

A doctor came up with my X-rays in hand.

"Well young man, you've just fractured your tibia."

"What does that mean in English?" In 15 National Hockey League seasons, I'd suffered an assortment of sprains, separations, hip pointers, cuts, and the like, but I'd never once sustained a serious injury. My nose has been broken so many times that it looks like it's looking for my ear. Sprained, broken, torn, cut – these were words I was used to. "Fractured" meant something else altogether.

"It means that you have a cracked bone in your leg."

"What does *THAT* mean?"

"I can't really say right here; your doctor will have to look at it." I looked over at Jeannette and she was biting her lip. She looked a lot more worried than I felt.

"Well, tell me what you'd do." I figured his next answer would ease her concern, and mine.

I was wrong.

"If it were up to me, I'd have to operate because the bone's displaced a little bit."

"Great. Just what I need." And a new reality came rushing in. This could be the career.

Heading into the 1987–88 NHL season, I was faced with several decisions. The first was: Would I play for Team Canada in the Canada Cup series planned for the coming September? I was the only player who had played in all three previous series ('76, '81, '84) and I'd been invited to the 1987 training camp. My former roommate and now my Managing Director, Serge Savard, called me about it in June.

"All of us – Bob Clarke, Glen Sather, and myself – feel you can make a big contribution to this team," he said.

My first reaction was no. I had respectfully declined a similar invitation the previous February to take part in the two-game Rendez-Vous '87 series against the Soviets and the seven days off in Florida had done me a world of good.

"Serge, I'm 36 and I really liked the Stanley Cup win in '86. I don't want to be dragging my ass next May, especially if we've got a shot at another one." I was not in the best of moods when he called; we'd lost to Philadelphia in six games the previous spring and still couldn't believe it. I felt we'd outplayed them in four of those games but that's the way it goes sometimes.

He left me with an open invitation and the whole summer to make up my mind. Throughout the summer, I fluctuated a bit. The original intention was that 1987–88 was going to be my last season, even though I had a full year and an option year remaining on my contract.

Playing for a Stanley Cup winner would be the ideal way to bow out, especially since I had bowed in on a Cup champion in 1973. A Canada Cup championship would also be a nice touch and I liked the idea of playing with Wayne Gretzky, Mike Gartner, and Mario Lemieux. Who wouldn't?

Yet the lure of polo was strong. I'd played all summer, enjoying myself immensely, including the Polo for Heart tournament in Toronto in June. There was another big tournament scheduled for Labour Day weekend and I wanted to be there.

All of these thoughts flashed through my mind as I was checked into Room 1820 of the Montreal General Hospital that Sunday night. I was downstairs getting more X-rays when Dr. Eric Lenczner, the club's orthopaedic surgeon, showed up at the hospital. He spoke with Jeannette and Celia Allard in my room and we all met there when I came back upstairs.

I was hoping that the second set of X-rays meant they had their doubts about the resident's initial prognosis. After all, if I had been injured so badly, how come I was able to climb back on my horse and finish the game?

Dr. Lenczner is a soft-spoken, bespectacled man who looks just like a doctor should, equal parts concern, friendliness and seriousness. He held up the X-ray and I saw the break.

"This is what we call a depressed tibial plateau fracture," he said.

"It is a serious leg injury. For most people, we would treat this with a series of casts and immobility. But you're a professional athlete and you need to get that leg strong again, in the shortest time possible. I'll operate first thing in the morning."

I looked over to Jeannette and she was shaken. She looked like I felt. Dr. Lenczner continued:

"Your tibia has been displaced and driven down toward your foot." He pointed to the image on the X-ray:

"I'm going to have to elevate this joint here that's depressed, back to normal level. I'll put in some bone underneath to support it, and then fix the whole thing together with a couple of screws here."

Screws was another forbidden word. Pro athletes with pins and screws in their legs usually became ex-pro athletes. Quickly.

"You can't put it in a cast or a splint?"

"I'd rather not. You want to be able to exercise your leg as soon as possible. Anyway, it wouldn't be one cast, it would be a series of casts and I would worry about circulation problems and possible muscle atrophy. The operation is the way to go."

Months later, he told me what we'd both been thinking all along and were afraid to discuss openly. My hockey career lay in the balance. Most people suffering this type of injury would expect a recuperation and rehabilitation period of six months or so. They would eventually be able to walk and function normally. But an NHL defenceman places a much greater strain on his legs than most people.

"After I operate on you tomorrow, you are going to start exercising your leg almost right away. I'm going to put your leg in what we call a Continuous Passive Motion machine. It will strap onto your leg and what it does is slowly deep-bend your knee and leg in a curl. And then it will very slowly straighten it. You'll be able to set the machine to operate at an almost imperceptibly slow speed, which takes several minutes to bend and unbend your leg, or faster if we want it to."

I had a lot of things to think about that night and it didn't help that the telephone never stopped ringing. The word was out: Larry Robinson had broken his leg and was probably out for the season. Jeannette was very upset and tried to contact Donny Cape. When something needs doing, Donny has an amazing way of seeing that it gets done.

He was on holiday at Robert Parker's Concord Hotel with his wife and two daughters. He was out when Jeannette called so she left a message with his wife, Heather.

He called after midnight: "What's happening?"

"I broke my leg playing polo. Doc Lenczner is operating in the morning."

"I'll be right there."

The Concord Hotel is on Lake Kiamesha in the heart of the Borscht Belt, the Jewish resort area of the Catskills about an hour's drive north of New York City. At a good speed, it's a six-hour drive from Montreal, most of it on winding Catskills highways after you leave the New York Thruway at Kingston.

Donny walked into my hospital room at 5:30 A.M.

"What did you do? Fly?"

"Not to worry, I'm here aren't I?"

A few hours later, Dr. Lenczner was back and running me through the operation again. After he left, neither Donny nor myself trusted each other to speak. We sat in silence for about 30 minutes, scared stiff. It's one thing to have the luxury of contemplating retirement at leisure; it's quite another to have your career end with no control, the decision out of your hands. Yet, at the same time, this was the first time my love for my career was being tested.

If you'd asked me on Sunday morning, August 9, 1987, I'd have probably said I was looking forward to bowing out gracefully after a final season. On Monday morning, August 10, as they were wheeling me into the operating room, I was suddenly determined to play as long as good health would help me. Then and there I decided to set a record for recovery.

"Are you nervous Doc?" Lenczner was beside the gurney as they wheeled me into the OR and I was groggy from the medication I'd been given.

"Damn right."

"Good. We're all nervous before the big games." And then I went under.

If the best laid plans of mice and men had been upset by the polo accident, my unshakeable optimism went the same route a couple of days later; I went through a mild bout of depression. The reality of the task ahead came rushing in when I saw the scar on my leg. All I could think was that I had places to go, things to do, and here I was lying around in a hospital room, of no use to anyone.

My leg was in the CPM machine 24 hours a day as Dr. Lenczner had said, and there was no major discomfort. The inactivity, however, was driving me crazy. Down at the Forum, hockey players from all over the NHL were congregating as the Team Canada camp got into full swing. The Montreal Expos were in the thick of the National League East pennant race. My polo buddies were having a good summer. Everybody else was active, *DOING* things. And I was lying in a hospital bed.

My hospital stay lasted nine days. Before I went home, though, I would have to get up. As long as I live, I'll never forget that experience. And I'll forever understand the trials and tribulations of convalescents in hospitals.

The simple act of standing up was total disorientation.

The blood rushed into my foot, I went very white and broke out into the kind of sweat you get after a strenuous hour-long workout. I moved all of about five or six feet to the wall opposite my bed.

"Find me a chair, I've got to sit down!" Nausea and exhaustion rolled over me in waves. Until now, I'd been fortunate. There'd been relatively little pain when I broke the leg, and little residual pain after the operation. That's why I was so unprepared for this.

I'd been all positive energy. I was going to get better, work out like a madman, heal my leg, and go back to playing hockey like nothing had happened. Nothing would hold me back.

As I was helped back to my bed, I remember thinking: "On the other hand, maybe this is a lot worse than I thought." Then and there I knew that the next few months would represent something very special.

TWO

The Canada Cup

T WO VISITS were of special significance to me when I was
    in the hospital.

The first was expected: Gaetan (Gates) Lefebvre, assistant
to the head sports therapist of the Montreal Canadiens. You
might remember Gaetan; he's the dark-haired, mustachioed
trainer who stood on our bench pumping his arms in victory
when we won the Stanley Cup in Calgary in May, 1986. It was
a source of some unhappiness among the veterans when Gene
Gaudet, a former colleague of Jean Perron at the University of
Moncton, was parachuted in over Gaetan after that season.
Gaetan's main function then became working with injured
players who couldn't travel with the team, while Gene Gaudet
travelled with the team. Most heartbroken was Mats Naslund;
he'd lost his backgammon partner.

"Looks like it's you and me, Bro," Gates said, looking at my
injured leg.

"When do we go to work?" All of this inactivity was driving
me nuts.

"As soon as you go home. We'll start right away."

"I'll be working out at home?"

"No way. At the Forum. Everyday. It's all taken care of.
We'll get a program going and you'll be there everyday to work
out. I'll even come get you until you can drive yourself."

The second visit was totally unexpected. The visitors were
the Washington Capitals' Mike Gartner and Scott Stevens, and

Rick Tocchet of the Philadelphia Flyers. All three were attending the Team Canada training camp at the Forum. Gartner had been a teammate on previous Canada Cup and Wales Conference all-star teams.

To say I was moved by their visit would be an understatement. It showed that the three are class individuals; that almost goes without saying. Gartner and Stevens I knew; Tocchet I'd only known as an opponent the previous May when he'd played a leading role in Philadelphia's 4–2 series sweep over the Canadiens in the Wales Conference Final. He's a tough, clean hockey player who would fit in beautifully with the Montreal Canadiens (or and other team), cut as he is in the "tough and clean" Mike McPhee, Cam Neely mold.

It was nothing they said because we just exchanged pleasantries. But just the fact that these three fine players had taken time to visit me in hospital seemed to bring the 1987 Canada Cup and other such competitions into sharper focus for me.

One thing most NHL fans have trouble believing is how career-long rivals can suddenly come together and play well as teammates on an all-star team or a national team for a special tournament or series. Guys who've slugged it out for years – Canadiens and Nordiques, Rangers and Islanders, Flames and Oilers, or Capitals and Flyers–are thrown together and forced to forge their own harmony and team ethic in a very short time.

The biggest thrill is walking into that dressingroom for the first time, knowing that you've been singled out for your talent and the perceived contribution you can make to this special group.

No matter who you are – Wayne Gretzky, Guy Lafleur, Gordie Howe, Frank Mahovlich, or Marcel Dionne – you feel it on Day One of a Canada Cup training camp. This is invitation-only. RSVP: Right now.

Each individual walking into that dressingroom feels it, acts it, knows it. This is the supreme honour, better than the individual merit trophies, because you know you've been handpicked to form a very special team. But moving from a group of highly motivated, highly talented individuals on that first day of camp, to a cohesive team unit in which all participants have clearly defined roles, can be a gigantic undertaking.

Sometimes it comes together quickly and naturally, like Team Canada 1976. Other times it takes a little more work, like Team Canada 1984. But please note that each team won its edition of the Canada Cup, rumoured disunity or not.

Occasionally, though, past antagonisms are stronger than anything; Chris Nilan of the Montreal Canadiens and Team USA slugged Rick Vaive of the Toronto Maple Leafs and Team Canada in the lobby of the Montreal Forum in 1984. (Still, they were on different all-star teams then so maybe it doesn't count.) Claude Lemieux of team Canada and Chris Chelios of Team USA, both Montreal Canadiens, postponed their regular-season loyalties during the 1987 Canada Cup and whacked each other around gleefully during that one.

My first Canada Cup training camp was an adventure. I was still relatively new to the league and I was invited to training camp after a strong Stanley Cup series. *Sport Magazine* voted me the player of the Stanley Cup final, our four-game sweep over Philadelphia, and awarded me a car.

I faced that August's training camp with some nervousness because I honestly didn't know how I'd fit in. My first experience with a group like this had been at the 1974 All-Star game in Chicago. Bobby Orr had been selected to the East team but was injured so they asked Carol Vadnais. He was hurt too, so Scotty Bowman went to Serge Savard but the Senator begged off. I was next in line, as a replacement-to-a-replacement. We lost 6–4 to the West.

The Chicago game was my only experience of this sort so I had my reservations about suddenly playing with staunch rivals, especially those from Boston, Buffalo, and Philadelphia. One guy who'd probably help break the ice was Philadelphia's star left-winger Bill Barber, who'd been my teammate in the OHA with the Kitchener Rangers. More than 30 of us reported to the Montreal Forum; 22 of us would "make the team."

The all-star roster was impressive; Buffalo's French Connection line of Gilbert Perreault, Richard Martin, and

Rene Robert, as well as Danny Gare; Philadelphia's Barber, Reggie Leach, and Bobby Clarke; Toronto's Darryl Sittler and Lanny McDonald; our own Peter Mahovlich, Guy Lafleur, Steve Shutt, and Bob Gainey. Throw in some "no-names" like Bobby Hull, Marcel Dionne, Jean Pronovost, and Phil Esposito and you didn't envy the task facing opposition goaltenders.

On defence, we were even more solid. Although Ken Dryden was injured and would miss the series, we were strong in nets with Gerry Cheevers of Boston, Dan Bouchard of Atlanta, Chico Resch of the New York Islanders, and Rogatien Vachon of the Los Angeles Kings between the pipes.

On the blue line were the other two thirds of our own Big Three, Guy Lapointe and Serge Savard. Joining them were Paul Shmyr; Carol Vadnais; Jim Watson; Denis Potvin, the man everyone said would be the next Bobby Orr; and, bad knees and all, the current Bobby Orr.

My memories of that first Canada Cup focus on Bobby Orr, the player who single-handedly redefined the game as it is played in North America today. At age 27, Bobby Orr should have been at the peak of his fabulous career as we prepared to "defend" the first-ever Canada Cup. Unfortunately for hockey fans all over the world, crippling knee injuries had reduced the Bobby Orr who reported to training camp that August to a mere shadow of his hockey playing talent. Which meant that he was a dominating, soaring hockey player who could still take over the game on occasion.

The asterisk became a famous punctuation mark in 1961 when Roger Maris hit 61 homers in 162 regular-season American League games, breaking the record 60 set by his New York Yankee predecessor Babe Ruth in 1927. Baseball purists everywhere wanted an asterisk placed beside Maris's feat in the record books, because Ruth had accomplished his feat at a time when the season was 154 games long.

Many hockey fans who still wax nostalgically about the 1972 Soviet-Canada series forget the double asterisk. Asterisk one is the fact that Bernie Parent, Bobby Hull, Derek Sanderson, and J.C. Tremblay had signed with the brand-new WHA and were not allowed to play. Asterisk two is that the incomparable Bobby Orr was recovering from knee surgery and missed the entire series. Also, other players of ability, guys like Jacques Laperriere, Walt Tkaczuk, Dallas Smith, and Ed Giacomin preferred not to play.

So, in truth, Canada was not represented by its very best because three, if not more, impact players weren't available. The Soviets were very good in that series, but even they would admit that it would have been a quite different result if powerful skaters Orr and Hull, then at the peaks of their careers, and a puck-control man like Tremblay, had played for Team Canada on that big international rink in Moscow. A goaltending tandem of Parent and Dryden would have been stronger, too. Hull had been my childhoood hero; Orr was but four years older than me but it seemed that I had been hearing about him all my young life.

It was a thrill to be in the same dressingroom with this true superstar; but it was also here that you acquired a firsthand appreciation of why the fabulous Robert Gordon Orr had come down from Mount Olympus to rejoin the rest of the human race.

His knees were criss-crossed with incision scars. Many hockey players have scars; in fact, it's the rare hockey player who has not been under the knife at one time or another. But this was different. Many of his new teammates could only quietly shake their heads at the tracks on the knees that had hobbled the world's greatest hockey player. You couldn't help looking, and such was the esteem Bobby Orr was held in by his fellow professionals that there wasn't a guy in the room who didn't wish Bobby's knees were a hundred percent, even though it might mean Stanley Cup final money taken from our pockets.

We were all aware that a Bobby Orr comes along only once in a generation, if not a lifetime. And we sensed that this Canada Cup would be his first and last. Moreover, we were aware that he knew this far better than we did.

How good was Bobby Orr? We'll never know. Injuries had slowed him so much, even in his early years in the league. Although I was only four years younger than Bobby, he'd been starring in the NHL for going on seven years and had won five Norris Trophies as top defenceman before I played my first game in 1973. Along the way, his knees had absorbed a fearful pounding.

Still, playing on two badly damaged legs, or one good one depending on which sports cliché you prefer, he was capable of astonishing feats. I remember one night at the Forum in my second year where Yvan Cournoyer got a breakaway. We called Yvan "The Roadrunner" for the obvious reason; with his huge thighs driving like pistons, he was capable of exploding over the ice surface at high speed. On this night he was clear of all opposition by almost a full zone.

Bobby Orr caught him before he could get a shot away, even though Yvan had enjoyed a 20-foot head start. Guys on our bench sat with their mouths wide open. Cournoyer skated back into the play as it moved up ice into our zone with a tight little smile on his face. He and Bobby were good friends off-ice and you could almost hear him thinking, "Dammit, that's one I owe you! If I ever can figure out how I'm going to repay you for it."

What kind of competitor was Bobby? He singularly elevated the game to another plateau. I'll never forget the All-Star game where he went down to block a Bobby Hull slapshot. Once a game started, he seemed to be on a higher plane than the rest of us and he played there, most often by himself.

Elmer Ferguson of the *Montreal Star* was in his late 80s when I came to Montreal; he'd covered the meeting in November, 1918 that had led to the formation of the NHL. He had seen everybody who had played the game up until that point.

Everybody.

He wrote of Bobby:

"He has speed afoot, hits the ice with such power he uses up four pairs of skates per season. Orr may, indeed, be creating a new concept of defence play. The day of huge, slow-footed defence players passed with the era of such as the late Harry Mummery, the Rangers' Taffy Abel, and Ching Johnson, among others.

"There has been a steady swing toward puck-carrying defence players, and Orr has added a new dimension to this trend. He may become a model for defence players of the future, featuring speed, fine stick-handling, and scoring ability."

Today's young hockey fan wouldn't have had the opportunity to read the insights of Ferguson, a man who spent a half century chronicling the exploits of hockey players and the National Hockey League. But watching Paul Coffey, Ray Bourque, Chris Chelios, Peter Svoboda, Craig Hartsburg, Gary Suter, Scott Stevens, and Denis Potvin ply their trade in the last decade, and noting the transition and the game that has resulted, we can all attest to the wisdom of his words.

Bobby Orr, like few hockey players in his generation or those before him, changed the game irrevocably.

I arrived in the Ontario Hockey Association with Kitchener several years after Bobby had left the Oshawa Generals. I had just two years on defence, under the demanding but patient coaching of Dan Dexter in Brockville. He had converted me from centre to defence because of my size and skating ability, because Bobby Orr had shown the hockey world that some of a team's best skating talent belonged on the blue line. Prior to his arrival, defence was where the slower skaters were relegated, those who might not be able to keep up with the puck as forwards. After Bobby Orr, the revamped hockey wisdom had it that your best skaters usually played centre or defence.

When I played in the OHA, everybody was being compared with Denis Potvin, then a 15-year-old defenceman. But Denis, himself, was being compared with Bobby Orr wherever he went because he was such an offensive force in our league. That bothered him immensely because "I have always wanted to be the first Denis Potvin, not the second Bobby Orr." He must have said that a hundred times in junior and many times that in the NHL. But each time he met a new reporter, the "second Bobby Orr" question resurfaced and it rankled.

His frustration came to a head at the 1976 Canada Cup. After we had won the series, the journalists voting for the MVP award selected Orr. They were voting with their hearts to a large extent, but you couldn't take away from Orr's contribution. He had played superbly on an all-star defence anchored by people like Potvin, Guy Lapointe, Serge Savard, and yours truly.

That burst the bubble for Denis and he made a few comments in the heat of his disappointment and damned himself in the process. Those comments turned off a lot of people, myself included. I knew Denis from his Ottawa days and knew that he was a really nice guy, articulate and intelligent, but from then on he was diminished in my eyes. It also hurt him with the general hockey media; I'm convinced of it. Even though he was a deserving Norris Trophy winner on three different occasions, and instrumental in four straight Stanley Cups by the Islander between 1980–84, it seemed to me that the hockey press always tempered their compliments when it came to Denis, especially the media outside New York. It seemed they had him tabbed as a "Me-firster," and damned with faint praise the contribution he made to one of the best teams in NHL history.

When Denis finally surpassed Bobby Orr's career point total of 915 during the 1985–86 season, there was little reaction in the hockey world, unlike what you might see and hear when a Wayne Gretzky passed a Marcel Dionne or a Gordie Howe. The consensus seemed to be: "So what? Bobby accomplished what he did in 250 fewer games." And Denis Potvin's feat (he now has become the first defenceman in NHL history to surpass 1,000 regular season points) was diminished in the process, which is highly unfair. He was one of the true impact players of his generation and deserved the recognition that went with it.

Why many hockey observers had elephant's memory about Denis's remarks was the fact that Bobby Orr was on his last legs at Canada Cup 1976. Although he was not officially retired until after the 1978–79 season – and from Chicago Black Hawks, not Boston – he played relatively few games after the 1976 Canada Cup. His fine performance with that team proved to be his last true hurrah and those selectors who voted him the series' MVP must be applauded for instinctively knowing it at the time. They were saying: "Potvin and Robinson will have their turns. There will be other Canada Cups, other international series. This one's Bobby's." And they were right on.

Now that I've ended the suspense and you all know who won the first Canada Cup, let's backtrack to training camp, 1976.

With Hull and Orr, and even missing Ken Dryden, we were probably the strongest Canadian team ever assembled and we knew it. But we were not marked with the cockiness or uncertainty of our predecessors in 1972. That narrow victory over the Soviets had sounded warning bells in North American hockey and it was a sober group that congregated in Montreal that August. The city was on a high; the Canadiens had won the Stanley Cup in May, the Olympic Games had just ended, and everyone was looking forward to extending the spirit of international competition with another September Showdown with the Soviets.

The coaching staff, Scotty Bowman, Al MacNeil, Don Cherry, and Bobby Kromm, had assembled a multi-talented group. The emphasis was on skating and offensive skills because we had played the Soviets a lot since the 1972 series and had come to realize that intimidation didn't work, even in our smaller rinks. During the previous Christmas Holidays, the Soviet Wings and Red Army had taken part in Super Series, eight games against NHL opposition. The Wings beat Pittsburgh, Chicago, and the New York Islanders in close games before Buffalo hammered them 12–6. The Red Army beat the New York Rangers and the Boston Bruins handily before tying us 3–3 in the famous New Year's Eve game. They then dropped a 4–1 decision to the Philadelphia Flyers in a game where they left the ice in the first period and threatened to go home after Ed Van Impe hammered Valeri Kharlamov to the ice and went unpenalized by referee Lloyd Gilmour.

So we were anticipating a fast-paced international game, international-quality officiating, and any kind of psychological ploy by the men with CCCP on their shirts. It was the Canada Cup; there were teams from Sweden, Finland, the

U.S., and Czechoslovakia also included, but we treated it like 1972 all over again; just you and me, Russki!

Funny thing was, nobody told the other four teams that they were considered the appetizers for a Canada–USSR main course. Bobby Kromm, Detroit's coach and a veteran of international hockey, was a voice in the wilderness as we prepared for the tournament.

"The Czechs are the team to beat this year," he said.

"They're a solid, veteran crew who have been together for a long time and have quality goaltending. The Russians are in transition; they've substantially changed the 1972 team, even though Tretiak makes them a formidable force to reckon with. And they've left some top talent at home; Kharlamov is hurt and they've left his linemates Vladimir Petrov and Boris Mikhailov back in Moscow, as well as Alexander Yakushev and Vladimir Shadrin."

We played several intra-squad games as the team was being formed and then lined up for a couple of games against Team USA. We handled them fairly easily, even though they showed us more than we expected, a compliment to the fine coaching job of Bob Pulford, then the GM of the Los Angeles Kings. Pete LoPresti of Minnesota was especially tough in nets and NHL journeymen Fred Ahern, Steve Jensen, and Gary Sargent showed unbelievable (to us) tenacity.

Then we made a strategic mistake. We played an exhibition game against Czechoslovakia. First and foremost, it appeared that Alan Eagleson wanted the Canada Cup to make money. So an extra game against the Czechs might be a good idea because the gate was sure to be profitable. The folly of this "bottom line-first" thinking would be most graphically demonstrated in 1981 when we gave the Soviet a free exhibition game in which to figure out Wayne Gretzky.

The 1976 Czechs were a veteran team, anchored by the "jovial bear" 34-year-old Vladimir Dzurilla and Jiri Holocek in goal, Milan Novy and Jiri Bubla on the blue line, and the Stastny brothers, Jaroslav Pouzar, Ivan Hlinka, Frantisek Cernik, Oldrich Machac, and Vladimir Martinec up front.

We blew them out, 11–4. In retrospect, I draw two conclu-

sions from that game. The first is that they played possum and
lulled us into a false sense of security. The second conclusion
is that playing us when it didn't count allowed the Czechs to get
their awe of Canadian hockey out of their system. Whether we
were aware of it or not, the Europeans then still looked up to
our game, and especially our star players. Even though several
Europeans toiled in the NHL, and much larger numbers were
involved in the WHA, this was still prior to the airlift that
would change NHL hockey forever in the late 1970s.

That healthy respect was evident in our first official tournament game against Finland, in my backyard, at Ottawa's Civic
Centre. We won 11–2, driving one of the top-rated goalies in
Europe, Antti Lappaenen, out of the nets with a three-goal
burst by Rick Martin, Phil Esposito, and Bobby Hull in the first
seven minutes of the game.

The Finns spent most of the game standing around and star-
ing, as if they couldn't quite believe they were actually playing
these legends.

We were brought back down to earth in the second game, a
4–2 win over Team USA, in which we took an early 3–0 lead,
watched them make it 3–2 on second period goals by Steve
Jensen and Fred Ahern, and then put it out of reach with an
empty-netter by Darryl Sittler.

One thing the coaching staff had noted in the first two games
was that we were weak defensively up front. We had a talented
cast of goal scorers – Martin, Esposito, Sittler, Lafleur,
Perreault, Dionne, Leach, Mahovlich – but few gave any
indication of a desire to backcheck. Our defence was strong
and mobile but was tiring out against a long succession of 3-
on-2s and 2-on-1s. We'd also missed the presence of the injured Bobby Clarke in Game Two and would be without Philadelphia's excellent defensive defenceman Jim Watson for the rest
of the series, the result of a broken cheekbone suffered against
the Americans.

We needed a defensive forward and went to the man who has
defined the position, Bob Gainey, and a player who has since
been known for scoring, Lanny McDonald.

There has been a succession of solid defensive forwards in

the history of the league gut until Bo came along, nobody was good enough at this thankless task to force the league to provide a trophy that would mean recognition for his labours.

It was decided that he was going to dress for the game against Sweden and was reunited with Darryl Sittler and McDonald on a line that had shown a lot of promise before the tournament began.

The game was played at Maple Leaf Gardens and the loudest ovation was a surprise to Team Canada members, including Sittler and McDonald, both true blue-and-white Leafs. The loudest pre-game applause was for defenceman Borje Salming, who skated out on the Gardens ice for the first time in the yellow-and-blue uniform bearing the Tre Kroner, the Three Crowns of Team Sweden. Nowadays we've grown accustomed to the cheers team USA's Chris Chelios and Chris Nilan or Team Sweden's Mats Naslund receive at the Forum. But back then it was still something new. We didn't particularly resent it, especially since Salming was proving himself to be one of the best defencemen in the NHL, but we were surprised by it.

It's funny how a strange or opposition rink affects you as a player. Before the 1976 Canada Cup, I always hated playing at Maple Leaf Gardens. Players get this feeling, almost like a rink has square corners. That changed during the Cup, and I've liked playing there ever since. Another factor is that I've always been well received by the Toronto fans, a knowledgeable crowd.

One of the reasons I hated the place was the bad ice. In those days Toronto had a slower club so they used to put a lot of water down between periods. They probably turned down the refrigeration too, to slow it down even more. I remember Scotty Bowman going out there with a squeegee before a period started just to prove his point. The referee came out and made the maintenance people literally mop up the excess water into pails. This was a playoff game so the TV audience got to watch a mopathon while the colour man worked overtime in the broadcast booth.

The referee was talking to one of the maintenance guys when I went sloshing by in the pre-period skate:

"What kind of bush move is this?"

"Bush move nothing, it's too warm outside," the maintenance guy replied.

It was about 55 Fahrenheit. I've noticed in recent years that as the team speed of the Maple Leafs has improved with guys like Russ Courtnall, the ice has been a lot faster. Even when it's 55 degrees outside.

On this night in September, 1976, the ice was fine and Bob Gainey was about to make converts of millions of hockey fans who had yet to realize his enormous contribution to the Montreal Canadiens.

From their very first shift, Sittler, McDonald, and Gainey were a natural combination; they meshed beautifully. And we needed them because the free-wheeling Swedes showed us plenty in the first period, testing Rogatien Vachon on several occasions. They outshot us 15–8 in the first and Rogie was brilliant on a breakaway by Anders Hedberg, but we led 1–0 after Phil Esposito banked one in off Bobby Hull and past Hardy Aastrom, the Swedish goaltender.

Bobby Kromm had been quite explicit in the previous practice and Scotty had repeated the message in the pre-game meeting: "The Swedes like to open it up early, get the jump on you, and then skate away from you the rest of the night. If we can hold them even, or take a lead after the first, they don't have the game to play catch-up." The Swedes had shut out the U.S. and tied the Soviets in their first two games of the series.

Kromm was right again. We pressed them a lot more in the second and Lanny put the puck right on Bo's stick. 2–0. With that line checking, and the aroused Bobby Clarke spearheading a furious forechecking assault with his line, the Swedes were back on their heels. Aastrom stopped Bobby Orr twice close in, Esposito hit the crossbar, and then, with 20 seconds left, Pete Mahovlich fed Marcel Dionne a wonderful pass and it was 3–0.

We won it 4–0 and darned if Bo didn't get another goal, this time on a set-up by Sittler. We were looking good – three games and three wins – and the Czechs were up next in Montreal, the same team we'd squashed in exhibition in the same building a mere ten days before. And right behind them lurked the Russians.

What happened next was a huge surprise. First, we lost 1–0. Second, this was one of the most exciting hockey games ever played and would overshadow all previous and subsequent games in the first Canada Cup.

Vladimir Dzurilla and Rogatien Vachon. This game will always belong to them. It is theirs, they earned it.

For 55 minutes the game was dead-even on the scoreboard, 0–0. We clearly had the better of the play in the first and second periods, and people like Esposito, Hull, Leach and Orr were sent away shaking their heads. Then Oldrich Machac took a blast from the blue line on a power play, and Rogie's skate came out of nowhere. A little later it was Vladimir Martenec in on a breakaway and the crowd gave Vachon a standing ovation after a great save. Then it was Milan Novy and he, too, was stoned.

Finally, at 15:41 of the third, Novy got another break and it was in. We had lost 1–0 and the Czechs were on their way to the best-of-three final. We would have to tie the Soviets back in Toronto on Saturday night to qualify.

We beat the Soviets 3–1 but the score doesn't really tell the tale. Gilbert Perreault played great, scoring our first goal and setting up the second by Hull, and Bill Barber got the clincher. Rogie Vachon was unbelievable again, stopping Helmut Belderis cold on a breakaway and Vladislav Tretiak was outstanding in the Soviet goal, especially in the first period when we had 18 shots.

In a way, the best-of-three final against the Czechs was an anti-climax. We beat them 6–0 and 5–4 in overtime to win the series, the latter on an overtime goal by Darryl Sittler. The second game was exciting in that we were leading 3–2 midway through the third period and appeared to have it locked up and then the Czechs scored two quick goals to go ahead before Bill Barber sent it into overtime.

But that championship game will be forever overshadowed by the one we lost; that 1–0 loss is on my list of the Top Ten games I've ever played in.

On the same list is a game in 1984 that also was a first-round game and not a championship round match up. It's strange how public memory works. Years after the fact, people still mention that great 1–0 game against the Czechs in the Canada Cup final. The same goes for the "great overtime championship game against the Soviets" in Calgary in 1984. That 3–2 win against the Soviets got us into the final where we beat the Swedes two straight, but those two games have faded from public memory.

Before I jump ahead eight years, I should go back to 1976 for one last image. That was in our victorious dressingroom, watching the media horde gather around Bobby Orr. Bad knees or not, Bobby was sky-high, a permanent grin etched on his face.

"This is great," he kept saying over and over and laughing, the perpetual kid. This was to be his only chance at international hockey.

"I love it. We were great. The Czechs were great. This hockey was great."

Bobby had finally found the league that matched his sublime talents; the supreme irony was this would be his only opportunity to play at this level.

Robert Gordon Orr would finally retire in 1979, his third "season" with Chicago Black Hawks, a victim of one too many knee injuries. That year would also represent a watershed for the National Hockey League and the style of game that was played there, as well.

The catalyst for this change was an NHL marketer's dream called the Challenge Cup. Ever since John Ziegler had become president of the NHL, the league had run hat-in-hand after the U.S. networks. We'd been made to look small by this shameless pandering to the TV people in New York and have yet to secure the elusive "network connection" that these people have actively sought for more than a decade.

The U.S. networks hesitate to carry a sport nationally that will almost guarantee small ratings in the Sunbelt. I've always been convinced that given enough exposure to hockey these people could be won over, but there isn't a major network around that will take the chance. That didn't prevent NHL marketers from imitating other sports. Bring hockey to the Big Apple in a week-long, media-hype Super Bowl format, they reasoned, and the spectacle will take over.

The NHL expansion of 1967–68 had been a move by a league in a desperate search for a network TV contract. Oakland and Los Angeles would heighten interest in California, Minnesota and St. Louis would start midwestern rivalries with Chicago, and Pittsburgh and Philadelphia would fill in that wasteland from New York to Detroit. Later would come Atlanta and Washington in a bid to succeed on the other side of the Mason-Dixon line. You could almost see the stars in the eyes of the NHL governors, especially the American ones, as they daydreamed about a coast-to-coast network of U.S. teams linked by satellite dishes.

Everywhere else in sport, television was the driving force behind expansion or the formation of new leagues. The American Football League, made successful by a network contract with NBC, had first forced the mighty National Football League to play an inter-league championship game called the Super Bowl, and later to merge.

Major League baseball expanded twice during the 1960s TV decade, in 1961 (Houston, New York Mets, Los Angeles Angels, and Minnesota) and in 1968 (Montreal Expos, San Diego Padres, Seattle Pilots, and Kansas City Royals). The NBA competed with the ABA for televised pro basketball. It was "Have TV Contract: Will Travel."

Try as hockey might, though, the sport just couldn't get the ratings and hockey found itself outside the Network Fishbowl, looking in. Enviously. Hoping against hope that Georgia boys would suddenly lace on skates, and that Californian beach boys would trade in their surfboards for hockey boards and a rough game played on an ice surface, 200 feet by 85 feet.

It was up to the 1979 Challenge Cup to deliver the final message loud and clear: No sale. Ken Dryden and I sat talking about it in New York before we went out to practice one morning. He wrote this in his book, *The Game:*

The Challenge Cup was the bottom, on the ice and
off – Madison Square Garden, the Waldorf-Astoria, the
Russians; a week in the Big Apple, big corporate clients wined
and entertained. It was like Super Bowl week, its model. ". . .
one of the world's most dynamic sports events," columnist
Dave Anderson wrote in *The New York Times*, but no impact
. . . It should be the talk of the town. Instead, it's hardly
mentioned except by the hockey community." And finally what
should have been clear was clear. It is easy to feel big when
you're not, if you surround yourself with others who are smaller. But if you pretend you are big, and surround yourself with
others bigger, you feel crushingly small. That is what happened
in New York.

It was embarrassing that few people in New York cared. It
was also embarrassing that so many real hockey fans outside
New York read far too much into what happened there that
week.

Instead of playing the Wales-Campbell all-star game in
February, the whole league was being given the week off while
an all-star squad played Team Soviet. It was set up as a best-of
three series, all three to be played at Madison Square Garden,
on February 8, 10, and 12, if necessary.

The marketer's dream was a player's nightmare. All over
the league, players wrapped up Saturday or Sunday games
and hopped planes for the Big Apple as we tried to put a
team together. New York was easy to get to from most U.S.
points; those of us who played in some Canadian centres
spent a lot of that Saturday or Sunday hanging around
departure lounges. This great idea was not shaping up as the
NHL braintrust had thought.

What made it worse was the media types having their usual
field day with headlines and deathless prose: Finally the NHL
couldn't use the excuse that the players weren't in mid-season
form. Finally, North American hockey would be represented
by its best players (even though Wayne Gretzky and Bobby
Hull were in the WHA). The game would be played on an NHL
rink in a time zone that favoured us.

It was all a crock, of course. The Soviets play together 11 months of the year. They are a team of sprinters, built for explosive production during short-term projects like tournaments. Their entire training is built around peaking for specific events, the Izvestia Cup in early December, the Olympic Games every fourth February, the World Championships in April and, if need be, the Canada Cup in September.

They had been practising on an NHL-sized rink for a couple of weeks prior to coming over, and even switched their day clocks to Eastern Standard Time to overcome jet lag.

On the other hand, we were from 21 different teams and styles of play. We were marathon men, built to withstand the rigours of an 80-game season and another 15 or so in the playoffs. Even our playoffs were marathons, best-of-seven affairs.

Best-of-seven is unheard of in international hockey. There it's one-game-takes-all, or on occasion, best-of-three.

Team Soviet had a unified, established coaching staff; we had six guys trying to coach the team. Right away we made a major coaching mistake, considering the fact that two staunch rivals, Montreal and the Islanders, were running the team: Guy Lapointe and Denis Potvin were brought in, even though both had suffered major injuries and hadn't played more than a couple of games between them during the previous month. And then I cracked a couple of ribs during the first game of the series and was sub-par as well, so our defence wasn't what it appeared to be on paper.

Another distraction was that it appeared that our coaches were developing an inferiority complex. Guys like Scotty Bowman, Don Cherry, Bob Pulford, and others seemed to be genuinely bothered by all the talk of "Soviet-style" hockey, or the "European flow game" or other hi-tech terminology.

It seemed that every coach in Europe was a college professor with 72 University degrees while our guys were former players who'd grown old and traded in their uniforms for suits. There was also the impact players like Anders Hedberg, Ulf Nilsson, and others had playing with Bobby Hull and the Winnipeg Jets of the WHA. Hull had made headlines with his comments about their "creative style of play" enriching a stale North American game that had deteriorated into goon hockey, a result of the Philadelphia Flyers' success earlier in the decade.

North American hockey was passé, the message was, and new, smarter professional coaches would have to be found if it ever was to return to the vanguard of the sport.

Bobby Hull was fairly complimentary about the Montreal Canadiens' style of play, but his comments were making a lot of ears burn in other NHL cities, especially when they were echoed by university coaches and amateur hockey officials on both sides of the border.

In my relationship with Scotty Bowman, he'd always been a very optimistic man, fully aware of his abilities and those of his players. But that week in New York, he seemed different. He was rattled and so, it seemed, was the rest of the coaching staff. And that would carry on to other international contests, whether they were games against club teams on New Year's Eve at the Forum, or all-star international matches. I began to get the impression that Scotty felt he had to prove himself over again each time we played the Europeans.

Whether we suffered from wild paranoia or just simple pessimism, you couldn't prove it from our first on-ice appearance. Just 14 seconds into Game 1 in New York, Guy Lafleur beat Vladislav Tretiak and we went on to win 4–2.

We took a lead in the second game, as well, but the Soviets rallied to beat us 5–4 and we were going to a third and deciding game. This is where the wheels started falling off.

First, the coaching staff decided to replace Ken Dryden with Gerry Cheevers, a mistake since Ken had been playing terrifically, his best international hockey in a long time. He had the kind of in-close style that worked against the Soviets, who liked to bring the puck right into the crease before shooting. Cheevers was more of an angles goalie, who moved out and away from the net to make his plays. The trouble was, the Soviets were very adept at drawing out such goaltenders and sneaking in behind for easy tip-ins.

They won 6–0 even though it was a tight 1–0 game for the

longest time. Cheevers let in a couple of long-distance shots in the third period and the media jackals started braying. "North American hockey takes it on the chin." "Soviets now confirmed as world's best" and on and on. The same press box experts who had been proclaiming us a powerhouse now jumped down our throats, telling us our game was "static," "outmoded," and a "relic."

Scotty and the other coaches didn't take it well, but they suffered in silence. And the NHL inferiority complex grew. The Canadiens got back a measure of satisfaction the following New Year's Eve when the Canadiens beat the touring Red Army team 4–2 in our semi-traditional holiday match. Scotty got his revenge too; his Buffalo Sabres hammered the Red Army 6–1. But CSKA ended their portion of the tour 3–2 with wins over the Rangers, Nordiques, and the Islanders, while Moscow Dynamo had two wins, a loss, and a tie in their four games.

The next NHL-Soviet match-up of any consequence – I purposely ignore the so-called annual world championships and the Olympic Games – came with the 1981 Canada Cup.

Politics reared its ugly head right at the outset and this would prove to be an omen of things to come. Because of the Soviet invasion of Afghanistan, the Canadian government withdrew our country's team from the 1980 Olympic Games in Moscow, and also ruled against the staging of Canada Cup II in 1980. Instead, we waited an extra year and played Edition Two in 1981. Gone were the Drydens, Espositos, Lapointes, Vachons, and Savards; replacing them were the Bossys, Gillies, Gretzkys, Liuts, and Hartsburgs.

The Canada Cup in 1981 was almost the complete opposite of its predecessor.

In 1976, the Soviets had been in a downward spiral. They won the Olympic title but went sour at the World Championships, losing to Poland (!), Czechoslovakia, and Sweden and finishing second. Veteran players like Shalimov, Maltsev, and Petrov were often injured and appeared near the end of their careers and then came news that Valeri Kharlamov, the diminutive winger who had electrified audiences in 1972, had been seriously injured in a car accident. New players like the Goli-kov brothers and Helmut Balderis were being worked into the new national team so the squad that competed in Canada Cup didn't have the cohesiveness of other Soviet teams we'd met.

Nineteen eighty-one was something else entirely. The Soviets had won the Challenge Cup in 1979 and then been upset by a bunch of U.S. college kids at Lake Placid in the fluke of the century. They came to Canada with a veteran team, one with revenge on its mind for the Olympic Games collapse and a strong desire to prove that the Challenge Cup had not been a fluke in itself.

Again ever anxious for a buck, we repeated the mistake we'd made with the Czechs in '76. We played the Russians in an exhibition game before the tournament opened and handled them easily. Wayne Gretzky set up shop behind the Soviet net and fed the puck out in front all night, to shooters with names like Perreault, Lafleur, and Bossy. This was something new to the Soviets; they'd never met a player with the skills to park behind the opposition net with impunity and hold an entire defence at bay while feeding his teammates with quality scor-ing chances in close.

This was also the year that we first met up with the KLM line: Vladimir Krutov–Igor Larionov–Sergei Makarov, as deadly a threesome as you'll find on a hockey rink. Put them on a front line with the talented Vyacheslav Fetisov on defence and Vladislav Tretiak in goal and you had a serious threat to our keeping the Canada Cup title.

As I said before, the second edition of the Canada Cup was the opposite of the first; we did well in the early round, only to have our heads handed to us in the championship game.

For some reason, Alan Eagleson and the rest of the Canada Cup braintrust had decided on a change in format for 1981. In-stead of two teams emerging from the round robin to play for the title in a best-of-three affair, they were afraid the Soviets might beat Canada in the first round, and then they'd be left with an all-European final. This time the four best teams, of six, would advance to a semi-final where first would play fourth, second would play third, and the winners would face off in a single-game final.

As it turned out, after struggling against the Swedes and the Czechs (both games ended 4–4), we beat the Soviets 7–3 in a meaningless round robin game, the last for both of us. There was nothing to prove in it since we'd both reached the semi-finals, so the Soviets sat out Tretiak and a couple of other players. And if 7–3 sounds like a decisive victory, the score was 2–2 going into the third where we blew it open with five goals. It was like Game Three of the Challenge Cup, in reverse.

We edged the Americans and the Soviets downed the Czechs in the semis and a one-shot, winner-takes-all Canada Cup final was scheduled for Montreal, September 13, 1981 – five years to the day after our 6–0 win over Team Czechoslovakia had given us a 1–0 lead in the best-of-three 1976 series.

The 1981 game was different in many respects. First, it was scoreless after the first. Second, it was Canada that would get blown out. The game was 25 minutes old when Larionov put the Russians ahead but we came right back with a Mike Bossy score to equalize.

Then it all fell apart. Sergei Shepelev made it 2–1 and the Soviets added another six goals against a beleaguered Mike Liut to win the title. At the other end of the rink, Tretiak was a fortress, turning back our attacks like a mediaeval castle.

From his viewpoint in the opposition net, he had this to say about that game in his autobiography, *Tretiak: The Legend*:

> . . . I gave my all in that game, and so did the rest of the guys. What's the matter with the Canadians? I thought. Presumably they were over-eager; they wanted so much to make a brilliant showing in front of millions of their fans. In the early going they had numerous scoring opportunities but they couldn't put the puck in my net. Usually professionals fight to the end, but once we'd scored a few goals, I saw something I'd never seen before – the Canadians seemed to give up. They hung their heads and, like an army given the order to surrender, they lost

their hearts. I felt sorry for their goaltender Mike Liut. His team had left him to be torn to pieces by our forwards. The fans were in a rage. The final score was 8–1.

I couldn't have said it better myself.

Looking back on it, that loss was probably one of the best things that could have happened to North American hockey; it finally laid to rest all speculation that the Soviets were a "one-team" wonder, able to produce a great national team every generation or so. By 1981, nearly all of the 1972 series players were gone, replaced by bigger and better players who were learning and adapting all the time.

And by 1984, the changeover was complete. Maltsev, Petrov, Mikhailov, Yakushev, Vasiliev, Tretiak, and Kharlamov were gone. Their replacements, believe it or not, were even better, with the notable exception of the nets where the Soviets have yet to replace Tretiak.

Canada Cup III saw the format altered yet again. Alan Eagleson, his face still red from the 8–1 pasting in Montreal in 1981, took the best elements of the previous two editions for what has since become the standard Canada Cup format. After the round robin, Teams one and four and two and three would meet in sudden-death semi-finals with the winners advancing to a best-of-three final round. Nor more one-shot finals!

Also, after two editions in eastern Canada, the tournament was moving west. The majority of the important games would be played in Edmonton and Calgary.

Team Canada was going to be quite different, too. Glen Sather of the Stanley Cup champion Edmonton Oilers was in charge and nobody could ever accuse Slats of being a shrinking violet. The fur flew when he announced the roster of players invited to training camp: there were eight (count 'em) Oilers and that upset a lot of people, particularly members of the New York Islanders whose Stanley Cup reign had been ended at four straight that May by the same Oilers.

"Why bother asking for anybody else?" needled Mike Bossy.

"Why don't we make this the Edmonton Oilers versus the world and the rest of us will get on with our summer vacations."

Other Islanders had their say and, when training camp opened, there was a big rift right down the middle of the team. On one side, the Islanders; on the other, the Oilers. Right in the middle, yours truly.

I had developed a lot of healthy respect for both teams over the years. Montreal-Islanders had been an excellent rivalry for almost a decade – beautiful, tough hockey played with a lot of class and a minimum of brawling. Lafleur vs Bossy, Gainey vs Nystrom, Robinson vs Potvin, Lemaire vs Trottier, Billy Smith vs Dryden, right down the line; these were two highly competitive teams whose games were an exercise in mutual respect.

Unlike our rivalries with Philadelphia and Boston, which degenerated into goon hockey because that's what had made those teams, our contests with the Islanders were clean. Neither side pretended to intimidate the other. Neither side gave an inch.

Although we hadn't been playing against the Oilers for long, we had developed a healthy respect for them, as well, for many of the same reasons that characterized our relationship with the Islanders.

When we all got together in Montreal for training camp that summer, it was like the Trans-Canada Highway on a statutory holiday. Cars whizzing by on three lanes in either direction; and me stuck on the median, trying to get back into the traffic. Nothing closed the gap through training camp and our exhibition games. After practice and games, we'd shower and split off into separate groups.

I talked to Wayne Gretzky, always a most reasonable guy. A team man all the way:

"Look, this shit can't go on. We'll end up with another 8–1. You guys are going to have to bury the hatchet."

I talked with Mike Bossy, always a most reasonable guy. A team man all the way:

"Look, this shit can't go on. We'll end up with another 8–1. You guys are going to have to bury the hatchet."

Wayne's answer:

"It makes sense, but they don't want to talk to us. They're still mad because we took the Cup away from them and all they can think about is how they're going to take it back next year."

Mike's answer:

"It makes sense, but they don't want to talk to us. They're still gloating over the Cup final and it gives them great glee to laugh at our guys out there. Brent (Sutter) and John (Tonelli) are really upset. Denis (Potvin) isn't too happy either."

We were still divided when the tournament started and it showed. We easily handled the West Germans (there instead of the Finns) but then we had to play the game of our lives to tie Team USA 4–4.

Our next game was in Vancouver against Team Sweden and they handled us easily, 4–2. We were playing dull, listless, disjointed hockey. There was almost total lack of communication on the ice and the fans and media didn't like it one bit. Prior to the Vancouver game, Sather had given us a major league blast in practice, but it didn't seem to work. Our troubles seemed to go deeper than that.

We had a win, a loss, and a tie and the Czechs and Soviets were coming up. There was a very real possibility that we wouldn't make the top four and the semi-finals, let alone the final round for a re-match against the Soviets.

We returned to Calgary for the Czechoslovakia game. The night before the game, a number of us gathered at Yosemite Sam's, a popular bar and grill, and started talking out our differences. The Oilers and the Islanders agreed to disagree – during the NHL regular season. Here at the Canada Cup they were neither Oilers not Islanders.

Team Canada finally showed up for the tournament.

The next evening, we went out and hammered the Czechs 7–2 to squeeze into fourth place behind the Soviets, Swedes, and Americans. We could move up if we defeated the Soviets in the final contest of the round robin. If we lost, there was a terrific chance we'd play Team Soviet in a sudden-death semi-final.

We lost 6–3 and would play CCCP in the second semi-final.

The date: September 13, 1984. The third anniversary of the 8–1 drubbing at the Forum.

Within the team, there finally was a feeling of unity and it must have been the same kind of "screw'em" attitude that characterized Team Canada '72 after they were booed mercilessly in Vancouver. The negativity and braying in the Canadian media reached new heights; we were dragging Canadian hockey to the lowest depths, we were unworthy representatives of our country, we were clearly second-best and probably heading for third.

The attitude was reflected in the crowd at the Calgary Saddledome when we took to the ice for the start of the game. There were large sections of empty seats, some 13,307 fans attended the game in an arena which then held more than 16,500. A lot of hockey fans chose to stay at home and watch us lose on television, it seemed.

Strange as it seems, we didn't particularly care if the building was empty. We'd decided to play this one for ourselves.

And play we did . . .

This game was right up there with the 1–0 loss to Czechoslovakia in 1976; play going from end-to-end, both goalies – Vladimir Myshkin and Pete Peeters – turning back every thrust.

In the first period, the Soviets pressed, figuring that if they took the lead, we'd never catch up. Try as they might, they couldn't score on an aroused Peeters. That period ended in a scoreless draw and normally offensive defencemen like Paul Coffey, Raymond Bourque, and myself spent most of it behind our own blueline, manning the parapets.

Between periods, Sather came into the room and quietly said:

"I know they have a quality offensive team, but so do we. If we hang back waiting for the breaks, they're going to get them before we do. Let's start taking it to them. Let's move the puck up ice a little quicker and see how they like playing defence."

We pressed right from the opening faceoff of the middle period and, sure enough, it was Myshkin's turn to be tested severely. They started running around in their own end and a Soviet was penalized. On the resulting power play, the Oilers' Coffey carried the puck into their zone, swept a one-handed pass toward the Islanders' Tonelli and his high wrist shot flew in over Myshkin's shoulder 1–0.

The place erupted and we were Canada's darlings again.

We pressed for the rest of the period, outshooting the Soviets 17–6 and would have had a three-or four-goal lead had it not been for Myshkin. For one period, the ghost of Tretiak played in the Russian net.

In the third period, the tables turned yet again. The Russians began pressing again and I was sent off for hooking. While I sat in the penalty box, Sergei Svetlov tied it on a backhander that hit Peeters in the shoulder and squeezed into the net just under the crossbar.

Anxious to make amends, I made a big mistake on the next shift and we were suddenly down 2–1. Sergei Makarov came down on me at the blueline and made a beautiful fake to the outside, which I fell for hook, line, and sinker. As I floundered, he cut back inside and went in alone on Peeters, beating him with a magnificent deke and a backhand into the deserted net.

The Saddledome went into shock; so did we. For the next five minutes, we were barely hanging on and the real possibility of a 1981 replay loomed large. Wave after wave of red-shirted attackers rolled into our zone and we were barely able to clear the puck. All was quiet on the western bench.

Then, almost imperceptibly, it started to change. Mark Messier skated through the entire Soviet team, only to have Myshkin stop him at the post. Gretzky moved up ice on a 2-on-1 that misfired but the Soviets were becoming noticeably less anxious to press to the attack. As they fell back, we pressed forward. We were into the 13th minute when the reward came. Gretzky, playing like he was possessed, and Messier, kept the puck in the Soviet end, dumping into the corners and bringing it out each time they battled with Soviet defenders. They fed wingers and defencemen for shots that went wide, or off legs, but each chance was getting closer and closer.

Finally, Gretzky picked up the puck in the corner, skated behind their net, faked right then came back to the left. He threw the puck out into the slot, right onto Doug Wilson's stick. Doug cranked it, and it was 2–2.

When the siren went to end the third period, the score had not changed.

I had sat in our dressingroom in Montreal in similar situations – before we went out and played the Soviets in the 1981 Canada Cup final; after the third period of the seventh against Boston in the 1979 NHL semi-final; after the second period of the sixth game of the Quebec series earlier that same year.

What goes through your mind in situations like this? Nothing and everything. I've seen players who can blank out what's happening by super concentration on the task at hand. Unable and unwilling to focus on negative thoughts, they go into a little trance, visualizing the play that will win it for us in the upcoming period.

I have seen others in a state of semi-shock brought on only by what can be termed "fear of failure." Are the real successful "money" players those able to master their emotions and talent in moments of crisis? Or are they athletes whose pathological fear of failing drives them to new heights? In Montreal, where the media and fan pressure is overwhelming, where failure is nothing short of public disgrace, the temptation is to answer the latter.

Glen Sather came into the room.

"You have several advantages over those guys," he began.

"You're playing on your own rink. And you're playing against a team that doesn't know what overtime is all about. They've never had to play overtime before.

"Take the game to them."

We did. Glen hadn't stoked our flames with burning oratory, he didn't have to. We knew it would be an awfully long winter if we lost to the Soviets in the semi-final.

When the puck dropped, we pressed forward and began an

assault on Myshkin and friends. But a funny thing happened; the Soviets who'd never played overtime before were matching us stride for stride. While we pressed and held a territorial edge, we were afraid to really step on the gas because whenever we did, they popped out of their zone on potentially lethal counter-attacks.

And that's just what happened at 11:45 of the period. The puck popped out of their end and two Soviets were bearing down on Paul Coffey.

In the past few years, I've heard the "experts" criticize Coffey because he's an offensive defenceman. "He's always caught up ice," "he can't move players out from in front of his net," or "he only cares about his point totals." (The point totals dart is a favourite of the Gretzky denigrators too.)

Drivel.

When I hear the crap about Paul Coffey today, I hear the voices who used to downplay Bobby Orr's contribution to the Bruins. Paul Coffey is a defenceman who scored 126, 121 and 138 points in 1983–84, '84–'85, and '85–'86 respectively. Going into last season, he had 669 points in seven seasons. He had twice won the Norris Trophy.

Most importantly, he had played on three Stanley Cup winners.

The bottom line is that Paul Coffey is a fine defenceman and probably the best player in the game today when it comes to the transition game. Coffey has the uncanny ability to make a defensive play in his own end and start the puck back the other way before the other team can react. Our transition game is like basketball's – the quicker you can move from offence to defence, or vice versa, the more successful you're going to be. An Edmonton trademark when Coffey was there was Coffey breaking up the play in the corner or in front of the net and Gretzky, Messier, or Kurri speeding away across the other team's blueline scant seconds later, after a long pass from Coffey.

In basketball, the transition player is revered – Michael Jordan, Larry Bird, Sydney Moncrief. In hockey, he's often dumped on by the so-called purists who don't realize that the game has left them behind.

We won that game thanks to Coffey's transition skills.

As the two Soviet wingers bore down on him, the crowd, and our bench, held their collective breaths. The three were about ten feet inside our blueline when one Russian tried to pass across to the other, right to left. Coffey got his stick down, intercepted the pass and, before the Soviets could react, was steaming away down to the other end.

Where the Soviets just had a 2-on-1, we now had a 5-on-3. The puck went into the corner to Myshkin's left as they struggled to contain our pursuit. Rugged John Tonelli of the Islanders won yet another battle along the boards and got the puck past to Coffey. With a Soviet taking a desperate lunge at him, Coffey let it fly.

The chest-high shot flew towards the net. Mike Bossy of the Islanders, posted off the crease to the goalie's left, had it hit his stick and deflect down into the goal. Islander to Oiler to Islander. Bossy from Coffey and Tonelli and 12:29 of the fourth period. Team peace had been made and Team Canada now was on its way to the final against Sweden, an anti-climax.

When the craziness died down, I remember someone telling me we'd outshot the Soviets 41–23 and thinking: "That was the hardest 23-shots-against game I've ever played in my life. Right up there with the hardest 13-shots-against game New Year's Eve in Montreal, a few years back."

Yosemite Sam's was never livelier than that night. As I left with Mike Bossy to head back to the hotel in the wee hours of the morning, I didn't realize that this would be my last international confrontation of such magnitude.

Two and a half years later, another Stanley Cup under my belt, I was invited to take part in Rendez-Vous '87 in Quebec: a Challenge Cup finally done right. I opted instead for four days in the Florida sunshine, a highly effective mid-season rejuvenation for these old bones.

And when Canada Cup IV came along, I'd opt for a horse and end up watching on TV as Mario Lemieux joined Wayne Gretzky in that special league where only two now play.

As they say, hindsight is 20/20.

THREE

Training Camp

1971.
1975.
1987.

In a career that has spanned 17 seasons of professional hockey, I can say that I have seen a lot of training camps. For a variety of reasons, these three stand out.

1971 because it was the thrilling first; an incredible adventure for a green kid from Marvelville.

1975 because this is where one of the very best NHL teams ever to play this game first began to come together to challenge the record of the 1950s juggernaut.

And 1987. A training camp like no other in the professional hockey career of Larry Clark Robinson.

My 1987 training camp officially began early on August 22nd when Gaetan Lefebvre pulled up in my driveway at the wheel of a brand new white-and-blue van. The vehicle was a loaner from Terry Snyder, a friend of Donny Cape.

"It's yours to use until you're better," Terry had said.

"Enjoy."

I settled in the back of the van, Gaetan took the wheel and we headed for Montreal. My first training camp meal of 1987 was take-out at McDonald's on the way in. As it would turn out, Gaetan Lefebvre would be my nursemaid, chauffeur, psychologist, and physiotherapist, and I've probably omitted a few of his other roles.

When I had returned home four days before, I was still weak enough to need a wheelchair to get around. I set up shop in my son's bed with the CBM machine; the device did its work well and within a couple of days I was on crutches. Dr. Lenczner had been adamant:

"Get all the movement you can. I want you to be working that leg 24 hours a day on the CBM and then putting as much weight as it will bear when you're on crutches. It will seem difficult at first and pain will be your guide. But you'll have to work it."

So here I was at the Forum training room, barely two weeks after the operation.

"We'll start nice and simple," Gaetan said.

"The exercise bicycle only, for now. It will help work the leg, especially the joint, and it won't hurt your cardiovascular system either. You can get a lot of exercise without putting a lot of weight on the leg."

My road back to the NHL was pedalled on a stationary bicycle. Every day, twice a day, I would report to the Forum weight room and put in my time on the bike. Exciting it wasn't, and it was nothing like my very first training camp with Montreal Canadiens. First and foremost, a training room with exercise bikes and Universal and Nautilus equipment was unheard of in September, 1971 . . .

My first training camp actually began three months before that, on June 10, 1971, the day of the National Hockey League entry draft at the Queen Elizabeth Hotel in Montreal, and eight days after my twentieth birthday.

My wife Jeannette and I had been back home in Metcalfe, staying with my parents to save money, for about a month when draft day came. Both of us had summer jobs, I was working on the farm and Jeannette was a waitress in Ottawa, to make ends meet and keep our infant son Jeffery in formula and diapers. We were glad to be home from Kitchener, relieved that my season with the OHA Rangers was over and anxious to get a little rest from the very new and difficult task of raising a baby boy. Mom pitched in and helped a great deal.

But both of us were also keeping an anxious eye on the calendar. As far as we were concerned, only one date of the 365 in the year meant anything: June 10, a Thursday.

During the season with the Rangers, I'd heard that scouts were expressing some interest in me and by the halfway point of the year, there was mention of it in the local newspaper, the *Kitchener-Waterloo Record*.

. . . During recent times when Rangers have managed only two wins and a draw in ten games, one player in particular has done his share and maybe more in an effort to pull Kitchener up in the standings.

That one player – none other than Larry Robinson, a sort of mini-Wilt Chamberlain who hails from Brockville, Ont.(sic).

In fact, last weekend when Rangers were having their times against Toronto and Peterborough, it was Robinson's tidy defensive play that had a couple of professional scouts waxing their palms. One of them said during a between-period press room session that Robinson may surprise a lot of people in the ranking of amateur draft selections next June.

You know, he (Robinson) doesn't appear like he's accomplishing much with his loosey goosey style. He's deceptive though, a lot of forwards have trouble beating him and offensively he can bring that puck out when the heat's on.

That kind of support was encouraging and there was more of it as the OHA season wound down. As a result, I looked forward to the draft with equal parts nervousness and anticipation. The 1971 draft was going to belong to several people: Sam Pollock, whose Montreal Canadiens had manoeuvered themselves a number one pick with his typical foresight; Guy Lafleur, the blond right winger who had scored 130 goals with Memorial Cup champion Quebec Remparts and who was going to be Pollock's pick; and Marcel Dionne, the OHA's scoring machine who had personally given my own Kitchener Rangers an early summer vacation. It was very much Lafleur's and Dionne's draft but I wanted a piece of it.

Each player has his own opinion of his abilities. These do not always mesh with those of the scouts who have seen him play, or the teams that are getting ready to roll the dice in hockey's version of a Las Vegas craps game.

I'd played only one year in the OHA but I knew I had done well; I couldn't remember ever feeling overmatched, even by the players the scouts and press were touting as top picks. But I'd only played one year in the OHA; and that could work against me. The negative opinion would be that it was a fluke season. The positive response would be "he developed late" or "he should have been in that league earlier."

I chose the optimistic route and reasoned that I'd be fairly well considered. I might even go somewhere in the first three rounds, where the money was. I guessed. I assumed. I reasoned. I felt.

But, like most of the 200 or so amateur hockey players being considered that day – and only 117 would be drafted – I didn't know. Guy Lafleur knew. Marcel Dionne knew. Jocelyn Guevremont (No. 3), Gene Carr (No. 4), and Rick Martin (No. 5) knew.

It being a short drive from our farm in Metcalfe to Montreal, Dad gave us the day off and we went to the draft. We were a little late, thanks to Montreal's infamous traffic, and most of the first round had been completed when we walked into the room.

What a shock to discover that I'd been here many times before! The farmer boy from Marvelville via Metcalfe strode resolutely into the 1971 National Hockey League Amateur and Entry Draft, President Clarence Campbell presiding, and turned to his father in surprise:

"This is a cattle auction!"

In the centre of the room were numbered tables, each bearing the emblem of an NHL team. Around each sat team executives and a number of scouts. Sitting outside this bull-pen and looking on anxiously were the "cattle," strapping young men in new, ill-fitting suits or blazers and slacks. You had never seen so many flowered shirts and paisley ties outside San Francisco.

Nattily attired in pinstripes, Mr. Campbell was on a raised platform, addressing each team spokesman as his turn came up, much like the auctioneer who would have cattle paraded for inspection before a group of farmers.

When I entered, Sam Pollock was already making his second choice of the first round, number seven overall.

"The Montreal Canadiens select, from the Flin Flon Bombers, forward Chuck Arnason." Mr. Campbell then repeated the draft selection as a member of the NHL staff wrote the name on a card and slipped it into a slot under the Montreal Canadiens logo on a huge toteboard.

A couple of unfamiliar names, Larry Wright of the Regina Pats and Pierre Plante of the Drummondville Rangers were selected next by the Philadelphia Flyers before the Marlies' Steve Vickers was picked by the New York Rangers.

Again it was Sam Pollock's turn. Six NHL teams had not picked yet, and Sam was on his third selection of the first round. And three more were coming in Round Two, which meant that six of the first 28 picks were his. Not for nothing they called him Trader Sam or the Godfather.

"The Montreal Canadiens select, from the Ottawa 67s, a forward, Murray Wilson." Terrific pick, I thought to myself. With his speed and determination, Murray will fit right in with the Canadiens in a year or two. He had been a terrific high school athlete in Ottawa, starring in many sports. But this is Montreal; he better get used to the idea of playing in Halifax for a couple of years. If he'd been drafted by L.A. or Oakland, he'd probably be on the big club in October.

Chicago Black Hawks followed with Dan Spring of the Edmonton Oil Kings before two more familiar faces, Steve Durbano of Toronto and Terry O'Reilly of Oshawa, were picked by the Rangers and the Bruins respectively, to end the first round.

During the short pause between rounds, I looked around the room, occasionally nodding or waving to teammates and opponents I'd known. We were studies in feigned nonchalance – occasionally we would lock eyes and roll them upwards, as if to silently say across the room: "What a crock of shit, this is," while deep inside a little voice was saying "Pick me! Pick Me! Pick Me! I don't care if I have to go to Oakland and war funny white skates, pick me!"

Names, familiar and unfamiliar, were called out on the tinny P.A. system and were posted on the toteboard. Here and there, burly guys stood up and shyly made their way to the team tables – Ken Baird, Henry Bouchard, Bobby Lalonde, Brian McKenzie, Craig Ramsay. The last three I knew well. Lalonde was the tiny centre from Montreal with terrific speed who, despite his size, could take a hit. Brian McKenzie had been overshadowed by Marcel Dionne at St. Catharines but could play, and Craig Ramsay was an excellent two-way player, the kind the Peterborough Petes have been turning out since Adam and Eve were picking apples.

Once again, Clarence campbell said:

"The next selection, number 20, is Montréal's. Are you ready Mr. Pollock?"

There was a residue of nervous laughter, not the least which seemed envious. Most of the audience was remembering how the draft had started about 90 minutes before, while Dad and I were still trying to figure out Montreal traffic.

Going into the draft, the Canadiens had made it abundantly clear that Guy Lafleur would be their number one pick. They had ensured that with separate deals involving the Seals and the Kings the year before. A day before the draft, Jean Beliveau, the Canadiens' captain and inspiration for 11 years, had retired. He graciously offered his famous number four to Lafleur, who wore that number with Quebec. Beliveau had been known as the Man Who Built the Quebec Colisee in the early 1950s. Lafleur was the Man Who Filled it in the 1970s.

So when Clarence Campbell announced that the first pick of the 1971 draft belonged to Montreal, Sam Pollock paused dramatically, and then called "Time out." Everybody cracked up.

That was about 90 minutes ago. His one rare bid at comedy a mere memory, Sam's famous "all-business" look had return-ed. The only thing Mother Nature has to compare is a Great White Shark which has just received a gilt-edged invitation to a feeding frenzy.

"The Montreal Canadiens select from the Kitchener Rangers, defenceman Larry Robinson."

"Hold me up Dad. I think I'm going to faint!"

When you are 6′3″, your jaw has a long way to go to hit the floor. How wide open was my mouth? Picture a three-car garage. In a dream state, I felt myself getting up and making my way to the Canadiens' area. People, players and parents, scouts and well-wishers, were shaking my hand as I went by but it was all a blur. I kept mumbling "thanks" and floated along through a sea of outstretched hands at a speed that approached single-frame advance. Inside, however, my mind was on fast forward.

"The Montreal Canadiens! The Montreal Canadiens? Not on your life? J.C. Tremblay. Terry Harper. Jacques Laperriere. Guy Lapointe. Serge Savard. Pierre Bouchard. I'm going to spend my life in the American Hockey League," if I was lucky; the Canadiens also had a busload of talented young defencemen playing in Halifax.

Then the positive voice kicked into the Great Mental Debate. "If you throw in the towel before you even get to training camp, you'll never make it, dummy! Might as well start scouting the real cattle auctions for stock of your own; you'll be a farm boy all your life."

The rest of the day was out of focus. Although the press really concentrated on Guy Lafleur and Marcel Dionne, the rest of us Montreal picks were interviewed and photographed by the large corps of Montreal Canadiens media watchers. I remember a photographer posing all of us for a photograph on an escalator – Arnason, Wilson, Lafleur, Robinson, Deguise, and Robert Murray, a defenceman drafted from Michigan Tech. (Not the same player as the Bob Murray from the Cornwall Royals who has been with Chicago for 13 years, this Bob Murray eventually played four years with Atlanta and Vancouver before retiring.) All of us, Lafleur excluded, would play for the Halifax Voyageurs the following year.

Frankly, I don't remember much else, including my return home for the post-draft family celebration. Jeannette's father had a big grin on his face. A staunch Toronto fan, he'd joked with me about getting drafted by the hated Montreal Canadiens and how he would disown me. But neither of us had believed it for a moment; I fully expected to end up somewhere in the West Division. Los Angeles. St. Louis. Oakland. Wherever. But Montreal?

I wish I could say it was an idyllic summer, one full of those "lazy, hazy, crazy" days that Nat King Cole sang about.

These days, a professional hockey player is only too glad to emerge from the endless winter and our marathon season, cast away the NHL stress, and spend the off-season rejuvenating physically and mentally. The summer that works for an NHLer is the one where all the physical and psychological aches and pains are melted away, and the player is delivered to training camp in September, fully restored and ready for another eight months of the grind. Summer is usually too short, especially if you're on one of the better teams and your season ends in late May.

That summer was too long for me, about a hundred days too long. I couldn't wait for training camp at the Forum in September.

But first, a slight formality. I had to undergo the transformation from draft choice to official Montreal Canadien. About three weeks after the draft, the telephone rang in Metcalfe.

"Larry, it's Claude Ruel. It's time for us to get together and talk contract."

"Okay." I was big on dialogue in those days. I'd only been dreaming about this call for weeks, rehearsing the conversation over and over.

"How about the day after tomorrow?"

"No problem. I'll drive into Montreal and we'll take care of it."

"No, I'll come out and see you. It will give me an excuse to get out of the city."

"Okay. I'll give you directions . . ."

"I don't need them." Claude Ruel was Montreal's head scout and Sam Pollock's RSM, Regimental Sergeant-Major, able to fill in anywhere. A former head coach of the Canadiens who would serve a second stint at that position in the early 1980s, he was tabbed to assist Scotty Bowman in the coming season. Bowman was replacing Al MacNeil, who'd replaced Ruel himself and coached Montreal to a surprise Stanley Cup a month before. Claude spent that summer handling a lot of administrative chores, an unofficial assistant GM.

Claude Ruel had a unique gift, however. He was probably the premier talent scout in all of hockey, a squat fireplug of a man who'd been a blue chip defensive prospect in junior hockey until he left an eye at the arena one night. There wasn't a rink between Victoria, B.C. and St. John's, Nfld., that he couldn't find, one eye or not. And there wasn't a hockey prospect he couldn't figure out.

I hung up the telephone and turned to Jeannette: "That was Claude Ruel. He's coming here the day after tomorrow to sign my contract. We'll have to do something special for supper."

My parents were away and Jeannette was going to have to hold the fort in the kitchen. A lot of things had happened in the last 12 months of our lives – my high school graduation, marriage, the early arrival of Jeffery, and our first season away from home in Kitchener with the Rangers. We'd made do during the eight months in Kitchener and Jeannette will be the first to admit that cooking was still new to her and not one of her basic skills. We opted for simplicity; pork chops and potatoes. It was also a favourite of mine.

On the day that Ruel was expected, Jeannette stayed home from work and took up residence in the kitchen in the morning, her nervousness culminating in a mess of burnt potatoes. There was still the scent of seared spuds in the air when the doorbell rang early that afternoon.

Claude Ruel, and my first contract, were on the threshold.

We spent the rest of the day negotiating. Actually, that's a bit misleading – most of that time was taken up with Claude patiently explaining to me how professional contracts worked. Agents were becoming common in pro sports around that time but players who used them still were in the minority. It had never really occurred to me to even look into the matter.

On the other hand, Guy Lafleur had Gerry Patterson negotiate his contract and Arnason went to the top man, Bob Woolf of Boston, to negotiate his deal. I opted for pork chops and potatoes.

Once most of the basic legal niceties were explained, Claude began negotiating with me. Actually, he seemed to be negotiating with himself.

"We'll give you $6,500. With all of the people we have in Montreal, you'll probably end up in Halifax for a couple of years. But when you move up, the money will be there."

"Okay." I resolutely drove a hard bargain.

"No, no, no, that's not enough. I can't offer you that if you'll be unhappy in a year or two. I want you to be happy and I should be fair." He offered $7,000.

And I was ready to sign for $7,000.

Once more, "No, no, no, that's not good enough. We'll pay you $7,500."

I finally agreed to the contract (he finally let me agree) and signed – $7,500 a year with a $7,000 signing bonus. Forever the gracious rural host, I asked him to supper.

"No thanks, I'm on a diet," and he left. Feeling rich and a touch extravagant, Jeannette and I celebrated my first deal with pork chops and burnt potatoes. That "poor man's steak" turned out to be particularly significant; a year later, the Canadiens signed John van Boxmeer out of Tier Two Junior in Ontario. This was the same player who had not been able to crack the Kitchener Ranger line-up the year I was there. His deal was 50–50, $50,000 to sign and $50,000 a year.

I was so mad that during the first intra-squad game at the 1972 camp, I ran him on the first shift. But I'm getting ahead of myself.

Almost three months to the day after I was drafted, I stood stripped to the waist in a line-up of other similarly semi-attired young men at the Forum. Training camp had finally arrived and here was the skinny kid from Marvelville via Metcalfe goggling at the beefcake in the room.

I was what you would call wiry back then. A touch over 6′3″ and 193 pounds. If that doesn't sound comparatively small, I've played at 215 to 220 pounds, 22 to 27 pounds heavier than that, during most of my career. I wasn't weak because I tossed around bales of hay and played ball all summer but, to be honest, I was shy about my weight. I saw these other guys with their shirts off and they were all muscle. I began wondering what I was getting into, to tell you the truth.

If I had any illusions about my place with the big boys, it didn't take too long for them to be dispelled. I was pure rookie and ticketed for Halifax. My first brush with the fabled Canadiens tradition came in the guise of a pair of dusty old shinpads. As I put on these relics for the first time, I made two quick discoveries. The first was that they were about four inches too short and those four inches would take place between my skate and my shinbone! Here I was, a defenceman who would be on the receiving end of slapshots and sticks. I prayed as I put them on.

The second discovery was the number nine written in magic marker on the inside of the pads. Only one player had worn that number with Montreal during my lifetime: Maurice Richard. After that first practice, I nervously noted out loud that while I was thrilled to be wearing the Rocket's pads, I was not looking forward to the broken leg I'd soon be faced with.

Eddy Palchak, the club's equipment manager, was characteristically blunt: "Why didn't ya say anything today, rook? Ya mighta been hurt."

Lesson One. Guy Lafleur's equipment all fit on Day One.

Lesson Two. They'll listen to a rookie if he makes sense.

Lesson Three came on the ice. Those naked muscles I'd seen at the team physical were the real McCoy. At Brockville and Kitchener, I'd played against some big boys and held my own. Most of the larger guys there were not known for their speed.

Here they were bigger. And they were all fast.

Michael Poirier got me going. A free agent rookie, he was one of the best men on the ice in training camp and practices. But come game time, he tightened up so bad, it was unbelievable. Nerves took him right out of hockey. At the 1971 camp, he didn't care who he hit and proved it by whacking around a couple veterans in a scrimmage. That inspired me and I hit somebody in front of the net and the next thing I knew, Claude Larose was taking a run at me.

"Rookies don't run veterans," he hissed.

"Wanna bet?" I retorted with no little conviction.

I resolved to keep hitting guys when the opportunity arose, rookie or veteran, and to keep my head up at all times. Nothing untoward happened during the rest of the training camp, but Poirier's example served me well. I was seen by the veterans and not in a negative light. The league had been stocking up in the beef department, Boston and Philadelphia leading the way, and big guys were welcome in most training camps.

I remember discussing this with my roommate Serge Savard a couple of years later. We'd been talking about another rookie who'd come to camp in the mid-70s, and I turned the discussion to my arrival.

"Did I make an impression?"

"Sure you did. We saw this big guy coming in who could skate well, wasn't afraid to go on offence, and who wasn't going to get pushed around by teams like the Bruins and the Flyers. This kind of player we could use. Especially since I was a defensive defenceman who preferred to lay back and let the other guy take the puck up ice."

I couldn't know that then. I was sent to Halifax about midway through the camp and was out of the Canadiens picture for a full year. I was determined to learn as much as I could so my second Montreal Canadiens camp would be more eventful. But as far as Montreal was concerned that first year, I was "out of sight, out of mind."

Nineteen seventy-five, four years later, it was a different story. While I'd been fortunate to win a Stanley Cup in 1973, my first year (half-year) up with Montreal, that was with a club in transition. The 1972–73 edition of the Montreal Canadiens was definitely competitive and had to be considered among the favourites for the post-season championship. But it had a lot of company in the NHL penthouse.

When we came together in September, 1975, there'd been a major transfusion. The transition Canadiens were gone – Frank Mahovlich, J.C. Tremblay, Dale Hoganson, Marc Tardif, and Rejean Houle to the World Hockey Association;

Michel Plasse, Chuck Arnason, Chuck Lefley, Bob Murdoch and Wayne Thomas via trade; and Henri Richard and Jacques Laperriere had retired.

In their place were young veteran forwards like Lafleur, Shutt, Gainey, Tremblay, Risebrough, Lambert, Wilson; a solid defence headed by Savard, Lapointe, Robinson, Bouchard, Van Boxmeer, and Awrey; and anchored by the goaltending of Dryden and Larocque.

And to come were Pierre Mondou, Bill Nyrop, Rod Langway, Brian Engblom, Mark Napier, Doug Jarvis, Pat Hughes, Cam Connor, and Rejean Houle (returned from the WHA).

When we reported to camp that year, the Broad Street Bullies were the reigning NHL champions. Clarke, Shultz, Kelly, Barber, Leach, and company had stampeded through the league for two straight Stanley Cups. Whatever got in the way was summarily dispatched. Goon hockey was in.

As Serge Savard was saying, the veterans were glad when big rookies like myself showed up at training camp and proved that they would eventually belong. In the early 1970s, spurred on by the success of the Flyers, teams were scrambling to beef up. Our camp featured a whole slew of family-sized forwards and defencemen – myself, Butch Bouchard, Rick Chartraw, Bob Gainey, Peter Mahovlich, Yvon Lambert. The newcomers were no midgets. They included Glenn Goldup, Sean Shanahan, and Mario Tremblay.

If you get the impression that I am criticizing Philadelphia, nothing could be further from the truth. Working entirely within the rules, the Flyers built a goon team. They essentially had seven or eight highly skilled players surrounded by enforcers and plumbers. They were skilled down centre with Bobby Clarke and Rick MacLeish, two excellent hockey players, and Orest Kindrachuk, a very hard worker who was vastly under-rated. They had some excellent wingers in Bill Barber, Reggie Leach, Simon Nolet, Bill Flett, and Gary Dornhoefer. And they had the incomparable Bernie Parent playing behind the Watson brothers, Tom Bladon, Moose Dupont, and Ed Van Impe on defence.

Another plus was behind the bench; Fred Shero, Freddie the

Fog, knew how to squeeze the very last drop of effort out of these guys. He knew they weren't figure skaters; he took the components of that team and arranged them so they worked best. He devised a system that maximized their strong points and minimized their weak ones; each player had a role inside that system, including Dave Schultz.

Once the system was in place, Shero made sure that the players stuck to it and the club's work ethic, enlisting the able help of team leader Bobby Clarke and veterans like the Watsons, Van Impe, Dupont and Dornhoefer.

So the Flyers may have appeared as goons to the world, but underneath that surface was a solid, well-coached team of guys who would make sacrifices for each other. Unless you could penetrate that, beat them decisively, and cause them to start doubting their team unity, you were not going to get far against Philadelphia in the long run. With Clarke as captain, it wasn't going to be easy to get them down on themselves; he simply refused to let it happen.

Thus, we prepared for the wars. Our reasoning was simple: if we could eliminate the Flyers' physical edge, or contain it, our superior hockey skills would allow us to beat them. If we could strip away Fred Shero's system, the flaws underneath would be exposed. As good as Clarke, MacLeish, Barber, and Leach were, Lafleur, Shutt, Mahovlich, Cournoyer, Lemaire, et al were better. And it was time to prove it.

The war came early. It couldn't even wait for the season to start.

We had home-and-home exhibition games scheduled with Philadelphia on Saturday and Sunday, September 20 and 21, respectively. This was midway through camp; we'd still play another five or six pre-season games before the 1975–76 NHL schedule got under way.

After three or four years of training camps, I'd come to expect a certain number of pre-season melees and brawls. It was a time-honoured way for rookies to make their point quickly, and quite often these practice games would be punctuated by a series of brisk and enthusiastic scraps. I remember my very first exhibition game was against Boston, the

Big Bad Bruins of the 1970s. The game was in the Garden that night and some of the veterans had come down with the Boston flu so they flew in myself and Kerry Ketter to play. Ketter had been signed as a free agent and wanted to make an impression.

He did, on Johnny McKenzie, the bronco-busting left winger they called Pie because of his big, round face. Ketter's first order of business was to rearrange McKenzie's features with a judiciously applied cross-check. You didn't usually do this to the Bruins, and never in their own rink. As gloves flew and white and red shirts converged, my reaction was "Oh oh, here we go."

I might have said you didn't do this to the Bruins in normal times, but pre-season never was normal times. The veterans grew to expect the unexpected from rookies out to make names for themselves. That is why smart coaches, faced with a traditional rival in an exhibition game, would not dress some of their more valuable commodities, preferring to load the line-up with lots of healthy, young impressionable types who were very anxious to please.

And while veterans snarled meaningfully at the newcomers, they usually gave them a wide berth.

Pete Mahovlich explained this September silliness in one word:

"Hormones."

"Hormones?"

"Yup, hormones. They still got 'em. Us older guys have had them leached out of our system by all of these years of 100-game seasons. These rooks are full of hormones; it makes 'em crazy. Us veterans have more sense than to go around fighting in pre-season when we don't even get decent meal money."

That's why it was somewhat strange that when the Flyers lined up against us for the Forum game that Saturday night there was nary a rookie to be seen. This was a veteran team facing us, one that appeared determined to deliver a message or two. Like "we have the Cup and we're going to keep it."

For one night, they kept it, as the Canadiens and Flyers played a mid-season game in shirt-sleeve September. They edged us 5–4, Dave Schultz scoring the winner, and there was an uncommon amount of talking, post-whistle milling about, and stickwork. Schultz, as usual, was in his element, cross-checking Yvan Cournoyer to the ice. Yvan had just been appointed team captain on the retirement of Henri Richard and this was Schultz's way of challenging the entire team.

Doug Risebrough was the only one who picked up the gauntlet. He jumped on Schultz's back and hung on for dear life in a lightweight-heavyweight mismatch. Riser would be instrumental in the away game the following night.

On Sunday our line-up was definitely aimed at countering a physical threat: Sean Shanahan, Glenn Goldup, Pierre Bouchard, and Rick Chartraw were front and centre and got lots of ice time. All four were over six feet tall and averaged about 205 pounds in weight.

It was a long, long game, about three hours old and late in the third period when it erupted. We led 6–2 at that point and there had been about 80 minutes in penalties assessed so far, ten minutes for a first-period fight in which Charty had handled Schultz. Doug Risebrough and Bobby Clarke were skating back to their benches when they exchanged words, and then punches. Dougie was whaling the tar out of Clarke when Schultz led the Flyers off the bench. We flew off ours and fights broke out everywhere.

Chartraw grabbed Schultz and quickly made it 2–0 for the night while Butch Bouchard mopped up the boards with Jack McIlhargey; everywhere you looked, red shirts were hammering white and orange. When it was over, the Spectrum was strangely quiet. Referee Bruce Hood handed out a total of 322 penalty minutes, 250 alone for that fight, and ended the game right there.

But it was too late for Philadelphia; we had ended the Broad Street Bullies. Never again would they dictate their system or style of game to us, and eventually the rest of the league.

That's why I'll never forget Training Camp 1975. We dispelled one myth of invincibility, and went on to create another one in its ashes. We left the Spectrum that night knowing we'd done something very special. The 1975–76 Montreal Canadiens, free to play Firewagon Hockey, went on to a record-setting 60 wins, 12 ties, and 8 losses. This is one record that will stand for a very long time.

And then there was training camp, 1987. It's easy to get introspective when some upheaval takes place in your life. The event, big or small, tends to give you focus. At this camp, I felt a lot of memories coming back as my rehabilitation got under way.

I shared the Canadiens' dressingroom with Team Canada members in my first days back; I reported for Montreal's training camp a full three weeks before the team. The first hurdle would be a least as important psychologically as physically, Dr. Lenczner told me. Would there be pain when I started on the exercycle?

I felt no pain at all.

For the first week, all I did was ride the bike and do some light exercise on the trainer's table. I'd arrive at the Forum at about 8:30 every morning and lie down on the table. Gaetan would strap a weight to my lower leg and I'd do leg raises, two sets of ten. Then it was over on my stomach for leg curls, bringing my leg in close and trying to touch my buttocks with my heel. Then there'd be more leg raises, sitting on the edge of the table this time.

The plan was to build up my leg strength without sacrificing flexibility. Stopping myself from limping was another priority. The worst thing about a major physical injury is dwelling on it and its consequences. The worst thing about limping is thinking about it. If you don't believe that, try to consciously think about something as automatic and mechanical as walking, as you do it. Skipped a few steps, did you? It's like your brain takes your legs off automatic and puts them on manual.

I tried not to think about it. I tried not to limp.

Dr. Lenczner explained that because I hadn't been using my leg for so long, I had to be reprogrammed; the brain messages being sent to my leg weren't right. In essence, my brain was telling my leg: "You can't step on it, you can't step on it."

Now I had to adjust to the doctor saying: "Your brain is wrong. It's okay. You can use your leg now." It was the weirdest feeling.

About five or six weeks after the accident, I was down to one crutch.

"Try it without the crutch," Dr. Lenczner said.

I put the crutch aside and began walking. It was the strangest sensation, not knowing if the next step was the one where the leg would collapse and I would fall crippled to the floor. As I left the doctor's office, and my crutches for the last time, he was adamant.

"I don't want you exhausting yourself by walking too much. But when you do walk, I don't want you limping." For the first couple of weeks after that, I would limp some days, and not limp on others. I had been told not to think about it, so I didn't. There was a surefire way of knowing whether I had been subconsciously hobbling; my hip would start to ache from the undue stress caused by an unnatural stride.

Months later, after I'd returned to the NHL, I'd occasionally get a stiff hip or stiff back. Gates would become my instant chiropractor – a little twist, a crack and the hip would snap right back.

By the time my Montreal teammates reported to camp in mid-September, I was already working out on several exercise machines, doing more and more reps (repetitions) of leg raises, extensions, and curls at higher and higher weight levels. My injured leg was responding beautifully but the big test was yet to come; all of this effort and energy would go for nought if I couldn't skate when the time came.

Gaetan, Donny, and I got together in early October.

"I feel ready," I told them, "and I think I should do it somewhere quiet. I don't want TV crews out here for a Hollywood production of 'Larry's big skate.'"

Donny got us some early ice time at the arena complex in Dollard-des-Ormeaux, a West Island suburb about halfway between my home in St. Lazare and downtown Montreal. On October 16, we snuck into the place at about 6:30 in the morning. Gates tied his skates and was waiting for me on the ice when I walked out of the dressingroom. As I stepped onto the ice for the first time, he got down and salaamed. Meanwhile, Donny was hovering in the background like a Secret Service agent, making sure no spies were hanging about to sell valuable videotapes of The Great Return to the other 20 NHL clubs.

It may have been a little silly, but I preferred the privacy. I wanted to know how the leg would act before the general public found out.

We skated for about 30 minutes on that first day and it felt pretty good. I moved lazily through some broad circles, left and right, traded some passes with Gaetan and shot some pucks just to get my mind off the mechanics of skating.

The next day we were back, this time for an hour, and the same the day after that. Donny and Gaetan started skating me in shifts as my strength and confidence returned. We'd skate forward and backward, passing the puck, making quick turns and cuts. That was a particular strength of Gaetan; this trainer was fit and able enough to work out alongside you, on ice or off. My convalescence was not a solitary affair and that shortened it considerably.

I'd been on skates five or six times before my celebrated return at the Forum. I was a little cocky in front of the cameras, knowing that most of the journalists were looking for signs of the injury. I was feeling good after two months of pedalling and leg exercises and a week of skating on the sly. I'd also worked on the weights quite a bit during the layoff.

I came off the ice and some of the TV guys admitted amazement:

"Which leg did you break anyway? It doesn't show."

And then I started to practice with the team. What a shock. My legs were fine after all that work but it felt like I wasn't holding a hockey stick. My co-ordination was way off, the extra weight training had added strength but sacrificed co-ordination and flexibility. I immediately dumped the weights and began an elaborate series of stretching exercises, just to get the feel back.

As my training camp progressed, so did the 1987–88 NHL season. I watched the Montreal Canadiens, one of three or four bona fide Stanley Cup contenders, get off to a dynamite start, spurred on by the early-season excellence of defencemen Chris Chelios and Petr Svoboda.

It was going to be a memorable season.

FOUR

Where Is This Place, Anyway?

EDDIE MACCABE of the *Ottawa Citizen* had the most fun with it.

"A guy your size just couldn't come from any one place, he has to have come from three or four. At least."

I grew up in the Ottawa Valley, about 20 miles south of Ottawa. The 1987–88 Montreal Canadiens guide says I was born in Winchester, Ontario. Newspaper articles in the past have described me alternately as "Metcalfe's finest," "the Winchester giant," and "the Captain of Marvelville." There has been passing mention of other Valley centres such as Russell, Edwards, and Kenmore too. I'm everybody's boy.

Eddie wrote this in April, 1973, three months after I had been called up to join the Montreal Canadiens. If you ever want to find my hometown, you won't go far wrong with these instructions:

". . . Back in January, when he was called up to Montreal, we made a note of it and mentioned he was from Metcalfe, where his parents live now. A lady called to set us straight. He's a Marvelville boy.

'I can believe it,' he says. 'I was on TV and mentioned I was from Metcalfe, and I heard from them in Marvelville.'

"You can understand we just had to see this place with such cresting community pride.

"Well sir, you take Highway 31, the goat track which runs south toward Morrisburg, out about 12 miles from Ottawa.

"Make a left then, going east, into Metcalfe, and stop at Stanley's General Store and Post Office. You'll notice a sign in the window urging the citizenry to save their Canada Packers labels to help get a new coffee percolator for the community centre. That's the place. They'll direct you from there, advising though, that the road is 'all boiled up.'

"Go on east from Metcalfe a bit and you'll come to a crossroads, turning south to Kenmore. Go on down there, right through Kenmore, cross the bridge over the Castor River and you'll come to a sign that says: 'Pavement ends.'

"That's true. It surely does. Now take a left and go a few miles down a dirt road until the road ends, and then take a right, going south. A few more miles down this narrow strip of boiled mud and you'll come to a little red brick building with a tiny bell tower on it. It's on the left there . . . you can't miss it.

"The stone in the wall says the building goes back to near the turn of the century but there's a new sign over the door proclaiming the modest structure as the Marvelville Community Centre, 1967.

"Wellsir, right there is where Captain Marvel must have gone to school. Down the road about another 100 yards there's a crossroads. There is a sign up . . . Marvelville . . . and when you look closely, it used to say Marvelville Grocery, but the Grocery has been painted over.

"There's a gas station there, a modest two-pumper . . . and that's it. Up the road a bit, a few farms . . . and that's Marvelville . . . maybe fifty proud souls in all, not counting the stock of course.

"Along the way, we had asked for confirmation of our direction, and about the state of the road, and we were told:

"'Just go right along there . . . and don't worry about the road. If you get bogged, any one of the lads down there will get you out.'

"So that was a comfort. Everybody knows the people of Marvelville won't see a lad stuck. But they're fearful proud of Larry Robinson, and don't be transplanting him to Metcalfe."

I'm grateful to Eddie MacCabe for those wonderful instructions and impromptu road guide to the Ottawa Valley. And I'm also eternally thankful that his "Captain Marvel" nickname never caught on; I've had enough aggravation with Big Bird. Imagine trying to live up to Captain Marvel. Or the Captain from Marvelville.

I think the best way to clear up the confusion is to say that I was born in Winchester – obviously Marvelville was too small to have a hospital – grew up in Marvelville and moved to Metcalfe with my parents at age 18 when my Dad sold the farm to my brother, Brian.

The way this story begins is with Larry Clark Robinson coming into the world June 2, 1951 at Winchester, Ontario; son of Leslie and Isabel Robinson, younger brother to Brian and Carole, and (later to be) older brother to Linda and Morris.

This same Larry Clark Robinson would grow up to be your typical farm boy, through and through.

My uncle Ray and my Dad had dairy farms about half a mile apart. In those days, that's how you survived on the farm; you shared machinery, helped each other do the hay and sow and harvest the crops. My grandfather also lived with my uncle; they had an extension on the house.

Farm life is healthy and I've tried in recent years with our horses and home in St. Lazare, Quebec, to give my kids an idea of what it was like for the five Robinson kids to grow up in Marvelville. But what they experience a little bit with my five horses on our farm bears little resemblance to growing up on a dairy farm. My kids are "countrified city kids"; that might be the best way to describe them.

Farm life was healthy and invigourating for the simple reason that there was much more opportunity for work and play. You have to be physically involved on a farm, whether as a parent or a child. Reality and priorities come early in a farm childhood. There's no question of putting off milking until tomorrow, or postponing harvest or seeding because your favourite TV shows are on. My brothers and sisters and I all worked on the farm with Mom and Dad. That meant chores and special responsibilities before and after school.

I was driving a tractor at age seven, which I think explains my love for tinkering with cars and machinery. And I was milking cows at age ten, which also probably explains my love of animals. It's significant that Dad let me drive the tractor three years before he let me milk a cow. He always said we should stay away from the livestock until we were mature. That kind of logic may seem strange for a city person but on the farm it makes a lot of sense.

One of the rewards of hard work on the farm is that when the work is done, you have the whole outdoors at your beck and call to play in. And play we did.

Every winter, Uncle Ray had a natural rink on a large pond right behind his house. That's where all of the Robinsons started skating. When I was four years old, Dad got me my first pair of skates and my eyes must have been as round as saucers when he first laced them up for me.

I didn't even need the skates for Lesson One. Dad took a chair out onto the pond, sat me in it, and pushed me all over the place while I howled with glee. Lesson Two saw me finally on my feet, pushing that chair everywhere while my feet got used to skates and my body got used to a new kind of balance. Lesson Three began the day the chair disappeared and I've been skating ever since.

Most of the skating I did in the early years was not on man-made rinks, but on ponds and creeks. We'd get onto the creeks and skate for miles and miles. These little creeks snaked among the farms and townships and you could skate along non-stop for a couple of hours . . .

That is also where I discovered what cold and wet could really be. Back in those days, we meant something else when we called someone a "fluid skater." I got my share of soakers creek skating, after going through the ice in certain places. But, like my brothers and sisters and cousins, I eventually learned where the springs were. We'd skate for a mile or so, realize there was a spring coming up around the corner, climb up on the bank and walk around, and resume skating when we were past that point.

I'd skate for miles and hours as a kid, the farm version of power skating. There were no DayGlo orange road pylons or "instructors" for us. We became natural skaters because skating was a natural way of covering distance in the wintertime, like walking would be during the summer. When you didn't have to think about your skating any more, you were a good skater.

But even then, my mother says, I was more enthusiastic about skating and hockey than my brother and sisters. Whenever the work was done or I'd come home from school, I'd strap on a pair of skates and hit the ice.

My first real hockey rink was a local rink down behind the schoolhouse in Marvelville. A couple of families with other hockey-mad young boys were nearby: the VanDongens were of Dutch ancestry and lived on top of the hill; the Martels were French-Canadian and resided just down the road, near the school. We were the rink-making committee.

The group of us would anxiously await the first snowfall so that we could go out and "start" our rink. As soon as it got cold enough, we'd be out tamping down the snow. First, we'd wet it down with a hose and then the guys would trudge back and forth, packing it down. After that, another guy would be hosing it down again to get the base down. Then we'd usually spend all night watering the rink.

We'd get the key for the school from the local General Store and we'd sit in there and have hot chocolate and talk, or sleep if the next day was a school day. One guy would go outside and flood for an hour and we'd do it in shifts right through the night. If it was a real cold night, by morning we'd have a real good sheet of ice. And then, of course, all the locals would show up.

That was Murphy's Law, as it applies to outdoor rinks. It states: Everybody else will show up and start skating on the rink five minutes after you've spent all night watering it, or clause B of Murphy's Law on outdoor rinks: everybody else will show up five minutes after you and three of your friends have just finished scraping off a foot of snow.

It was amazing how good their timing was.

We didn't really care though. We just wanted to play hockey. We played hockey all winter and when spring brought the thaw, we'd all be out looking for all the pucks we'd lost in the snowbanks alongside the boards during the winter. Everybody had their initials carved on their pucks to make for easy identification.

The biggest disaster that could befall us in those days was an unseasonal thaw. We wanted the cold weather to last as long as possible because we depended on it to play hockey. This may seem an alien concept for kids who've grown up in arenas, but we didn't have that luxury. It was outdoor rinks, or nothing.

When the weather warmed, or before it got cold enough to flood our own rink, we'd play ball hockey on the road, just like city kids. Or, very much unlike the city kids, Brian and I would also play in the barn as soon as the hay got down to where we had room. The barn being a constricted space, we'd play Showdown. Or One on One. You'd get back 20 feet with a rubber ball . . . one guy the goaltender and the other guy taking shots. You'd score 10 or 20 goals and then switch around. We played a lot of barn hockey.

The operative word is play . . . as opposed to the work ethic that they push so hard in kids' hockey today. Adults had no place in our games. They were kids only, until I joined a real team, that is.

That happened when I was about eight years old. Until then, I'd never played any organized sport. I didn't even know what it was to play left wing, right wing, or whatever. When we kids got together, if there were six guys up, we'd play three aside; if there were ten guys it would be five aside. Our game was a scramble, everybody after the puck. You'd never hear one kid yell at another: "*PLAY YOUR POSITION!*" In those days, your position was wherever the puck happened to be.

Today I see well-meaning adults trying to show five-and six-year-old mites their "position" before they can even skate or hold a hockey stick. I see seven-and eight-year-olds spend most of their ice-time in rigidly controlled practices, repeating endless nonsensical patterns around those orange pylons. I see all of these "very serious" little boys going about the business of learning the "very serious" game of ice hockey, yelled at by coach and parent alike because they zigged when they should have zagged in their exercise. They also have rigidly controlled age classifications; the result often is that brother two or three years apart in age are usually kept separated during their entire hockey careers.

I remember the great times Brian and I had, and later with Moe, and wonder how minor hockey got so stupid in a hurry. In our day, whole families played together and, in fact, Brian and I would anchor the defence of the Metcalfe Jets Junior team in our teens. Today, that is almost impossible as I found out during the years Jeff played minor hockey. With such an influence on arena hockey, few kids are used to playing outdoors or will bother to play pick-up outdoors anymore.

It is in the big cities and suburbs that you can see the influence of over-coaching at a young age as kids who should be having fun in free-for-all hockey, are heard constantly exhorting their teammates to "pick up your wing" or "stay in your position," even in pick-up games at the park.

In a lot of those same big cities, the huge increase of two-income families means that a lot of parents get home at 6 P.M. or later, either picking up their kids at some after-school activity or from the babysitter.

The kid who would come home in my day, drop off his schoolbooks on the kitchen table, chug-a-lug a glass of milk, and hardly be able to holler out "Bye Ma! I'm goin' down to the rink!" over a mouthful of apple, grabbing stick and skates as he slammed the door behind him, has gone the way of the dinosaur. Between 4 and 6 P.M. or school dismissal and suppertime, hockey rinks were hives of activities with multiple games in progress and the happy whoops and shouts of boys of all sizes heard above the flat smack of wood on wood or body on boards.

Drive by an outdoor rink at the same time today, and a few listless kids might be skating around in solitary little groups.

If those factors aren't enough, municipal labour disputes affect outdoor hockey for kids too. Disagreements between municipal administrations and their blue-collar workers have played a large role in a decrease of quality outdoor facilities. These disputes often have led to the latter doing a terrible job of maintaining outdoor rinks during the winter. "Want us to work late at night watering the rink? That's double overtime boss!"

The moment those magic words "double time" ring out, the municipal government that was just elected on a promise to keep expenses down, decides that outdoor rinks are no longer a priority.

So even if today's kids are as hardy as we were and want to play outdoors, far from adult supervision, they'll have a hard time finding rinks that are properly maintained. The paradox was that "our adults" gave us kids much more credit for common sense and a whole lot less supervision, and we did not prove them wrong. Nobody worried about how much water we might use making our rink, or that kids had the run of the schoolhouse overnight while we were flooding the rink. For us, going to school was fun. Making the rink was fun. Playing unsupervised hockey was fun.

That was the advantage of growing up in a so-called "backward" rural area. Farm duties taught us to be serious beyond our years. Our parents, neighbours, friends, and teachers trusted us. That was how we could get the run of the schoolhouse overnight to flood the rink.

Another major reason was the trust shown us by two people who played important in my formative years; Flora Fader and Graham Marcellus.

I am one of a dwindling number of Canadians who can proudly say they began school in a one-room schoolhouse. These rural institutions have since gone the way of the dodo, and in many ways, it's a shame.

Flora Fader taught me the basics of the three Rs (reading, 'riting, and 'rithmetic) in grades one through three at Marvelville school. She was a patient and loving teacher and was loved by her students.

After that, Graham Marcellus took over. He was a man who made each class different and interesting and who always had time to spare for his students.

When the time came to go to high school, off I went to Osgoode Township High, a regional secondary school with about 300 students. A disappointment greeted a sports-mad Larry Robinson upon his arrival: Osgoode High had no gym! What a crisis! By my junior year that was remedied and we were all so grateful we went out and won the Ontario high school basketball title to celebrate.

However, football was the "in" sport at Osgoode and what a team we had! I played corner linebacker and tight end (practically all of us were two-way players) on a team that must have set some sort of record for Canadian high school football. In my senior year, Osgoode High never surrendered as much as a single point during the season. There is an asterisk: we beat Ashbury College school 27–7 that year but it was an exhibition game. We went undefeated, untied, unscored upon; people in the Valley still talk about that team.

Osgoode couldn't do as well in track and field, although we showed well. Here our small enrolment hurt us; other schools could afford to hire competent and experienced track coaches, we couldn't, and I essentially had to teach myself the events I competed in: the high jump, triple jump, shot put, and discus throw. What we didn't have in facilities or training techniques we always made up for in close team ties, enthusiasm, and a willingness to work. I'll never forget Osgoode High. It was a great character builder.

But I'm getting ahead of myself a bit. My first hockey was played with kids of all ages and it was the most natural thing for me. That changed when I began organized hockey. First of all, Marvelville really wasn't even a town. Basically it was just the general store. The population of Marvelville was 2; the couple who ran the local store-general store and the post office. When Brian was 12 and I was 8, we went up to Russell and joined the league sponsored by the Lion's Club. Service clubs – Kiwanis, Rotary, Optimists, and many, many others – are the lifeblood of amateur sport all over North America, especially in non-urban centres. A major factor in my development as an athlete was my home life. My parents believed a good word was worth 10,000 technical explanations. They never criticized; they never pushed their children. In their matter-of-fact way, they accepted the fact that Brian, Moe, and myself were sports-mad and did all they could to help.

I mentioned growing up on a farm and priorities. Now that we were playing organized hockey, there were scheduled practices and games and Dad gently readjusted our responsibilities. This meant he often was left alone with chores; to cover for his sons who were in Russell playing or practising, while Mom had to put down whatever she was doing to drive us over. But they never complained; in fact, they went out of their way to show their pride in our accomplishments. I don't think I've ever told my parents this but my accomplishments have always been their accomplishments; I could never have done this without them.

That first year, the Russell league was the equivalent of a suburban house league. Boys came from all over the area to play Saturday morning games at the Kinnaird Arena, named after a great man, a country doctor named Francis Kinnaird. One of the most giving persons I've ever had the privilege to meet, he was the typical country doctor, up at all hours to travel remote backroads in the dead of night, dispensing medicine, care, and good cheer. And when boys were stuck and couldn't get to hockey games, it was Dr. Kinnaird who arrived at their doorstep with mock impatience: "Come on, young man. Your game is waiting."

The first real organized minor hockey I was involved with was the peewee Russell Lions, starting when I was 9 and right up to age 12.

We wore Chicago Black Hawks uniforms which suited me in more ways than one because I was a big Bobby Hull fan. Mom recently showed me a picture of me at age seven or eight – and I was wearing a Montreal Canadiens uniform. I can't remember the sweater or ever cheering for them because they won all the time. I always liked to cheer for the underdog.

Carson McVey and I played together in peewee. We were about the same age . . . and were considered good players so we were often invited to play with bigger boys. That really helped both of us improve. Carson was one of the first ones to go and play in Ottawa. He ended up playing for a Minor Bantam team there; they got full uniforms and we were really envious because in Russell we got our socks and sweaters given to us and that was it.

That hint of poverty, and our rural roots, proved to be the only motivation the Russell Lions would ever need. We'd play exhibition games against teams "with all of the equipment" and were glad to beat them handily. We always had a really good team and nothing got us up more than watching a fully-equipped team skate out against us.

As I grew up, this "Poor Boy, Rich Boy" thing became more pronounced. Whenever we went into a tournament, the opposition usually had a good laugh at us: "Where are you from? Ah, yer the Russell Lions Club. The Farm Boys. Arentcha supposed to be home milkin' tha cows or sumptin?" Yuk yuk yuk.

Us big, hick, farm boys were taken as everybody's patsies. We would find ourselves competing in the A or B Division with everything stacked so the local team would win. Unfortunately for the home team, we rarely co-operated. The Russell Lions won a lot of tournaments. In my last year as a Peewee, we won six tournaments out of eight entered. We won 26 games in a row at one point and I think we might have lost maybe five games all year. Strangely enough, there was little emphasis put on winning, for us anyway. We were just a group of kids from the country around Russell getting together to have fun and all the coaches knew it.

The Russell Lions weren't overly humble or too competitive but we loved to stick it to the big city boys from Cornwall, Kingston, and Ottawa. The scenario was a familiar one to us.

I'll never forget one tournament in Cornwall. In our very first game, we were scheduled against Montreal Rosemont, a powerhouse from the east-end of that city. In today's system, based on population and the number of players available to an organization, Rosemont would be classified Peewee AAA and we'd be Peewee C and wouldn't get within four or five categories of each other.

But here we were in Cornwall playing Rosemont in our first game. We beat them 2–1. In game two, we faced Cornwall and the arena was packed with 1,000 or so locals screaming for their kids. I'd never seen so many people in one place before.

No matter, we beat them 3–1 and advanced to the finals against a team from the small Quebec town of Thurso, just across the border from Ottawa.

This Thurso team apparently had this blond kid who was unstoppable, but we'd never heard of him so we weren't fazed in the least. We showed it by going out and taking a 1–0 lead in the first minute of play.

This kid, Guy Damien Lafleur, scored the next five goals of the game and Thurso handled us easily. All I really remember of him was a slapshot he scored on from centre ice. Now that impressed this 12-year-old; especially when it was another 12-year-old who did it. The Lafleur kid was someone with a future. Everybody said so and he looked like he knew it too.

On the other hand, I loved the game so much I never really noticed how good or bad I was. Our team was good; our record proved that. But we had a lot of good players. I've already mentioned Carson McVey; and we also had Donny Honey who scored a lot of goals, a Gretzky type who could really handle the puck and shoot. He was from Russell. He was a really good hockey player and everybody expected him to go far. Then there was Barry Graham, a smallish defenceman with a booming slapshot. He ended up playing with the Ottawa 67s for a couple of years.

The thing that held it all together was our coach, Bill Linegar. He had the unique ability to make us work hard and come together as a team, without ever putting undue pressure on any individual. All of the Russell Lions became proficient two-way players under the teaching of Bill "Back check" Linegar. Nobody played a one-way game with Bill. Even in the summertime, a group of us could be hanging around shooting the breeze and all it would take to have us all rolling on the floor would be some joker imitating Bill's famous "back check, back check, back check!" that boomed out at us during all of our games.

Here imitation was the sincerest form of flattery and the utmost respect; his players loved Bill Linegar and it was a huge shock to me ten years later when he died in a car accident. He, like Dr. Kinnaird, was a very popular man in the Russell area.

One question I get asked a lot, especially by parents of hockey-playing youngsters is: When did I, as a young boy, start realizing that I had something special in hockey?

The answer is very simple. I never really did.

I played many sports well because I enjoyed them. It was in my competitive nature to always want to do better than the next guy. Having read that, you'd assume that this competitive streak would cause me to pay special attention to my progress up the sports ladder. I really didn't. Looking back now I figure it was because love of competition had my total concentration; I loved playing sports so much, and competing against other top athletes, that I never had time to really take stock, or think about the consequences of continued improvement. This single-track focus just meant that I was happy.

I firmly believe that this world is populated by two main groups of people: doers and watchers, and their behaviour patterns are determined at an early age. Athletes who start watching themselves, or pay too much attention to personal results will soon find themselves on the sidelines, watching others. Even to this day, I have trouble watching a game on television or in the stands. If you can be playing, why watch? I don't know if that attitude will change once I've retired.

Another question then arises about my abilities as a boy player: If I didn't pay particular notice to my athletic prowess, did other people? Did some super talent scout or some adult come along at one time and proclaim: "Kid, you're pretty special. You may have a shot at the Big Time."

Carson McVey and I often played with the bigger boys and that was a sign that we were progressing well ahead of our group. But we were also physically bigger than the boys our age and that was a factor too, so we didn't think about it much.

In retrospect, I have to admit it must have happened, but I have no recollection of a specific incident or it ever happening that way. I must have heard this kind of talk at times because I won quite a few trophies when I was young. But I never thought or told anyone that I was going to be a hockey player, or football player, or whatever. I was never one of those kids who dreamed of being a player . . . I was having too much fun doing what I was doing. With Carson McVey, Donny Honey, and Barry Graham as teammates and Bill Linegar as coach, it was easy to spread the credit around for team successes.

That is a recurring theme with me. I strongly believe that the very successful athlete is so because he or she is one-track minded, or single-minded. This kind of athlete rarely attempts to think about his or her athletic talent, let alone try to analyze or dissect it. This causes all sorts of misunderstandings, for example, with media.

Their way of thinking, or mind-set, is different. Reporters who have to deliver the sports world to their readers in story-length chunks, see everything in terms of drama, "the thrill of victory, the agony of defeat."

Why? Because, frankly, it is convenient. It allows them to deliver the news in precisely-timed, bite-sized chunks. So and so won. So and so lost. And now, the highlights . . . . Athletes are expected to deliver short bite-sized quotes to punctuate the action footage.

It also reflects on how journalists learned their craft. Drama, tragedy . . . these are the bases of the real news story. A dramatic lead paragraph is going to make you want to read on. A tragic picture on page one will get more people to buy newspapers than not.

Although professional players become accustomed to playing the media game, that's all it is: a game. We don't see it as reality, this post-game thrusting of microphones in our faces as we stand there naked and dripping. We learn to answer basic "support-the-replay-image" questions with short, trite statements.

When I broke my leg, Montreal's hockey press corps was genuinely concerned. Many of them took the time to tell me so.

However, somewhere in their group sub-conscious, they must have been a little happy because my "tragedy" represented "good copy." They were already anticipating their "near tragedy" articles about the "Big Bird pondering shattered leg and possible end of career." It was, no pun intended, a break from the hockey season routine.

I don't and can't think like that. Neither do any of the athletes I've played with or against.

Newspaper writers, and to a lesser extent the electronic press people, are taught to think negative thoughts. What if he won't come back? What if the number one draft choice doesn't pan out and the general manager has to resign? What if Player X has lost a step and must be traded?

Otherwise what would they write about? The game? Nearly everybody has seen it on television anyway, especially these days when at least half of our games are on TV in Montreal. What could the print people add that the public hasn't already seen live and on six different kinds of replay?

The athlete's mind-set is fixed on the here and now. The day-to-day and the everyday. The game that must be played. The next shift. The opponent. The score. The standings. Positive thoughts foster a team consciousness and that team consciousness fosters victory. Victory leads to success. If you understand these fundamental differences, you understand why athlete and reporter often will not mesh. Neither resents the other, recognizing that they both have a job to do. There is genuine mutual respect.

But their terms of reference are very different. I think that this helps explain why a lot of the very best hockey players, Maurice Richard, Gordie Howe, Bobby Hull, Frank Mahovlich, Bobby Orr, and Wayne Gretzky were considered bad or boring interviews. They did things naturally and were not ever going to be persuaded to waste a whole lot of time trying to analyze their talent. Or trying to dramatize it, either.

They really didn't know what to say about themselves because their hockey abilities to them were just as natural as eating, sleeping, and going to the bathroom. They were happy that they scored three goals; they were glad that this performance helped their team win; they liked the fact that the season was going well because this was what they were paid for. But for the life of them they couldn't begin to explain the processes that led to their talent and refused to situate this in the dramatic scenario that the writers sought.

As kids, we had our own dramatic scenarios. We'd often

dream out loud and even during competition. You might be Bobby Orr carrying the puck down the ice or Bobby Hull winding up for a slapshot. I think we've all done that. But that was the extent of dramatizing for me. I played football; I was in track and field; I played basketball; I did everything.

I must have been a good hockey player when I was young and must have known it to some extent because at age 14, I was playing Tier Two Junior for the Metcalfe Jets, which meant I had gone from Peewee to Bantam and then on to Junior B in about 18 months.

We played in the St. Lawrence Junior B League in the Ottawa Valley. Metcalfe, Maxville, Prescott, and Cardinal were the teams. I played on a line with Barry Graham and Allan Duncan. Erwin Duncan, a cousin of mine, was coaching at the time. He and his twin brother Ed had achieved fame down our way for their hockey feats with the renowned Inkerman Rockets of junior hockey years before.

Erwin Duncan, like Bill Linegar, believed in the serious or work ethic side of hockey. He knew the game and was very tough on us. I got the impression that he was preparing us in case any of us advanced beyond Junior B. I played for Metcalfe for two seasons, all the while trying to catch on with other teams.

When I was 16 going on 17, I wangled a tryout with the Ottawa 67s of the OHA. I figured I might have a good chance, seeing that this was a new franchise in the Ontario Hockey Association. I lasted a few practices and was sent down to practise with their Junior B team instead. "Enough of this," I said to myself, "I've just played two years of Junior B. I want Junior A."

I then called and asked for a tryout with the Junior A team in Cornwall. When I got there, the scourge of the '60s reared its ugly head; a couple of team officials decided my hair was way too long and took me into a room and cut it. I was almost bald when I emerged and I was doing a slow burn. The more I thought about it, the hotter I became and I eventually just walked away from Cornwall, vowing never to play for those idiots.

Back I went to Ottawa. I practised with the team for a couple of days and was invited to an exhibition game, guess where? They had scheduled an exhibition game down in Cornwall. However, that day turned out to be one of those miserable fall days eastern Ontario is famous for — driving winds and frozen rain making driving treacherous — and my Dad and I arrived in Cornwall a few minutes late. The coach was angry and had a few words for me: "You aren't playing, kid!"

I ended up watching the game in the stands with my Dad. During the game, a gentleman named Dan Dexter came over to where we were sitting.

"Larry, I know who you are and I'd like you to come play for me in Brockville." Dexter was coach of the Brockville Braves of the Central Ontario Junior A Hockey League and the team was managed by Eric Colville.

Later that September, at the club's training camp in Athens, Ontario, Dexter took me aside and said: "You're built like a defenceman."

I'd spent most of my career playing forward and loved playing centre. But if Dan Dexter said I looked more like a defenceman so a defenceman Larry Robinson would be. I ended up making the Brockville Braves and playing there for two seasons.

It was slow going at first, and I was terrible on the blue line. I had all the habits of a forward and got caught up ice a lot. I felt like a traffic cop out there, directing opposition forwards around me in all directions while I looked on helplessly. Throughout these travails, one thing remained constant; Dan Dexter's faith in me. He gave me lots of ice time and worked me very hard in practice. A former defenceman himself, he had a lot to teach and the foremost lesson was to "forget the puck, start playing the man."

Forwards usually have eyes only for two things, the puck and the opposition goalie. A forward moved back on defence has to improve his eyes first, learn to see more of the ice surface and the game, before he can ever improve any other part of his game enough to cut it on defence. Once he's improved his vision, he can then begin to learn the different ways to move the puck out of his zone without danger, and how to judge the impending loss of possession by his teammates.

That done, a good defenceman will often find his feet skating backwards and into a defensive position almost before his eyes and mind have told him that his team had lost the puck and it's time to retreat and defend. Once a player reached this point, playing defence became fun.

In my first year at Brockville, we lost in the playoffs and the Hull Olympiques went on to represent our league in the Eastern Canada championships against the Sorel Black Hawks. At that time, league champions were allowed to reinforce themselves for provincial and national championship tournaments by adding two or three players from teams that had been ousted from the league playoffs.

Hull selected me and I played for them as a forward. You never lose your touch, I guess, and even after a year of playing defence I was able to score a goal, seven seconds into my first shift.

We had a lot less luck as a team because Sorel was a powerhouse that featured the late, great Michel Briere, the Pittsburgh Penguins centre who died after a car crash after only a year in the NHL; Dave Schultz (yeah, *THAT* Dave Schultz); Richie Leduc, who would star in the World Hockey Association and also play a bit in the NHL with Boston and Quebec; and Bill Hogaboam, who would play for Atlanta, Detroit, and Minnesota. They blew us out.

In my final year with Brockville, we lost a rollercoaster seven-game final series by the M & W Rangers and they picked me and two other teammates to play with them against the P.E.I. Islanders. Again we lost, but this time it worked to my advantage.

I was seen by Barry Fraser and Punch Sherer and invited to the training camp of the Kitchener Rangers that coming fall. I was heading for the OHA, only a step away from a career in professional hockey.

And that would be some accomplishment for a boy from Marvelville. Back to Eddie MacCabe, to finish off the chapter that he started.

"So here you are . . . a big, open-faced kid, soft-spoken, a ton of ability, proud of his farm upbringing . . . a bona fide Canadian Captain Marvel(ville).

"Now . . . you won't find Marvelville on your road map . . . or maybe on any map. It's not in the Canadian Almanac, but it does get a mention in the Railroad Guide.

"But even without that, Marvelville is on the map now. Larry saw to that."

But before I could move to the OHA, and then on to the NHL to put Marvelville on the map, my life would change dramatically.

FIVE

Jeannette

T HE WONDERFUL thing about adolescence is that you can take it slow, postpone becoming an adult, or speed up the process and grow up ahead of your peers.

In my hockey career, I've met people who fit into both groups; in fact, some guys were so good at taking it slow they were still teenagers well into their 30s.

I didn't have that luxury, although I would like to think that I've kept a youthful outlook on life.

One thing happened to me when I was 17 to speed up the maturation process. That "thing" was meeting Jeannette Lamirande when a friend and I crashed a party in Marvelville. I was home for the summer after my first season in Brockville and it was one of those idyllic times; I worked a bit at a summer job, played a lot of ball, and "hung out" with a few friends.

There was a family that lived just outside Ottawa in Alta Vista called the Godwins. I think I was 12 years old before I found out that they weren't related to us. I always thought they were cousins or something like that. My Mom and Dad used to raise chickens on the farm and sell eggs in the Ottawa area. Anyway, this is how they met the Godwins and they struck up a lasting friendship. Their kids were basically the same age as the Robinson kids so I grew up playing with their two sons, Howie and Teddy. (Also among their customers in the suburb of Vanier was a Lebanese-Canadian family, the Ankas, who had a son called Paul who was about eight or nine.)

Teddy and I were close and spent a lot of time at each other's homes throughout my childhood and especially during my adolescence. In fact, the first time I ever got drunk in my life was with Teddy—we guzzled copious amounts of lemon gin and I was so sick I still can't face that drink to this day.

As I mentioned elsewhere, I also grew up with the Van-Dongen boys in Marvelville and I remember in late 1968 one of them telling me that a new family had moved into a farm not far from where we lived. They were the Lamirandes.

Gerald Lamirande was a former Royal Canadian Air Force corporal who had always wanted to move to the country after he retired and that's what he did. The Lamirandes rented an older farm just down the road and settled in: the parents and seven kids—six girls and one boy.

He wasn't even intending to be a gentleman farmer, like many city folks who moved out our way. He just wanted to live out in the country where he could have a garden to putter around in. Unlike most other families in the military, the Lamirandes had been stationed in one place for years, Uplands Air Force Base in Ottawa. The expense of moving such a large family from base to base would have been too great, so the RCAF was glad to leave them at Uplands. But after 16 years there, Mr. Lamirande was looking for a quiet place in the country.

One night in late spring, Teddy and I had been out for a few laughs and were on our way home when we saw the lights on at the Lamirandes and heard the unmistakeable sounds of a party. I'd been away playing hockey all winter and I didn't know them; neither did Teddy.

"Peter VanDongen told me the Lamirandes are having some sort of party." I said.

"Who are they?"

"Apparently the old man was in the armed forces and they moved in a little while ago."

"So what's the big deal?" Teddy was always looking for the bottom line.

"They have six girls and I heard they're cute."

"Wanna crash the party?" Teddy had heard the magic words.

"You're on!"

As bold as brass, we drove up to the Lamirandes and knocked on the door. A girl answered it and with a quick "I'm Larry", "I'm Teddy" we blew right in. On this spring night, Larry Clark Robinson was the essence of 1960s cool. I had on this godawful gawky-looking sweater that an old girlfriend of mine had made and which was the in-thing then. It wasn't tie-dyed, but could have been for all the different colours and motifs that ran riot across it. Jeannette remembers it as some sort of paisley abomination; I vaguely recall the subtle blending of colours like purple, yellow, orange, green, and red.

I was making a subconscious fashion statement. Something along the lines of "he who dares to wear this shirt should be buried alive in it." On the 1960s fashion hit parade, it was number two to a pale blue Nehru jacket.

JEANNETTE'S STORY, OR A BRIEF INTERLUDE WHEN "THE AWFUL TRUTH" REARS ITS "UGLY HEAD"

I saw this shirt walk in on the body of this guy who was so tall I started looking for a stepladder. You couldn't miss that combination; you saw them (Larry and the shirt) coming from far off. Beyond that, I wasn't impressed; in fact I was angry that he and his friend had crashed our party. That was decidedly uncool.

Then somebody told me he was a good hockey player and that cinched it; my response was somewhere between ho and hum. I spent the rest of that party studiously ignoring him while he did what all uncool guys do at parties like that. He hung around in a corner with one of the VanDongen boys, Teddy Godwin, and my brother, Gerry. Poor Gerry Jr. Every-time some guy wanted to go out with one of the Lamirande sisters, he'd start hanging around Gerry first until the girl agreed to go out with him. Then Gerry would be minus a friend.

And that was the case with Larry. I'm sister number four; there are two younger than me, and originally Larry was interested in my younger sister, Pauline.

WE RETURN TO THE ORIGINAL NARRATIVE

I wasn't even trying to go out with my wife at the time; I wanted to take out her sister Pauline who was 15. Jeannette had a boyfriend, this guy from Ottawa who played in a band and she worked so she was very much the big city girl.

I never did go out with Pauline but Jeannette and an older sister, Nicole, started going to my games in my second season in Brockville. I introduced Nicole to a teammate, a New-foundlander named Jimmy Duhart, and they started going steady. They eventually got married and have a son and a daughter, like we do.

THE OPPOSITE, BUT EQUAL VIEWPOINT

A hockey player would not interest me back then. I hated hockey. Maybe I should say I *HATED* hockey.

My Dad was a big hockey fan. Toronto Maple Leafs were his team, and our livingroom was Riot Central on Wednesday nights when hockey was on television and my sisters and I wanted to watch a movie. Very few people could afford two TVs back then, not us for sure, so it was the Gerrys senior and junior against the women in the family.

Therefore it definitely was no big deal that Gerry had a new friend who played for the Brockville Braves. On top of that, I'd left school after Grade ten and I was working in Ottawa every day so there were few opportunities and no inclination to meet the guys around where I lived.

But it happened anyway. I broke up with my Ottawa boy-friend and one Friday night, Gerry asked me to tag along to a game so I started going to watch Larry play. Here I was at home on a Friday without a date. Friday nights are sacred to a teenage girl–staying home without a date is an admission that you have resigned from the human race.

Things just seemed to take off from there and it wasn't long before Larry and I were going steady. He definitely got me on the rebound, which for a defenceman probably makes all the sense in the world. It became a real family affair when Larry's teammate, Jimmy Duhart, asked if I had another sister who was shorter; together Larry and Jimmy resembled Mutt and Jeff. That's when I began bringing my older sister, Nicole, to games. Jimmy and Nicole are an old married couple now.

AND BACK, ONCE MORE, TO THE ORIGINAL NARRATIVE

It did not take long for Jeannette to change her mind about hockey and we were going steady. Steady actually might not be the word for it.

One day in the late winter or early spring the two of us had an important, if short, conversation.

She: "Oops!"

He: "Oops?"

She: "Oops!!"

Farm folk take life as it comes and tend to accept momentous news of this sort a little more stolidly than their city neighbours. Maybe it's all that animal husbandry on the farm. Still, "low key parent reaction" was not uppermost on the minds of two teenagers. There was the Big Problem, of course: How to tell Mom and Dad Robinson and (soon-to-be) Mom and Dad in-law Lamirande.

I wasn't overly thrilled with having to break this kind of news but that wasn't the major hurdle. Logistics was. The Robinsons had five children and I was number three. Our home, rural as it was, had turned into Action Central in those years and it seemed my parents were always rushing off here and there, driving one of us to some event or another.

"Come on, think Larry. How are you gonna let 'em know?" I plunged into my vast reservoir of logic and hit on the sure-fire way to break the news that Jeannette was pregnant and we had to get married.

I wrote a note and left it on the mirror in the bathroom; sooner or later everybody has to go to the bathroom. That's how Mom found out. To this day, my son Jeffery takes forever in the bathroom. I wonder if these two events are related.

The original plan had been to get married the following summer, a real June wedding after my year in the OHA. Instead, it was the Robinson family of three—Mom age 18, Dad age 19, and infant son Jeffery—who packed up their belongings and headed for the Kitchener Rangers training camp that September.

Here it was, the first time I'd ever been away from home and I was taking a wife and a baby with me.

It was time for a serious study of my short-term career prospects.

At the time Teddy Godwin was working for a printing company near Ottawa and convinced me that this industry represented a good career opportunity, especially since I was going to have a single shot at making a serious career in pro hockey. I had one year to prove myself in the Ontario Hockey Association; if I couldn't cut it with Kitchener, there were two chances of getting drafted the following summer—slim and none.

In those days, very few junior hockey players went to school; the practice and travel schedule was too brutal and week-long road trips by bus were not conducive to establishing good study habits. Many juniors supplemented their meagre hockey income with jobs usually found by team boosters, jobs that were heavy on manual labour and shift flexibility. Before I left home, I contacted the Rangers, explained my interest in printing and was told that they could line up a job for me at a printing place.

It didn't work out that way. I ended up slinging cases for Kitchener Beverages, the local Pepsi-Cola bottler. I had to pay $150 a month rent, feed myself, my wife, and a baby. At the time I was making $80 a week at Kitchener Beverages—whenever I could get there, because sometimes we'd get back at four in the morning and I wouldn't feel like getting up at eight o'clock and going to work to slug cases. I was also making $60 a week from the Rangers.

That's how I had to support my family all year. Our big supper once a week or so was pork chops with a bottle of wine we probably spent $1.20 on . . . that was our big "outing." We boarded with a Mrs. Vaillant, in a tiny apartment she'd had built on the top floor of her home.

Both Jeannette and I felt deprived of our youth. She'd had a job in Ottawa and the sense of independence that brings. I was used to going out for a beer with the guys after games, socializing. But we were the only married couple on the team, with a baby to care for. We couldn't afford the time or money to spend on the normal things that teenagers do.

JEANNETTE'S STORY

The baby was about three months old when we moved to Kitchener. We lived upstairs in a tiny apartment at Mrs. Vaillant's and it wasn't easy, especially with the baby crying a lot as young infants do.

Mrs. Vaillant was a saint. She lived with her brother and her daughter and was an immense help to a teenager who was growing up very quickly that winter. I didn't have my mother or Larry's mother around to help so Mrs. Vaillant really helped.

Larry would leave on long road trips, up to a week by bus all over southern Ontario and into Quebec because the Montreal Junior Canadiens were part of the league then. That was when I really appreciated living in with a family. I would watch television with them or have supper with them and feel at home and not so alone. Or stranded.

Mrs. Vaillant was a tremendous help the one time Jeffery got very sick. He was about five or six months old when he went through a spate of crying. After about a day of this, and a fever that didn't seem to go away, we took him to hospital where they diagnosed an ear infection and kept him overnight. He got better quickly but I was very grateful for Mrs. Vaillant's support—the first time a mom has to take a baby to hospital is very traumatic.

That year in Kitchener brought Larry and me closer together, closer than we'd been back home. And strangely, I probably saw less of him that year. I've already mentioned the road trips that could last up to a week. However, when the team was home, Larry was away for huge parts of the day. He'd just return from a road trip and then leave early for his job at Pepsi-Cola. After work there could be a practice or a game. If it was a game, he would not be home much before midnight, and then he would be up early again the next day to go to work.

The toughest thing was I wasn't able to get out to the games. There were other "couples" that we were friendly with, Anne and Ted Scharf and Bill and Jenny Barber, but they weren't married then and certainly had no kids. The other girlfriends would attend all the games and strike up their own friendships during the season, so they would always have someone to talk to when the team was away.

If I wanted to ge to a game I had to pay a babysitter and we simply couldn't afford it. Once in a while, Mrs. Vaillant would kick me out on a Saturday night with a firm "go to the game, I'll watch Jeffery" and it was like freedom from slavery. Then Larry and I could go out with everybody after the game and pretend we were a "regular" teenage couple for a while. We couldn't do this very often because we didn't want to impose on Mrs. Vaillant.

It was a long winter.

THE HOCKEY PLAYER RETURNS

On the hockey side, things went very well. As I mentioned before, I had one year of OHA action to make it or break it and I was definitely going to give it my best shot.

Kitchener GM Walter (Punch) Scherer helped a lot; so did the fact that Kitchener had only one veteran defenceman returning, Ralph Hopiavouri, and he underwent surgery on his elbow a couple of weeks before training camp opened. We arrived in Kitchener and were put up at the Riviera Motel, training camp home away from home for the Rangers—pool, air conditioning, TV, phones, as the sign said. Shortly after my arrival, Punch had a little talk with me.

"Young man, we signed you because we like what you did with Brockville," he began. "I know that you belong in this league and that you should have been playing here before now. Whatever the reason for it was, all that should be behind you. You have one year to make it and I know you can do it. We're just going to have to convince you." When I showed up at camp, I discovered that Punch Scherer liked me a lot; he kept mentioning me regularly in the *Kitchener-Waterloo Record* as a "can't miss" prospect.

That was not the normal way of doing things in major junior. Team owners and executives usually undervalued a player's contribution, especially for public consumption, because they didn't want that player to get too comfortable. They also didn't want an outbreak of superstaritis, and the subsequent demand in pay raise that inevitable followed the onset of the disease. Last but not least, there were another 20 or so sensitive egos to consider in the dressingroom.

Right away I could see that this league was faster but I discovered that was no problem. My size and skating ability served me well right from the beginning and I felt comfortable. However, this was the first time I'd ever really faced forwards who were equal to my defensive talent, and in especially large numbers. It seemed that every team in the league had top scoring stars who all eventually would move on to the National Hockey League or the World Hockey Association.

Reviewed 17 years later, with the help of a few yellowing scrapbooks, my year at Kitchener is a blur, with occasional images and incidents coming to sharp focus: my first game, my first game in Ottawa where they hadn't wanted me, games against players who would turn out to be future teammates, and my recollections of specific individuals.

My first game in Ottawa was very special. As hard as it was to get tickets at the Civic Centre, because the 67s were a top team and regularly averaged well above 7,000 fans in the 9,000-seat arena, it seemed half of Marvelville and Metcalfe was at the game that night. I was now Larry Robinson of Metcalfe, because my dad had recently sold the farm and moved there.

There were more than 9,000 in the stands that night when we came to town to face Potvin, Larocque, Wilson, and company and I was tighter than a drum. Ottawa had not thought I was good enough a couple of years before. And everybody was comparing 18-year-old Denis Potvin to Bobby Orr. There wasn't a defenceman in the OHA who couldn't get up for a challenge like that.

Denis was something special, everybody had to admit it.

He was in his third OHA season that year, and would play two more, having started as a regular rearguard with the 67s at age 15. Right from the start they'd run at him, and he'd never backed down, with 83 penalty minutes in his first year, 97 in his sophomore season. By the 1970–71 season, Denis was starting to fill out and it was *HIS* turn to run at other people as his PIM total nudged 200. More importantly, his 20 goals and 58 assists led OHA defencemen and won him a place on the first all-star team. Two years later, he would be a true phenomenon, a man among boys, with 35 goals, 88 assists and 123 points, and 232 PIM.

I didn't win all-star recognition in my year in the OHA but finished with a respectable 12–39–51 and 65 penalty minutes.

So here we were, two local boys lined up with opposite teams in our first OHA encounter. It was a much bigger deal for me because I had much more to prove. Denis had already played a hundred or so OHA games. When the game was over, I had no goals, no assists, and no penalty minutes. Denis had a minor, a major and an assist.

But we won 4–3 and I whistled all the way to Montreal as we bused out of Ottawa.

There are other players and games that emerge from that year. A game at Maple Leaf Gardens in which the Marlies (or was it the Argonauts) hammered us 15–7 sticks out. The Shutt-Gardner-Harris line ran amok that Saturday afternoon, netting five, three and one goals respectively. We were doing all right, tied at four after the first period when the roof caved in. You can't forget games like that one because you can never forget the look on the face of a goalie who's suffered through it. Neither Glen Seperich or Reg Logel would speak to us after the game.

More than anything or anyone, though, I remember Marcel Dionne.

The Black Hawks were a fairly solid team that had struggled at times during that season, although the same could not be said for their tiny captain from Drummondville, Quebec. The year before, he'd led the league in goals (55), assists (77), and points (132). Several quality players had graduated in the off-season so all Dionne did in my season was score 11 more total points (143) in eight fewer games.

We played St. Catharines late in the season in what was, for us, an important game. We were battling the Hamilton Red Wings for sixth spot and would play the Hawks and the Wings four times in the last ten games. In the first meeting, I can brag that I outscored Marcel Dionne. I scored a pair of goals as we trailed 3–2 and felt great when we'd gone ahead 5–4 after two. When the final siren went, however, St. Catharines had won 8–6. Dionne had an amazing 14 shots on net but scored no goals. In his defence, however, I must add that he registered five assists.

We made sixth place anyway, beating the Wings twice and, on the last night of the regular season, we downed the Hawks 7–4 in St. Catharines in a nothing game, on the surface anyway. Billy Barber scored three to finish the season with 47 goals and 57 assists and 104 points, which tied him for the team point lead with Tom Cassidy (42–62–104). We held Dionne to two goals and an assist, a major victory, and were looking forward to the playoffs where we would play the very same Black Hawks. We returned home feeling we'd delivered a major message by taking them out in their own rink.

Four games later, it was summertime in Kitchener as Dionne turned janitor and swept us away. In a scrapbook my wife kept, there's a picture from the *Kitchener-Waterloo Record* that perfectly captures the spirit of that playoff series. Taken in the last game, it shows Chris Meloff, myself, and Glen Seperich looking behind us near our net while Pierre Guite, Dionne, and Paul Shakes of St Catharines are all converging on a puck we can't see just outside the crease.

All Marcel Dionne did to the Kitchener Rangers was score nine goals and assist on nine others, for 18 points in four games. You didn't need Punxsutawney Phil or Wiarton Willie to look for his shadow that season. Marcel Dionne was the groundhog who made spring come early to Kitchener.

A few weeks later, Larry, Jeannette, and Jeffery Robinson were on their way back home. First, to enjoy the luxury of sleeping in for a few mornings while Mrs. Robinson Sr. spoiled her grandson rotten.

And second, to somehow make it through the nervewracking waiting period before the 1971 National Hockey League entry draft of June 10, 1971, at the Queen Elizabeth Hotel in Montreal.

SIX

Fare Thee Well In Nova Scotia

T HERE'S no disgrace in being sent to the minors if there's a purpose to the exercise.

When I was informed in late September, 1971, that I was about to become a Nova Scotia Voyageur, I fully expected it. Claude Ruel had been very clear about the matter when I signed my contract in June:

"A rookie coming out of Junior A has to show us something we didn't even know he had, if he's going to stay up with the big club," he said.

"Otherwise, he'll go to Halifax and play with our developing young guys in the American Hockey League."

In simple terms, I was being sent to the Voyageurs to go about the business of learning my business – how to become a professional hockey player. I accepted this and, strangely, even looked forward to it. I was thankful for the chance of proving myself in the AHL, much as I had done in the OHA at Kitchener. I couldn't complain about the people running the show, either. Al MacNeil, who'd been chased out of Montreal by an emotional outburst from Henri Richard, was coach and general-manager of the Voyageurs. A former NHL defenceman, he was recognized as a superior teacher and a quality individual behind the bench.

I called Jeannette back in Metcalfe after I got the word.

"It's U-haul time. We're heading east." The boy was going to learn to be a man.

In retrospect, I might have accepted the Halifax assignment too readily or even too lightly at the beginning.

I wasn't there a week when MacNeil suggested we talk, which meant mostly he talked: "How tall are you Larry?"

"Six-foot three, and a bit."

"What do you weigh?"

"About 195."

"When are you going to play like it?"

The message was clear; Montreal Canadiens had a third club for those draft choices who thought Halifax was a country club, where they could leisurely await recall to the Big Club. That was Muskegon of the International League. Muskegon was an industrial centre of some 46,000 souls, off Lake Michigan. It was where former pro prospects went to bury their careers.

"Unless you're going to be more aggressive, play tougher, we'll have to send you to Muskegon."

Montreal and Nova Scotia were not looking for a goon. Aggressive hockey didn't mean management wanted me to start fights; far from it. MacNeil made that point while first praising my offensive ability.

"First you play physical and you get more respect. That will force them to back off you a little bit. You'll get more room out there. And then your offensive game will open up."

Had MacNeil or anyone else said "Go out and beat up that guy," the answer would have been no. I wouldn't have done it. I'd never been an instigator. But if I was on the ice and one of our guys was in trouble, that was different. Today, some 17 years later, I still don't believe in premeditated hockey brawling.

In my last year at Brockville and my season at Kitchener, I'd accumulated 74 and 65 minutes in penalties, respectively. Broken down, there were probably four or five fighting majors, and a variety of minor penalties that defencemen take in the normal course of the season. (My highest-ever total in the NHL has been 76 minutes, in a full 80 games in 1974–75.) I'd played tough during those two seasons, without coaches ever complaining about my aggressiveness or desire. I always felt you could do both; play aggressively and still have low penalty-minute totals.

Like the NHL, the AHL in the early 1970s had toughened up, especially in Cincinnati, Richmond and Boston. Former NHL bad guy Reggie Fleming was a staple in Cincy, along with another bad apple called Keke Mortson and a genuine wild man in Rick Dudley. They held up their end in fight after fight. The Boston Braves had their share of beef, too, with players like Richie Leduc and Terry O'Reilly leading the way.

The Braves, of course, were the Bruins farm team, even though they were outdrawing the parent club at the Garden that year; the Cincinnati Swords belonged to Buffalo. Another tough club was Richmond Robins, the Philadelphia Flyers affiliate. As the Quebec Aces the season before, they had waged the Battle of Quebec with the then-Montreal Voyageurs. The animosity would linger on, even if the clubs had left Quebec for Virginia and Nova Scotia. Playing in Virginia wasn't going to soften up Dave Schultz, their hard-rock winger who had set a league record with 382 penalty minutes the year before in Quebec.

It didn't take long to realize that players on these three teams were trying to emulate their brawling big brothers in the NHL. But all four clubs were also at or near the top of the standings in their divisions because they had a lot of hockey talent as well.

Cincinnati had up and comers like Dudley, Butch Deadmarsh, Craig Ramsay, Terry Ball, and John Gould in their lineup. The Robins had future Flyers Schultz, Bill Clement, Bill Brossart, and Bob Taylor in theirs. The Braves looked like they were going to run away with the East Division early in the season on the strength of such talent as goalie Dan Bouchard, O'Reilly, Leduc, Fred O'Donnell, Gary Peters, Nick Beverley, Doug Roberts, Neil Murphy, Don Tannahill, and Ron Boehm.

Although we started slowly, the Voyageurs were no slouches. Up front we had Murray Wilson, Yvon Lambert, Chuck Arnason, Randy Rota, Germain Gagnon, Rey Comeau, Joe Hardy, Tony Featherstone, Chuck Lefley, and Larry Pleau (for parts of the season until they went up) and Ron

Busniuk. On defence there was Kerry Ketter, Mike Poirier, Bob Murray, Mike Laughton, Murray Anderson, myself, and Bob Murdoch. In nets were veterans Michel Plasse and Wayne Thomas. Michel Deguise, who'd been Guy Lafleur's goalie with the Memorial Cup champion Quebec Remparts, was our third goalie, on the outside looking in when the AHL season got under way.

I'd seen my share of fighting in junior hockey, but what went on in the American Hockey League seemed to be more systematic and premeditated. A major reason for this was the fact that this was the first league I'd played in where there wasn't an age limit. In junior hockey, we were all expected to move up and out by age 20.

Here, however, we shared ice with a lot of developing young stars who'd just graduated from junior ranks, but also with many much older veterans who were either minor league career professionals or former NHL players on the downside of their careers. Whatever the case, all of us were fighting for real jobs and real money and it made a world of difference.

The rough stuff was there right from the beginning as some teams seemed intent on delivering messages that would last the year.

Just a couple of games into the season, the Cincinnati Swords came visiting. Winger Joe Hardy joined us just before the game and scored two goals. Wayne Thomas was strong in net as we beat them 5–1. The game had long been decided when a couple of brawls erupted halfway through the third. Four genuinely tough guys went at it furiously at the Cincinnati blueline; their Fleming and Dudley, our Lambert and Busniuk. The officials finally got them to the penalty box and play was about to resume when Round Two began.

This was the first time I'd ever seen players destroy a penalty box. The fury of the fighting was such that the glass partition dividing opponents in the penalty area was torn out of place. The official timer and P.A. announcer literally had to dive onto the ice to avoid the war. Once the smoke had cleared, the four were sent to their dressingrooms, luckily on opposite sides of the building, and the game resumed.

However, they left us with a distinct reminder of their festivities.

During the brawl, one of the belligerents was knocked onto the timer's bench and managed to break part of the equipment there. As a result, the arena buzzer was jammed in the "on" position. For the last ten minutes, we found out what if must be like to live in a hive.

The buzzer got on everybody's nerves and may have contributed to another brawl, this time with five seconds left in the game. Keke Mortson got it going with Tony Featherstone, one of the best boxers in the business. I squared off against Ken Murray and Lynn Powis fought with Butch Deadmarsh.

Fighting was pretty much common currency back then; the fans certainly liked it, as they always have, and the media seemed to play it up more than they do today. Later that season, we played a 4–4 tie against the same Swords and Busniuk once again handled Fleming in a second-period fight. This was the same Reggie Fleming who'd brawled his way through the NHL with six teams, earning 1,468 minutes in penalties in 749 games.

By this time Busniuk was 4–0 against Fleming for the season and Cincinnati coach Joe Crozier was steaming after the game. It was hard to figure, the Swords had managed to come back from a 4–1 deficit with three third-period goals to tie us in our own building.

"I'm fed up with bigger teams full of lumberjacks taking advantage of my small hockey club," he ranted.

"We have 12 first-year pros on our club and they're not big in size when compared with the other teams in the league."

Then he made his big announcement.

"The Cincinnati Swords have retained the services of Rollie Schwartz, the United States Olympic Team boxing coach, to teach my players to look after themselves. From here on in, there will be a punching bag in our dressing room in Cincinnati and our players will be expected to make good use of it in their everyday training.

"Just because we're in first place in our division, the other teams think they can push us out of the rink. We rely on hustle and hard work to win games and we've been on the receiving end rather than being the instigators of these battles, as so many people think we have been."

Crozier's statements were absolute drivel. The Swords had many talented players who would eventually make Buffalo an NHL powerhouse through the mid-70s. But with Fleming, Mortson, and Dudley in their line-up, they didn't need to fear any team. As for pure hockey talent, we had much more; the proof was that nearly every member of the 1971–72 Voyageurs eventually made it to the NHL:

Michel Plasse	10 seasons and 299 games, a 3.79 career average with 6 teams
Wayne Thomas	8 seasons and 243 games with two teams, a 3.43 career average.
Murray Anderson	1 season, 40 games with Washington.
Kerry Ketter	1 season, 41 games with Atlanta Flames.
Bob Murdoch	11 seasons, 757 games with 4 teams.
Bob Murray	4 seasons, 194 games with 2 teams.
Chuck Arnason	6 seasons, 401 games (101 goals) with 8 teams.
Rey Comeau	1 season, 69 games with 3 teams.
Tony Featherstone	2 seasons, 130 games with 3 teams.
Germain Gagnon	4 seasons, 249 games with 4 teams.
Jocelyn Hardy	2 seasons, 63 games with 2 teams.
Yvon Lambert	10 seasons, 683 games (206 goals) with 2 teams.
Mike Laughton	4 seasons, 189 games with 2 teams.
Chuck Lefley	8 seasons, 407 games (128 goals) with 2 teams.
Larry Pleau	3 seasons and 94 games with Montreal and many seasons with New England Whalers of the WHA.
Randy Rota	4 seasons, 212 games with 4 teams.
Murray Wilson	7 seasons, 386 games with 2 teams.

Some 17 players from that edition of the "lumberjack" Voyageurs made it to the NHL. Crozier couldn't say the same thing about his Swords.

I was coming along, in my estimation and management's.

But it took a disgruntled goaltender in Montreal to lead to the furtherance of my education as a professional defenceman.

Hockey fans and even the media are rarely aware of the upheaval that is caused in the lower ranks of an organization when problems beset the Big Club. When someone with the Canadiens coughed, it usually meant several Voyageurs came down with pneumonia.

The latest viral strain was the sudden emergence of Ken Dryden in the latter stages of the last season. His arrival was not good news for Michel Plasse, Wayne Thomas, and Michel Deguise, young goalies all, in Halifax. Dryden's heroics the previous spring had relegated veteran goalie Rogatien Vachon to the bench. With only seven late-season NHL games behind him, Dryden played in all 20 playoff games en route to the Stanley Cup, and won the Conn Smythe Trophy as the league's top playoff performer.

The team's new coach, Scotty Bowman, saw no reason to change that arrangement and so, 11 games into the new season Vachon had played all of 20 minutes, the third period of the eleventh game of the year. He let in four Ranger goals in those 20 minutes, good enough for an 8–4 New York win, and delivered a post-game ultimatum: "Play me or trade me."

These words were not taken lightly in Montreal. Although Dryden went on to win the Calder Trophy as the NHL's top rookie that season, Vachon was a highly respected veteran who had posted respectable numbers of his own: A Vezina trophy shared with Gump Worsley as a rookie in 1968–69; a 1.42 goals-against average in eight playoff games that year as the Canadiens won the Stanley Cup under Claude Ruel; a 2.53 average in five seasons with Montreal; and 2.00 G.A. in 19 playoff games over three years during which Montreal had won two Cups. He was definitely a first-string goalie in a town where another number one had set up shop.

Worse still for his bargaining position, the Canadiens had yet another prized young goalie, Phil Myre, waiting in the wings and there was a very real danger that Rogie might find himself number three in their assessment.

His goalie pads still on, his shirt a wet bundle on the floor at his feet, and his pride stung, Vachon repeated his message to the huddle of reporters gathered around him in the dressing-room at Madison Square Garden: "Play me or trade me."

Three days later, November 4, 1971, Vachon was a Los Angeles King. En route to Montreal were veteran goalie Denis DeJordy, defencemen Dale Haganson and Noel Price, and forward Doug Robinson. Robinson, no relation, and Price were to report to Halifax. This trade would make a significant contribution to the Los Angeles Kings, because Rogie would play brilliantly there for many years, making the second all-star team twice. It would also significantly improve the Halifax Voyageurs.

That improvement came in the arrival of one player, Noel Price. Although Doug Robinson would make a real contribution to our fortunes until he was felled by an eye injury midway through the year, Noel Price turned a rookie team around all by himself.

The 36-year-old Brockville, Ontario native had already spent some time with Montreal, a total of 42 games worth in 1965–66 and 1966–67 before going to Pittsburgh in the Expansion Draft later that year. His arrival meant that Mike Poirier was on his way to Muskegon and winger Bernie Blanchette was ticketed for the Central Hockey League.

What it meant for me was that I now would be playing with a man with more than 15 years of professional hockey experience. Perhaps the best way to say it is the simplest: Noel Price taught me so much it was unbelievable. It was almost as if Sam Pollock had decided to get a private tutor for Larry Robinson in the Vachon trade. In reality, Price was obtained because the Voyageurs defence was so young and inexperienced. The only man on the blue line with experience, Bob Murdoch, was headed for Montreal as soon as he played himself back into shape after an injury. Bob would join Montreal and his buddy Ken Dryden just after Christmas.

Like his predecessor Frank Selke, Sam Pollock believed strongly in giving his young talent every opportunity to succeed or fail, quickly. The Canadiens prided themselves in having the best of everything – scouting, coaching, administration, support staff – at every level. They would draft more prospects, sign more free agents, and have more players under contract than any other team.

If those players didn't pan out, if the club decided that they wouldn't fit in well with the Montreal system, they were moved, either singly or in groups. The turnover was impressive.

Under no circumstances could a young player confuse the American Hockey League with the junior or college league he had played in the year before. The game was faster, there were players of all ages. But the most important distinction was sociological: All these people were adults. A year before, when the guys on the Kitchener Rangers went out for a beer after a game or practice, they might feel a little guilty because many were boys sneaking out to do something still new or, depending on their age and the provincial drinking laws, illegal. In the AHL, men went out for beers with teammates and thought nothing of it.

In our case, it was a much more comfortable environment after the year in Kitchener. There Jeannette and I had been the only married couple and the only parents. In Halifax, there were several couples and some with children. That made a huge difference to Jeannette.

The Voyageur family bond was strong, too, and lasting friendships would be forged during a single season. Most of the team members lived in the same apartment complex in Dartmouth: Tony and Elaine Featherstone, Murray and Cheryl Anderson, Mike Laughton and his wife lived on the same floor as we did, and a group of team bachelors, Chuck Lefley, Chuck Arnason, and Bob Murdoch lived downstairs.

That meant Jeannette and the others could share babysitters without breaking the bank and my wife could attend most hockey games. Another advantage was that the wives had each other for company when we headed off on our road trips. Unlike many other minor league clubs, we flew to a lot of destinations because we were geographically isolated from the rest of the league. We would often fly into Boston and then bus to Providence and other nearby points during trips that lasted between a week and ten days.

When we would leave, the wives would often stay together, to relieve their loneliness. One point outsiders never fully appreciate is the difficulty young families or couples in professional sport have in becoming acclimatized to a new city, especially when they move around from place to place in the early years of a sports career. The husband doesn't have a nine-to-five job and regular social contacts he can introduce his wife to; and she usually doesn't have a job because she's new to the city and, if she's from another country, doesn't have a Green card.

One sore point for many French-Canadians for years has been the stories of unhappy spouses forcing players to ask for trades out of Montreal, especially the case with the baseball team. Jeannette and I discovered how difficult it was to make friends outside hockey and we lived in places where we spoke the language. That changed as we became accustomed to Montreal and, later, Kirkland and the St. Lazare areas where we made our homes.

That having been said, imagine how difficult it must be for a young wife of a California-bred ballplayer who suddenly finds herself in a different language environment, 4,000 miles from her family, and in a sport where road trips spanning two and three weeks are common. To some, it feels like abandonment and all the best intentions and Berlitz courses in the world won't help.

In Montreal, players like myself, Bobby Smith, and Bob Gainey have taken the time to learn some French, likewise in Quebec with the Stastny brothers, and it's been appreciated by the fans and media alike. However, those who are quick to criticize other players who haven't done this are forgetting that it is usually not a finished product that arrives when a new player joins a team. That player may take three or four seasons to learn his craft, and that takes all his concentration, or it should. Those of us who learned French did so because we had one advantage many young players never have: time. All of us have been fortunate to enjoy lengthy, productive careers, well above average duration.

In Kitchener, Jeannette had spent the winter in near isolation with Jeffery while I either worked for Pepsi-Cola, days, and played hockey, nights. And although she never complained, I wanted to make sure that she'd never have to repeat that experience. One improvement right off the bat was that Jeffery was older and could play with kids his own age, like Corey Anderson.

Norma MacNeil, Al's wife, also helped a lot. Al was an original Maritimer, hailing from Sydney on Cape Breton, and the MacNeils had an ease of manner that made us feel comfortable and a part of the family. Several times during the season, Norma had parties or lunches for the players' wives and these were heartily appreciated by the players as well.

Keeping the home front stable and happy helped many of the younger players on the Voyageurs, and the team as a whole, develop in a more positive environment.

When I reported to Halifax as a rookie, I had lots of company; there were 13 first-year players on the team and, it seemed, nearly all of them on defence.

In reality, we weren't getting the fair test of our abilities the Montreal organization demanded because we didn't have anyone with experience to lean on in the crunch. That changed with Price's arrival. He took the Young and the Restless (Robinson, Ketter, Murray, and Laughton) under wing and began to teach us the basics.

Lesson one was: "Work on keeping the puck out of our net first, the rest will come, including the offensive opportunities you kids are always looking for."

Lesson two was: "Stay in control of your defensive zone; a defenceman who starts running around panics everybody."

Lesson three was: "Make your own play, nobody else's."

Price had been team captain of the Springfield Kings and anchor of their defence when the parent team announced the trade. We were new to the league and hadn't played Springfield often so few of us knew him well. For us it was a major revelation that a 36-year-old guy with a receding hairline, who was almost old enough to have fathered most of us, could still manage to contribute at this stage in his career. After all, weren't we all bigger, faster, and stronger than he was? And wasn't it true that he was only a year younger than our coach and general-manager, Al MacNeil, who had retired as an active player years before?

What we weren't was smarter, and we came to realize that after observing Noel Price over a few games. What we saw was economy of motion, a defenceman who never seemed to get out of position, and who would make the momentum of attacking forwards work against them. We saw a player who would instinctively always make the right play; the short clearing pass up the boards instead of the Hollywood "low percentage bomb" up the middle that alert opposition forwards might pick off; a rearguard who would rush with the puck only when there was an opening. We bigger, stronger faster defencemen were always getting into trouble by trying to make our own openings.

Within weeks of his arrival, we began to improve dramatically. A good offensive team had added defence and was chasing Boston for first place in the Eastern Division.

We started moving up on the Braves in the standing, a team we'd trailed by as many as 15 points just before the holidays, although they would end the season in first place, gaining home ice advantage in the Calder Cup playoffs.

I could feel my game improving as we went along, even though it appeared I'd suspended my offensive game to work on my defence. I finished the year with ten goals and 14 assists for 24 points, but I had most of those points collected by the midway point.

By the time the playoffs had arrived, my defensive game had improved vastly and Noel Price had all of us defencemen confident that we could handle anything the opposition could throw at us.

Hockey cliché number one has it that nothing wins playoffs like good goaltending. Against Boston, Michel Plasse delivered supernatural goaltending; he was on another planet.

He singlehandedly kept us in the opener for the first two periods, stoning the Braves time and time again in the early going before 14,000 frustrated Garden faithful. During a first-period Boston power play, Plasse stopped Doug Roberts in close and then robbed Barry Merrell and Tom Williams before the period ended. In the second period he sent Paul Hurley, Gary Peters, and Williams muttering back to their bench during another power play and then stopped Peters twice again before the period ended. Dan Bouchard was exceptionally sharp at the other end until Rey Comeau struck for two second-period scores and we led 2–0 going into the third. Boston finally broke the ice in the eighth minute, but late goals by Noel Price and Chuck Arnason put the game out of reach and we had the away game win we wanted. Plasse was almost perfect, turning back 40 of 41 shots directed at him.

In the next game, a Saturday contest before 12,900, he dropped the "almost." We took a 1–0 lead when Kerry Ketter beat Ross Brooks with a screened shot from the blue line at 17:58 of the first. That stood up behind Plasse's stonewall netminding. The best way to describe what he did to the distraught Braves would be to say he singularly and absolutely refused to allow a goal. Early in the second period, during a Boston power play, he turned back Richie Leduc, Don Tanna-hill, and Doug Roberts on close-in shots and that seemed to break Boston's back, even though the Braves fought to the very end. Bob Murray added an insurance goal into the empty net at 19:51 of the third and we were on the way home with a 2–0 series lead.

The key to it all was an aroused blue line corps. Al MacNeil essentially went with four defencemen – Price, Ketter, Murray, and myself – and spotted Murray Anderson at both forward and defence. Boston was becoming increasingly desperate as they saw the series slipping away from them, and I ended up scrapping furiously with Terry O'Reilly twice in the second period of Game Three.

But it was already too late for intimidation. Rey Comeau had another two-goal game and we won 4–2, even though Don Tannahill finally solved Michel Plasse with a pair of goals.

That was the best Boston could do in Game Four as well and we swept the Braves 5–2 in a game marred by two melees involving Boston players and Halifax fans. Doug Roberts got involved in one confrontation when he poked his stick at a fan behind the penalty box. Police had barely quelled that uprising when another incident began behind the Boston bench. The histrionics were far too little, far too late. We emerged from the first period with a 3–0 lead on goals by Joe Hardy, Tony Featherstone, and Chuck Lefley and then smothered the

Braves with our forechecking. Murray Anderson, in the second, and Germain Gagnon, in the third, rounded out the scoring and we were into the Calder Cup final.

Nothing much changed for us in the first two games of the final against the Baltimore Clippers, surprise winners over the Cincinnati Swords in the Western Division final. We threw a strong checking blanket on the Clippers in the first two games at Baltimore; Michel Plasse again was outstanding, allowing only two goals a game.

There was only a minor glitch – we were returning to Halifax down 2–0 in the series, victims of a 2–0 opening game and 2–1 (overtime) second-game losses. Pucks were hitting posts, crossbars, legs, and arms when they weren't going wide. We arrived home determined to rediscover the offensive touch we'd displayed earlier in the season, while retaining the staunch defence that had won eight of nine games against Springfield and Boston.

The offensive relief arrived in the person of my fellow draftee Chuck Arnason who scored three goals in a 6–1 win. That seemed to open the floodgates and Baltimore never again challenged as we closed it out with 6–1, 4–1 and 4–1 wins. In Game Five, Noel Price was once again a pillar of strength, scoring the game's opening goal, one of three we got while shorthanded.

The Nova Scotia Voyageurs thus became the first Canadian team to capture the AHL's Calder Cup and I had my first championship in professional hockey. The 6,633 fans at the Forum gave Al MacNeil a standing ovation when he was selected the game's first star for guiding the youngest team ever to the AHL title. The kids had come through, with Mike Laughton scoring a pair in the final contest, and Randy Rota and Murray Wilson adding singles. The biggest kid of the bunch, Noel Price, pitched in with two assists.

It was a typical championship dressingroom, full of half-dressed hockey players, team officials, media, and hangers-on. What quickly distinguished it as a minor league dressing-room was the interview Al MacNeil was giving to a reporter from the *Halifax Chronicle*.

"Great, great, it feels better the second time around," the

coach laughed, alluding to the Stanley Cup he'd won the year before in Montreal. Much better the second time around; for although it wasn't the Stanley Cup, there weren't any death threats either. The previous year's blow-up with Henri Richard spurred telephoned threats from the local lunatic fringe. Montreal police had plainclothesmen guarding the MacNeil family around the clock until the Stanley Cup final had ended.

MacNeil was reminded he was in the minors with the next question.

"How many guys will be back next year?" Championship teams in the bigs usually don't anticipate large-scale player movement.

"Oh, for sure we're going to lose some players," he replied.

"We can't help but lose them, they all played like NHLers. But we'll be getting some good players in the draft and we'll be in pretty good shape next year too."

He'd be proven right on that score, as future NHLers – guys like Steve Shutt, Dave Gardner, Ed Gilbert, John Van Boxmeer, Rick Wilson, and Michel Larocque – would wear the Voyageurs' colours in 1972–73.

As the champagne sprayed around the room and I listened quietly to those words, I was hoping that my first Calder Cup would be my last. I'd finished the playoffs strongly, with 2 goals and 12 assists and 31 minutes in penalties. I'd also put on about ten pounds during the year and become known for my aggressive, physical play in the heavy-going.

Besides, I had the word on my future from the Master, Noel Price.

"You're going to play for a long time in the NHL," he told me that night.

"A long time. I'll bet on it."

I wasn't going to quibble with his assessment: it would be nice to play my 1972–73 hockey season a little closer to home.

SEVEN

Transition

A BOY NAMED Robinson went to the 1971 training camp of the Canadiens. A year later when they called my name, a man answered.

It's quite amazing what a difference a year can make in the career of a young athlete. If attitude is everything, then I was an entirely different person when September, 1972 rolled around. This time I was going to get a more serious look and demotion to Halifax wasn't going to be automatic. But I wasn't kidding myself on one major reason why I was going to get a longer look in camp; players with names like Savard, Lapointe Dryden, Cournoyer, and Mahovlich (Frank and Pete) were otherwise preoccupied by the momentous eight-game series with the Soviet Union. Others like Terry Harper had been traded and J.C. Tremblay had defected to the World Hockey Association.

My summer started quite unlike that of most hockey players – I went out and got a job. Why would I go out job-hunting after nine months of stress and hockey? I had to. We were lucky to win the Calder Cup, but the extra month it took to end my season cost me extra money to stay in Halifax.

I've always made my living on low-temperature surfaces but this time I went from cold feet to the perpetual hot foot. While other hockey players were out golfing that summer, I was an employee of the Ontario Department of Highways, working from seven to seven each weekday building Highway

417 between Montreal and Ottawa – on the stretch between Russell and Maxville.

It was especially hot times for a guy who earned his salary on ice; when we were laying pavement in high summer it was often a hundred or more Fahrenheit. After a while I got so bored, I volunteered to wield a pick and shovel with the construction guys.

Like most professional hockey players, I followed that August's training camp for Team Canada with interest and, as the summer wound down, that September series helped me get psyched up for my own camp at the Forum.

A professional organization will reward their junior and middle managers who produce, especially away from head office out in the regions. When we won the Calder Cup in May, a number of the Voyageurs knew that this meant the parent club would have to take a serious look at us during camp. We had earned it by doing all that could be done at the minor league level – winning a championship.

Even before the AHL playoffs, players would talk; we all had a good idea which players would get more than a cursory look when they were finally called up. Noel Price and I talked about this a lot, and he was certain I would be with Montreal "within the year, at the very most, two." He would get his reward for tutoring our young defence, a couple of seasons of NHL salary with the expansion Atlanta Flames before he retired.

I remember another occasion in mid-season as a group of us sat around in Boston; Larry Pleau was with us then for a while before he was called up.

"You're going to play in the NHL some day," he said to me, "and you're going to be an all-star."

My reply was along the lines of an embarrassed "yeah, sure."

I appreciated the sentiments at the time but, until then, I'd never really thought much about it. There is no contradiction here; from the moment I was drafted I had wanted to graduate to the big club. However, at this point in my AHL career, I was focussing solely on my contribution to the Voyageurs. The time for the Montreal Canadiens, I was sure, would come later.

As for the all-star business, I wanted to be as good as I could be but I'd never seriously entertained the idea of becoming a star player. I'm sure I would have been happy to become an adequate NHL defenceman, perhaps above-average in some areas of the game. The word superstar was not in my vocabulary at the time, either.

But that's not to say that I took no personal interest in my achievements or that when I was playing I never picked up a newspaper to look at the stats and see where I stood point wise. All players like to do that. If you don't have any pride of accomplishment, then you probably don't have the drive to succeed in the sport. The fan who believes a player quoted as "Never reading the papers or checking out stats" is not living in the real world.

We're competitors; that's what got us here. Of course we're going to pay attention to what people are saying about our exploits and what our opponents did last night or the night before.

A simple explanation for my apparent disinterest in my long-term future, i.e., the NHL, was that I found the AHL exciting enough that first year. I had just left junior hockey and the AHL, with its plane travel to cities like Cincinnati, Boston, Richmond, Springfield, and even good old Hershey, Pennsylvania, was all new and exciting.

Also, it was the first time anyone had paid me serious money to play hockey. I was still so green I thought $7,500 a year was a lot of money . . . until I heard about Van Boxmeer and found out what top prospects really make. Until then, things like that had never bothered me.

However, after a summer of hot pavement, I had an entirely new outlook on life and hockey salaries. I was determined that this would be my last "summer job" between seasons. I would get better and so would the money. The only way to increase the money, of course, was to play where the big money was, Montreal.

Another major factor in my change of attitude in the 1972 camp was that this time I was going there as a member of a group. The year before I'd been an unknown commodity, a draft choice from Kitchener who might or might not pan out. I knew no one; no one really knew me. Just travelling to Montreal knowing that many of my Calder Cup teammates would be there gave me a big psychological lift. At the 1972 camp, our tight little group comprised Yvon Lambert, Murray Wilson, Chuck Arnason, Wayne Thomas, Michel Plasse, Bob Murray, Chuck Lefley, and Bob Murdoch.

The psychologists will tell you that a sense of belonging makes a huge difference for anyone involved in a new endeavour. Our attitude spoke volumes. We had won our championship; we were a force to be contended with. While we still might be considered rookies with the Canadiens and the NHL, we knew that several veterans were hearing footsteps and we were doing our best to tread as loudly as possible.

Training camp was a cat-and-mouse game; actually cat-and-cat might be a better description. We watched the veterans watching us in practice and scrimmages; every time Murray Wilson turned on the jets – a faster carbon copy of Frank Mahovlich – every time I muscled someone off the puck, or every time Michel Plasse made a flashy stop, messages were being delivered.

I played physically during the exhibition season and even chalked up my first major. Who was it against? the historians among you might ask. A replay of AHL hostilities with such notable young studs as Dave Schultz or Terry O'Reilly? Or perhaps a resident NHL tough guy like Dan Maloney, Keith Magnuson, or Brian Spencer? It came in a game against Toronto, against that noted goon Pierre Jarry. (I was as surprised then as you are reading this now. Pierre, a flashy centreman, would rack up all of 142 PIM in seven seasons and 344 NHL games.) But believe it or not, I had to fight him. He'd run Jacques Lemaire, just missing him with his stick. I followed in along the boards and hit him just as he turned. Then I turned myself, skating back to my position, and he came charging at me and threw his gloves off.

The only way to explain it is that it was Rookie Silly Season—two guys who normally would tiptoe around an ant hill were flailing away in hopes of landing jobs with the Big Club. I'd been told I had to play tougher; Pierre had probably heard stories that some macho type in the Leafs' hierarchy thought he might be "too delicate" to play in the NHL. It ended quickly; I grabbed him, held him out away from me and threw a haymaker that scraped the ice en route, cutting him for about five stitches. I banged up my knuckles pretty good.

After the fact, we both felt pretty bad about it. It was one of those dumb fights that didn't seem to have rhyme or reason.

But that was exhibition season, a time for transmitting and receiving messages, from management down to the players, and back.

Some messages were received loud and clear. Murray stayed, Michel stayed, I didn't.

I was surprised and angry when I first got the word: I was being sent down to Nova Scotia for the second straight year. After the disappointment wore off and when I'd had some time to think it through, it became startlingly obvious Canadiens management was not going to turn around and sit out Serge Savard, Guy Lapointe, Jacques Laperriere, or Pierre Bouchard to make way for me. They'd all proven themselves in the NHL, not the AHL. Also, Bob Murdoch and Dale Hoganson were ahead of me on the depth chart because they, too, had played a dozen or more NHL contests each.

Many of my Calder Cup teammates had graduated to Montreal or other NHL clubs, but the 1972–73 edition of the Voyageurs was no weak sister. Gone were Germain Gagnon, Noel Price, Kerry Ketter, Mike Laughton, Joe Hardy, Murray Wilson, and Michel Plasse. Back were Yvon Lambert, Murray Anderson, Wayne Thomas, Michel Deguise, Randy Rota, Bob Murray, and Tony Featherstone.

And joining us was the Draft Class of '73, two thirds of one of the highest-scoring lines in junior hockey: left winger Steve Shutt and centre Dave Gardner of the Toronto Marlies (their right winger Billy Harris had been the first selection in the draft), defenceman John Van Boxmeer of the Guelph Platers, and forward Ed Gilbert of the Hamilton Red Wings. Also reporting was Rick Wilson, a defenceman out of the hockey factory at the University of North Dakota and a 1970 draft; and Peter Sullivan, a 1971 pick from Oshawa. And back in the nets, yet another top junior talent, Michel (Bunny) Larocque, the best goalie in the OHA.

We were solid on defence with Wilson joining Anderson, Van Boxmeer, and myself. Bob Murray was returning from a bit of an adventure; a conditional deal during the summer sent him to the New York Islanders and he played with them throughout the exhibition season. However, he didn't make the club and was returned to Nova Scotia.

It was a more balanced Nova Scotia team that began the 1972–73 AHL season; our offence was not as potent as it had been the year before, but our defence was much better right from the start. A quarter of the way through the season, Randy Rota was leading the team in scoring with 13 goals and 10 assists for 23 points, good for sixth place overall in the league. And I was just a point behind, with four goals and 18 assists. Bunched up closely after me were familiar names like Featherstone, Lambert, and Gardner. Behind the blue line, Michel Larocque was leading the league with a 2.82 goals-against average in 17 of our 20 games played.

Another ten games later, four of the top nine spots in the AHL scoring race were taken up by Voyageurs – Lambert (4th) 15–24 – 39; Featherstone (6th) 20–17 – 37; and Rota 17–16 – 33; and Robinson 6–27 – 33 tied for 8th.

It was about this time that we heard about the Airlift – six of us were going up to Montreal!

For one game.

We were to bolster the Montreal Juniors of the Quebec Major Junior Hockey League who would be playing Moscow Selects December 12. Also joining the team would be four players from the Quebec university league. Picked to make the trip were Larocque, Robinson, Van Boxmeer, Rota, Gardner, and Lambert. As it turned out, Bunny pulled a muscle a week before the exhibition game and it was Michel Deguise who accompanied us to Montreal for the game.

The Montreal contest was the third for the Selects, a veteran team that included names like Shalimov, Terakhin, Volchen-kov, and Zinger. They had edged the Hamilton Red Wings 3–2 in their first contest, and then had cleaned an Ontario Senior Hockey League all-star team 8–2.

The Forum always seemed to bring out the best in Canadian-Soviet hockey encounters. Five years before, a junior team bolstered by goalie Jacques Plante and several Quebec Aces had edged the Soviet national team 2–1; all Jake the Snake did was stop Almetov, Mayorov, Alexandrov, and Krutov on breakaways! Two years after that, one of the strongest junior teams ever assembled anywhere, the Montreal Junior Canadiens – Marc Tardif, Rejean Houle, Gilbert Perreault, Rick Martin, Germain Gagnon, Richard Lemieux, and company – annihilated the Soviets 9–2 before 18,000-plus fans at the Forum.

So no matter which Soviet squad was visiting, you could always count on a top-level contest at Atwater and St. Catherine.

It turned out to be an eventful game, perhaps a pivotal one in my career, and certainly an exciting trip.

Although there were five collegians among the reinforcements, it happened that the Voyageurs got most of the ice time. John Van Boxmeer and I must have played about 45 minutes each and the forwards were not far behind. Yvon Lambert got a goal, assisted by myself and Dave Gardner. Randy Rota scored at 18:53 of the third period to deadlock the game at three, and both teams retired to their dressingrooms satisfied with the result.

We also retired to the dressingroom to discuss The Hit, one of three I've made in my professional career that people never fail to bring up in conversation.

Like many Canadians, I'd been glued to my TV set during the Canada-Soviet hockey summit in September and I noticed that when a lot of the Soviet players took a pass, they would reach back for it. In their style of play, with little physical contact on the big international rink, a pass thrown a little behind a player was a way of protecting the puck and preventing an interception.

On the smaller North American rink, we had a simple description for this type of play: suicide. Many promising careers had ended with a forward reaching back for the sucker pass and an opponent bearing down on him. I told myself then and there that if I got a chance to play against the Soviets, I'd watch for the first chance I got to step into the forward reaching back.

My opportunity came midway through the second period. The play had started with a lot of the Soviets' circular flow and sure enough, a winger popped out just over the right side of centre and the puck followed him. He had to reach back for it.

I never charged him. I even let up before I hit him. But he went down like he'd run headlong into a building. He was out cold. It is hard to describe the sick feeling I had when I saw his eyes roll up. I thought I'd killed him.

That possibility didn't faze the fans, though. I got ovations the rest of the night. They'd been screaming for Canadian defencemen to step into the fleet Russian forwards for years.

That hit also impressed someone in the Canadiens hierarchy because I would be up with the big club less than a month later.

If I survived.

The next morning, we six Voyageurs were to fly to Boston to rejoin our team. Montreal was reeling under a big snow-and-ice storm and raging winds, and as time went by, it appeared certain that we would miss our game against the Braves.

However, the wings of commerce cannot be stilled, no matter how ice-coated they are. With all of the assurances you get from professional flight crews that a raging blizzard is "routine," we got on the plane, it went roaring down the runway . . . hit a patch of ice and then did a complete 360. As we taxied back to the terminal, the flight crew was remarkably subdued. We were in such a state of shock we didn't dare talk until the aircraft was at "a full and complete stop" back at the gate. We waited another three or four hours before finally leaving and six hockey players were very quiet during the second takeoff.

We made it to Boston.

I rejoined the Voyageurs and played for a couple of more weeks. We had just resumed playing after the Christmas break when I heard that both Jacque Laperriere and Pierre Bouchard were injured. It was after a game in Halifax, and a bunch of us were going to a restaurant to eat when I got a call to go see Al MacNeil.

"They're calling you up."

I never came back down.

I'd been with Montreal for two weeks when Scotty Bowman said they were keeping me up for the season. Laperriere had been injury-prone that season, Bouchard had been out twice while Savard and Lapointe missed games with "routine" injuries. Also, Ken Dryden was knocked out of action for several games, and the club wanted as many defencemen around as were available.

Larry Clark Robinson, NHL defenceman. Finally. It had a nice ring to it.

Back in camp when I got the word that I was being sent down for a second year of seasoning I'd been understandably disappointed. But as the first half of the AHL season went by, it became increasingly obvious to me that the Canadiens had made the right move in September.

Had I stayed with the Canadiens, I would have spent a lot of time on the bench or in the press box with the Black Aces. That was the name given to the club's subs, or taxi squad, because when Montreal first started using different coloured practice sweaters to distinguish the various line combinations, the scrubbies wore black. "Riding the pines" had never suited me; I had signed a hockey player's contract, not a bench contract, and the 40 minutes-per-game ice time I was getting in Halifax was light years better than two Forum hot dogs and a couple of Cokes upstairs with the media.

In retrospect, and being honest with myself, I have to admit that my size and style of play raised expectations and most probably made evaluating me a chore. Was I an offensive defenceman, whose main strength was moving the puck up ice and feeding the forwards? Was I a defensive defenceman who used his size and reach to sweep his own end clean? Or was I the Intimidator, one of the biggest players in the league, ready to drop the gloves at all times and handle all comers? The truth was, I was all of these players, and none of them.

I had the bad habit of going in spurts, showing true superstar for a game, a half-game, or a period, then making a bonehead play, looking incredibly awkward, and getting down on myself for a week afterwards.

When I was sent down, Scotty Bowman had a few words of advice: "Polish up your work in the corners and your defensive game. But don't do it to the detriment of your offensive skills. All of these will prove very useful to you when you're with the Canadiens to stay."

I'd played fairly well during training camp and the exhibition season but I had a bad habit of chasing the puck. In the AHL, those were rookies or journeymen pros coming at us, not NHL superstars, so defencemen were more comfortable handling the puck. In the NHL, the opposition could be on you in a flash and the slightest hesitation usually resulted in an embarrassing, especially at my size, turnover.

Three months after my demotion, all of these points were covered in my parting conversation with Al MacNeil.

"There's nothing else you can learn down here Larry," he said.

"You belong up there and now it's up to you to prove it. You have the size and the skills to become a major force with Montreal in a short time. But your size will work against you some times. When you make a mistake, it will be magnified. Ride it out; you'll do well."

And when I left Jeannette and Jeffery for the airport, my wife had a simple good-bye: "We don't want to see you again. In Halifax."

My first game would be January 8, 1973, against Minnesota in Montreal. I was ready.

Al MacNeil had finished his little pep talk with me by saying: "Make your size work for you. Go up there and play tough, hit everything that moves."

I took him at his word. On my very first shift, the North Stars skated into our end and I ran Bob Nevin in the corner. Without pausing, I skated out in front and hit somebody there, and went right back behind the net and hit another guy. When I skated back to the bench, Serge Savard was sitting there with a big grin on his face.

"Welcome," he said.

Ken Dryden had perhaps the best seat in the house for my debut:

> When I walked into the dressingroom before the game, there he was, already half dressed, looking taller, more rawboned, more angular than he does now. With our defence depleted, seeing Robinson didn't make me feel any better. But he played a re- markable game – poised, in solid control defensively, moving surprisingly well, with only a hint of lanky awkwardness. And what I recall most vividly, a goalie's memory, was that he blocked shots. (It wouldn't last long. After the first burst of rookie's enthusiasm wore off, he became like the rest.)

When Bouchard and Laperriere returned, I became a Black Ace which didn't particularly suit me.

One thing did suit me, though. I'd been with the Canadiens about two weeks when Scotty Bowman called me into his office at the Forum: "Send for your family. You're staying with the Canadiens. And don't worry about your ice time; work hard in practice and you'll get your time in. Count on it."

It had been a Good News-Bad News farewell with Jeannette when I had been originally called up.

"Now I'll be able to watch you play on TV," she said. The Voyageurs games were never televised. "The bad news is now you're going to be on a permanent road trip as far as we're concerned." Our friends on the Halifax Voyageurs pitched in and Jeannette and Jeffery never wanted for company.

So it was a banner day when I called Jeannette two weeks later and told her: "Dad is coming down there to pick you up. You're moving to Montreal." He and one of my sisters-in-law drove down to Halifax to get my family and our things.

Everything seemed to be falling into place as the thaw announced an early spring a couple of weeks later. Although I was officially a Black Ace, I was getting lots and lots of extra work in practice with Floyd Curry and, later, Claude Ruel. Injuries to a variety of players had opened up spots on the club and a bunch of the Calder Cup Voyageurs were making a seri- ous contribution: Chuck Lefley, Murray Wilson, Bob Mur- doch, Michel Plasse, and Wayne Thomas.

Better still, this was a club on the rise with the potential for becoming a serious Stanley Cup contender: the Canadiens had gone 15 straight games without a road loss during one stretch of the season, clinched the East Division title with a couple of weeks left in the schedule, and easily handled their two main East Division rivals, the Rangers and the Bruins, en route.

Led by Jacques Lemaire, the Mahovlich brothers, Yvan Cournoyer, Marc Tardif, Henri Richard, Guy Lafleur, and Claude Larose up front; backstopped by the incomparable Ken Dryden and an unflappable Michel Plasse, who, himself, was spelled by Wayne Thomas, the Canadiens had finished the season with 120 points on 52 wins, 16 ties, and only 10 losses in 78 games.

That was one short of the league record the Bruins had set in 1970–71 with 121 points, and the 10 losses in 78 games was a league record.

What did it, of course, was defence; the regulars like Savard, Laperriere, Lapointe, and Bouchard spelled by the newcomers, Robinson, Hoganson, and Murdoch. The Canadiens gave up only 184 goals in 78 games, a 2.36 average, even though Ken Dryden only played 54 of those games. His G.A. was 2.26; Michel Plasse's was an astounding 2.58 in 17 games, and Wayne Thomas's was 2.37 in ten games played.

How good was that defence? The 184 goals against was 24 better than runner-up New York with 208, Boston was 51 back with 235 goals allowed, and the two challengers in the West Division, Chicago and Philadelphia, had given up 225 and 256 respectively.

We weren't shabby on offence either. Our 329 goals scored was second only to Boston's 330.

What made me happy was that Scotty was right about ice time. What had started out as a couple of shifts here and there in spot duty turned out to be 36 games for me before the playoffs. I ended that season with two goals and four assists, a meagre offensive contribution, but I was making all the plays defensively and feeling comfortable. However, when the playoffs arrived, the first-string defence was healthy and I was scheduled to watch from the Press Box.

In our own division, the Bruins and the Rangers would be

tough obstacles to our Stanley Cup quest. On the other side were Philadelphia and Chicago.

If you notice that I left out a scrappy young team called the Buffalo Sabres, you're right. But back in 1972–73, I had a lot of company. Punch Imlach had done a terrific job of molding a team in a very short time and the '72–'73 season was where it all started to come together for the Sabres. That was the year that the French connection line of Rene Robert, Gilbert Perreault, and Rick Martin came together; it was also the year that Punch convinced one of his old Maple Leaf defensive stalwarts, the highly respected Tim Horton, 42, to come and work with his kiddie defence: Jim Schoenfeld, 19, and Larry Carriere, 20.

In 1970–71, the Sabres had finished sixth in the East Division with a record of 16 wins, 43 losses and 19 ties for 51 points. In 1972–73, they were a solid 37–27–14 – 88 points, and finished two points ahead of Detroit in fourth to make the playoffs. This meant they would play the first-place team, Montreal, in the first round.

They were our first obstacle and an obstacle they proved to be. We opened up with a pair of wins at home, a tight 2–1 opener followed by a 7–3 decision, and then took the third game 5–2 in Buffalo.

At this point, most young teams would have folded, declared the season a success because they'd made the playoffs, and retired to the golf course. But this was a Punch Imlach team and he had hired Joe Crozier (remember the Olympic boxing coach at Cincinnati?) to do the job for him. With their backs to the wall, and us guilty of looking ahead a bit, the Sabres slashed us 5–1 at the Aud and we had to return to the Forum for the "inconvenience" of a fifth game.

We committed the cardinal sin of repeating our Game Four inattention and Punch Imlach zapped us again. With the game tied 2–2 in the last minute, Coach Crozier called over to Referee Bruce Hood:

"I want you to measure Ken Dryden's pads."

"What?"

"I want you to measure Ken Dryden's pads. They're too

wide and that makes 'em illegal. That's also a two-minute minor. Measure 'em and give Montreal a penalty."

When we were playing in Buffalo, a Sabres employee had measure Ken's pads and discovered that they were just under 10¼ inches wide. NHL rules stipulated that they could be no wider across than ten inches and new pads were always meticulously measured before the manufacturer delivered them. However, with much wear and tear, and a goalie kneeling on them for a season, they might flatten out some and, technically, become a little wider than they should.

The NHL rule, as Punch Imlach explained to his coach, was that a pad measurement had to be requested during play, but it could only take place during intermission.

Hood was angry, and so was his boss Scotty Morrison, the NHL referee-in-chief, but they had to measure and when the Sabres were proven right, we got the penalty to start overtime.

They didn't score then, even though Jim Lorentz was in alone on Dryden and hit the post, but about halfway through the period Perreault sent in Robert. He didn't miss and we were forced in a Game Six back in Buffalo. We eventually won the series 4–2 back at the Aud and would never treat the Sabres with a lack of respect again.

I brought up that series because it seems to be the forgotten match-up of that playoff year. Some 15 years later, people easily recall the Philadelphia series that followed, and the Chicago final afterwards, but Buffalo is never mentioned. What brought it back to me with crystal clarity was the news this year as I was writing this book that George Punch Imlach, an original, had passed away after a heart attack. He had coached Jean Beliveau in the Quebec Senior League, built a dynasty in Toronto, and put an expansion franchise into high gear. In short, he was a superb hockey man, in a class with Frank Selke, Sam Pollock, and the Patricks.

I didn't see much ice time against the Sabres and then Jacques Laperriere went down with another injury and I was pressed into service. I ended up playing 11 games that spring, and had five points on a goal and four assists.

The goal was a big one.

After the Buffalo victory, the Philadelphia Flyers swaggered into town in their orange-and-black uniforms and with their high-assed style of skating. Most power skating coaches will tell you that if you skate with your torso bent too far forward, your shoulders will be too far ahead of your knees and you will sacrifice power and drive to the struggle or remaining balanced. If you sacrifice power and drive, through proper leg extension, then you won't skate as fast.

Somebody forgot to tell the Flyers. Led by the indomitable Bobby Clarke, they swashbuckled into Montreal with their bums in the air, said "nice wall hangings" to the championship pennants that hung from the Forum rafters, and proceeded to kick butt. Ours. They won the first game 5–3 and I played a few shifts in the early going.

And now it was Game Two. If we lost this one, we'd be trying to even up at the Spectrum, where fans wore orange-and-black Nazi helmets and called their players "Hound dog," "Hammer," and "Moose."

"Hammer" and "Moose" combined to get things going early for the Flyers. About four minutes into the game, Dave Schultz and Serge Savard squared off and the scrap was fairly even until the Flyers winger landed a haymaker that cut the Senator for 12 stitches above the lip. Just over a minute later, Andre "Moose" Dupont scored on a screened 40-footer and the Flyers were off and rumbling. Things would get worse. Two minutes later . . . with Savard in the clinic getting stitched up, two of our remaining defencemen, Bob Murdoch and Guy Lapointe, took penalties within a minute of each other and Gary Dornhoefer scored with a two-man advantage at 8:12. Philadelphia 2, Montreal 0.

In the first game, Flyers' captain Bobby Clarke was all over the ice, winning important faceoff after important faceoff, forechecking like a hungry wolverine and making our lives miserable.

In Game Two, Scotty Bowman pointed to Clarke and turned to our captain Henri Richard and said: "He's yours."

Scotty was right. The 35-year-old Pocket Rocket, distinguished grey hair at the temples underscoring his venerability, was playing his 18th season and his 17th playoff. Starting with that game, and carrying through to the conclusion of the series, he was all over Clarke like a blanket. He took Clarke out of Game Two. When defenceman Barry Ashbee took his third minor of the game late in the first period, Guy Lafleur combined with the brothers Mahovlich on the power play and we halved their lead.

Things really looked up when Pocket Rocket scored just 25 seconds into the middle period to knot the score but the euphoria lasted all of 11 seconds. Cowboy Bill Flett scored at 0:36 and the Flyers had the lead once again. We struggled the rest of the way in a very even game and tied it once more on an Yvan Cournoyer goal midway through the third. And then, overtime.

Often teams will close up in extra time, hyperconscious of defence and unwilling to move to the attack until the defensive situation is fully secured. Not so on this night – both the Flyers and the Canadiens moved the puck up and down the ice with abandon and there were several good chances at either end early on in extra time.

We'd played about six-and-a-half minutes when Dornhoefer and I met at centre ice, in hot pursuit of a loose puck. I poked at it and it hit the boards and bounced out again as the Flyer winger skated by.

I was just on their side of centre and Frank Mahovlich was just ahead of me. I made like I was going to pass to the Big M. One of their defencemen must have guessed that intention and he angled toward Frank. Seeing that, the veteran hollered "go with it" to me and "picked" the defenceman, cutting him off and giving me a clear path down the left-side boards.

As I got over the blue line, I decided I would slap it at their net as hard as I could, hoping that the rebound would give goalie Doug Favell trouble and one of our wingers might get to the puck for a scoring chance. I wound up and cranked it; 206 angry pounds went into that shot.

The next thing I knew, the Forum was going crazy. I looked up and Favell was just sitting there on his knees with the puck beside him and forward Ross Lonsberry was patting him on the head in consolation.

It was a goal! I started jumping up and down like a berserk ostrich. Then I looked to my right and this mob in the home whites of the Canadiens was converging on me, and also dancing around like weird birds. I had scored my first NHL playoff goal, it was an overtime winner, and I had become a Sesame Street character to boot.

From then on, I was Big Bird. You win some and you lose some.

That victory ignited us, and especially Henri Richard. In Game Three he was outstanding, scoring the winning goal in a 2–1 victory. Butch Bouchard helped set the tone early when he easily handled Schultz in a first-period set-to and we could return home no worse than tied.

On to the Fourth game. With Kate Smith blaring "God Bless America" and the rabid Philly faithful giving their team – some idiot once said Philly was a bad sports city – a five-minute standing ovation before the puck was dropped, the Flyers were psyched and Clarke scored early. But that was it.

We turned on the jets and players like Rejean Houle, who were considered too frail to play against the Broad Street Bullies, rose to the occasion. Reggie, who had scored our opening goal in Game Three, repeated his feat in Game Four at 7:38 of the second period. Then with Barry Ashbee off with a penalty, Reggie and I set up Marc Tardif and we were on our way to a 4–1 victory.

Game Five was all Henri Richard. All he did was score the winner in a 5–3 victory, and overcome two gashes on his forehead. In the first period, I unleashed another of my "patented" slapshots and caught the Pocket Rocket flush on the forehead for eight stitches. He was sewn up in the clinic and re-emerged, only to have Clarke re-open the gash with a judiciously applied high stick later in the game.

We had won the series 4–1 but it wasn't easy. Doug Favell had played well in nets but if they'd had a top puck stopper like Ken Dryden, or Bernie Parent . . . they might have gone far.

We went on to defeat the Black Hawks in six games for the Cup, but all admitted that the Flyers series was much tougher, even though it was a game shorter.

Ken Dryden said it best.

"We all knew that Clarke and (Rick) MacLeish were really good players, but we didn't realize how good fellows like Dornhoefer and (Terry) Crisp were. Dornhoefer is a lot better than good. He's a complete hockey player. He's tough, he bothers you around the net, he goes both ways extremely well and he has a good shot. He does everything you'd want of a hockey player."

I agreed. Dorny had practically worn me out during the series. I could ride him into the boards and he'd be right back up again, and with the puck. He'd make me take him to the outside but he had a good inside move and caught me with it a couple of times. He always kept coming and forcing me to play him up high, which is tiring to say the least.

Dornhoefer and I would meet again in the 1975–76 Cup final. Before then, he and his teammates would reacquire Bernie Parent and win two Stanley Cups.

Two weeks after the Philly series had ended, I sat in a daze in the visitors dressingroom at Chicago Stadium. We had just skated off the ice with a 6–4 victory and Lord Stanley's hardware. The winner's share was $19,000 per man. Not a bad finish to a year that had started with these words: "Larry, we're sending you back down to Nova Scotia."

I had one more chore to finish before I could settle back and enjoy the off-season. I'd have to call the boys on the Highway 417 construction crew with my regrets: I wouldn't be joining them this summer.

EIGHT

Boston Then And Now

BIG. BOLD. Brutal. Boston. Buffalo. Broad Street Bullies. Black and blue.

Note all those aggressive B-sounds – you almost have to spit out those words.

Bounce. Boards. Bobby I. Bobby II. Bobby III. Butch.

If the National Hockey League was Sesame Street, B seemed to be the Letter of the Day during 1974–75, my first two years as a full-time NHL defenceman. Boston was about to go through a major transition, but before the Big Bad Bruins of Esposito, Orr, Cheevers, Cashman, and McKenzie bowed out, they were going to give it a great shot at one more Stanley Cup.

The Buffalo Sabres were moving up, anchored by bruisers Jim Schoenfeld and Jerry (King Kong) Korab on defence, the French connection up front, and a great supporting cast that included Craig Ramsay, Don Luce, Jim Lorentz, Danny Gare, Rick Dudley, and Bill Hajt. They were coming into their own and also would give the Stanley Cup a great run.

And, of course, the Broad Street Bullies were in their heyday, dictating a whole style of play (!?) to the rest of the league in their bid to become the first expansion team to win the post-season championship.

In Montreal we were undergoing a transition of our own but were always competitive, always ready to claim the Stanley Cup as rightfully ours.

These were the teams that dominated the NHL in the seasons of 1973–74 and 197475.

As a result, these were my first NHL rivalries.

It all starts and ends with Boston. In the intervening years, there has been solid rivalry with Philly, Buffalo, Edmonton, and Quebec, but winter in the Northeast means Boston-Montreal.

There has always been something special about a Boston-Montreal hockey game, especially in the last two decades. It starts with the emblematic – the horseshoe design of the Canadiens C, scoring a ringer on the hub of the Boston B. These storied team logos in conflict will always get the juices flowing for hockey fans. Red-white-and-blue against black-white-and-gold, Montreal's emotional fire engine red versus Boston's home whites, or Boston's sinister black versus Montreal's home whites; this rivalry was made for legend.

It wasn't always that way. Before my time, when the league had two unofficial divisions among its six teams; Montreal, Detroit, and Toronto at the top, New York, Boston, and Chicago at the bottom, it was Montreal–Detroit or Montreal–Toronto. But by the late '60s Toronto and Detroit had gone into decline – neither has yet fully recovered – while the Bruins were in full ascendancy. The Canadiens, of course, were where they always belonged, at the top, so it was natural that the two teams would clash.

During the early 1970s, Boston, Philadelphia, and Buffalo were our main rivals, but there was something special about the Bruins. First and foremost, they played in our division and the Flyers didn't. Second, Buffalo got good quick; there wasn't enough time to stoke the emotions that fuel a serious rivalry.

The Big Bad Bruins.

I've always felt that nickname has detracted from the fact that this was a very talented team.

The Bruins of 1972–73 and 1973–74 were getting a bit ragged in the leg, not long in the tooth as many media observers wrote. Phil Esposito, Wayne Cashman, Ken Hodge, Fred Stanfield, et al were all veteran hockey players but they were by no means the Over-the-Hill-Gang. They had a lot of hockey left when I started in the NHL.

The same could not necessarily be said about the youngest of the group, Bobby Orr. His knees were so brittle that even at age 24 and 25, most writers were openly wondering how long it would be before that last injury left him crippled and wheelchair-bound.

The Bruins and Canadiens did not like each other a whole lot, but unlike some other rivalries, we respected each other. We hated the Flyers because they were assholes; later we would hate the Noridques because the Quebec and Montreal media worked overtime at fanning the flames. The Bruins, though, we respected. That has carried on to this day.

You couldn't help but admire guys like Cashman, Esposito, and Orr. Bobby was the dominant player in the game and a gentleman who could give as bad as he got if things got a little tense. Cashman was tough and had to be; he spent a lot of his career playing with a bad back that would have hobbled lesser men. Even as much as Orr and Esposito meant to the Bruins, I think Cash and Terry O'Reilly have been the true heart and soul of the hockey club during my career.

Off the ice, they were both exemplary gentlemen. On the ice, they put their sticks right up under your nose, dared you to beat them: "Here you win games the old-fashioned way, kid, you *EARN* it." They were also guys who could leave the game at the rink: you could skate off and say "nice game Cash" or "way to work Terry" and you'd get a small smile and a nod. I've always felt that is the true essence of a professional athlete, the ability to leave the game between the buzzers and white lines. It isn't a sign of weakness to acknowledge your opponent's effort; it's a sign of strength. Your opponent makes you what you are; his presence honours you.

For two decades, the presence of the Bruins has honoured the Canadiens. And vice versa.

And it all goes back to Cash and Terry. These two guys were the most able, ferocious competitors around. But when the siren went, the game was over.

I remember talking with hockey writers in those days and

invariably the subject of Cashman's "stickwork" would come up.

"Cashman's always using his stick; it's always high; he always takes sneaky shots," they would say.

"Not really," I'd respond.

"Wayne Cashman is a firm believer in advertising. He'll show you the stick a lot, but he'll rarely ever use it that way."

I got to know Cash a bit better than you would most opponents because his wife bred horses and that always was an interest of mine. He was a fine gentleman then and 15 years later, is still very helpful to his centreman as an assistant coach with the Rangers.

If Cash believed the world would be a better place through advertising, Phil Esposito took him one better in proving the medium is the message. He'd never stop talking.

Esposito was always talking to you on the ice. He'd try to get your mind off the game and he'd be the first one to slip in behind you and put it in the net. He was a natural scorer, very good in close.

Let's call this following scenario "Phil Esposito's Ultimate Hockey Video: Or How to Talk Your Way to the Art Ross Trophy."

Lights, camera, action.

The Bruins are pressing on a powerplay in our zone and Esposito is leaning his bulk into me, attempting to screen Ken Dryden. This tactic generally works great for him around the league because he towers over nearly all defencemen and goalies. He sets up shop in the slot, declares it his turf, and scores on tip-ins, rebounds, wrist shots, deflections off his unmentionables, you name it.

In Montreal, he tends to get frustrated. Not only are Serge Savard, Rod Langway, and myself bigger than him, so is our goalie. That's not playing fair in his book. So he starts yapping.

"Come on, ref, dammit, he's holding my stick! Keerist, did you just see Savard kick my skates out from under me! He's *HOLDING* dammit! Look at that! Look at that! You gonna call anything tonight or do you have the weekend off?"

While all of this conversation is going on, the referee is in the corner trying to keep his eye on the puck as the Bruins attack furiously in a swirl of black-and-gold. In front of the net, 400 to 600 pounds of agitated hockey players are locked in furious combat for control of the slot.

The puck goes into the corner. . . Ken Hodge hammers into the boards with Jimmy Roberts. Phil yaks.

"He's got my stick! He's got my stick!"

The puck skitters behind the net . . . Guy Lapointe whacks Cashman and fires it around the boards. Phil yaks.

"That's *NOT* a *CROSSCHECK*? Why don't I go and get him an axe handle so he can do it right? You gotta union, ref?"

It flies back to the point where Orr knocks it down with a hand and winds up for a slapper . . . the scrum in front of Dryden, including Espo, discreetly moves en masse to the nearest point outside the path of Orr's blast. "We're just making sure you'll see the whole thing Ken," we are fond of telling our goalie in the dressingroom. He knows that we are fleeing for our lives and we know he knows. "Chickenshits!" is his favourite rejoinder when the topic comes up.

Meanwhile, now a bit to the side of the goal, Phil Esposito is still yakking.

"Yeah, this is the NHL. The National *HOLDING* League, you jerk!"

Orr shoots, it goes wide (whew!), hits the dasher board near ice level and caroms out of the zone.

A dishevelled Esposito gives it one last ty: "Sonnuvabitch! Are you ever gonna call anything?"

From the corner, where the referee has stood stoically observing all during the powerplay, comes a voice:

"Ahhhhhhhhhhh shadddduppppp, Esposito."

A glare of pure malice on his face, muttering a Sicilian hex to curse countless generations of the referee's family, Esposito lumbers to the Boston bench, an irritated grizzly. The play and the referee move up ice.

Fade to black. Rewind.

Flying Phil certainly had his success against us, like all other teams, but not as much. Savard and I handled him fairly well but the guy who drove him to distraction was Rod Langway.

Roddy had played middle linebacker at the University of New Hampshire and just loved the scrum. He literally could pick up Espo and turn him over, he was so strong. Needless to say, that upset Number 7 in all senses of the word.

When Boston played against us and Langway was on defence, you'd swear the volume had been turned up. And Roddy, in his best Bahstin "pahk yoah cah" accent could occasionally be heard to exclaim: "Ah shaddap, Phil!" He usually was smiling as he said it.

Strangely enough, the guy I had a few run-ins with in that group was The Quiet One, Ken Hodge. He was a big guy and used his strength to advantage, forever trying to push everybody around and with nobody ever really challenging him.

Ironically, he wasn't even a Bruin anymore when we had our big run-in. One night, when he was playing with the Rangers, I was coming down the slot and he put the stick on me and knocked the feet out from under me. I landed right square on my tailbone . . . I couldn't walk, I couldn't sit, I couldn't do anything for about two weeks.

I stewed and planned all sorts of revenge.

As I nursed my sore bum, I also nursed a grudge. The next time we returned to Madison Square, we collided at centre ice on the first shift and I hit him. He just stood there. So I dropped the gloves and started pounding the stuffing out of him and had him down when Greg Polis jumped me from behind.

I rarely get as mad as that but he had broken a cardinal rule. A guy as big as he is didn't have to use the stick. A little guy who uses his stick in self-protection you can understand. Sometimes. For several years, the Bruins had a little guy who used his stick a little too much: Bob Schmautz.

A solid hockey player in the Johnny McKenzie mold, Schmautz had good offensive skills and one of the best wrist shots I've ever seen. But he was bad with his stick; he'd jab it under your nose and if you came too close and got nicked it was too bad. You'd made the mistake of coming too close.

"One day, I'm going to catch you without the stick, Bobby," I said on more than one occasion.

It took a few seasons, but that day finally came.

Afterwards, Schmautz complained publicly in the Bruins dressingroom: "Why didn't one of you guys come help me?" Nobody said anything but you got the impression the rest of the Bruins had seen him taunting me with the stick for a long time and figured that his luck had run out or his time was up. You always stick up for a teammate: that's the game's cardinal rule. But some teammates you stick up for more than others. Lots of hockey players are made uncomfortable by the fact that they're taking the side of an acknowledged dirty player. Teammate or not.

If you could take away the Battle of Quebec hype, and that's impossible in a province where the dailies contribute a hundred pages of copy to the fire every day, it's rougher in a Boston-Montreal game. Rougher, not dirtier.

It's rougher but it's good, hard bodychecking. You get into a little rink like in Boston and there's nowhere to go. Literally "No Place To Go." The end boards, by regulation, are 60 feet from the blue line. But the rink isn't as wide as others so the corners are small. And the neutral zone between the blue lines is a rumour. If you hit your own blue line at full stride, you'll be crossing theirs in three to four strides – that's how close it is in the "Gahden." Slower forwards and defencemen can stay with you because they don't have as far to go. Playing the angles is much easier in such a confined space. But get a step on a guy and you're gone; there's no margin for error, no room to catch up.

Then the final ingredients: They're a physical team; we're a physical team. Nature takes its course.

In my first years there, the Big Bad Bruins were a team built for the building. Esposito, Hodge, and Cashman were not Nureyevs on skates; neither was their supporting cast of Fred Stanfield, Don Marcotte, Pie McKenzie, Ed Westfall, Don Awrey, Dallas Smith, Rick Smith, Ted Green, Johnny Bucyk, Derek Sanderson, and Carol Vadnais.

Of course, Bobby Orr had enough speed left over for two teams, but was forced to play in a building that would eventually contribute to his premature demise as an NHL pro. Playing in a bigger rink like the Forum for 40 games a year, instead of the Beantown Bandbox, would have added seasons onto Bobby's career because fewer opponents would have been able to draw a bead on him.

Another thing that might have contributed to shortening Bobby's career was the arrival of the World Hockey Association. Few can argue that the Bruins were most badly affected by defections to the new league: Gerry Cheevers, Ted Green, Derek Sanderson, John McKenzie, and Wayne Carleton, all in the same year. Other clubs would be hurt; Montreal would lose J.C. Tremblay, Rejean Houle, Marc Tardif, and Frank Mahovlich, but over two seasons. The latter three were still around to contribute to our 1972–73 Cup.

A more important defection hit Montreal in 1973–74 and it was to a law firm in Toronto. Ken Dryden and Sam Pollock discovered to their mutual chagrin that they had the same character and determination. Ken wanted more money than Sam thought he was worth; Sam offered less money than Ken thought he was worth. Neither budged and the only hockey Ken played that winter was as a defenceman on a pick-up team in a Toronto industrial league. That hurt us in the long run. Ken was one of the two best goalies in the NHL at the time.

Despite losing a raft of starters, the Bruins captured first place in the East Division, finishing with 113 points, 14 up on Montreal. Two Philadelphia Blazers, Bernie Parent and Derek Sanderson, returned to their NHL teams with mixed results. Parent, the other of the two best goalies in the NHL, would backstop the Flyers to a Stanley Cup victory over the Bruins; Derek would come back fighting and flighting. Trouble was, his most publicized fight was a dressingroom encounter with Terry O'Reilly, a teammate who objected to his carousing and substance abuse. Dandy Derek also got fined a significant amount of money for missing a team flight and a game and was a burnt-out shell of the player he had been two years earlier.

On the personal front, I had a good season but not a great one, ending up with 6 goals and 20 assists. A year later, that jumped to 14 goals and 47 assists.

The years 1974 and 1975 were learning experiences for me. After the auspicious beginning in 1972–73 and the Stanley Cup success, I set about learning my trade. The team was undergoing many changes; J.C. Tremblay left, and Jacques Laperriere retired after the 1973–74 season, another victim of a string of injuries. Dryden missed '73–'74 but returned a year later.

Meanwhile, the club was getting younger with the influx of Voyageurs and new draft choices: Steve Shutt, Doug Risebrough, Bob Gainey, Yvon Lambert, Bill Nyrop, Murray Wilson, Michel Plasse, and Bunny Larocque.

Philadelphia and Buffalo were on the rise. The Flyers, anchored by Bobby Clarke and the skills of the reacquired Bernie Parent in goal, and ably supported by the Wild Bunch, went on to win two straight Stanley Cups, beating Boston and Buffalo in six games respectively in 1974 and 1975.

The New York Rangers, read Walt Tkaczuk, eliminated us in six games in 1974. Bunny Larocque played his heart out in the semi-final but it wasn't enough. We'd finished five points up on the Broadway Blueshirts that season, the difference being five wins by us and five ties by them.

The final went true to form, the Big Bad Bruins offence versus the Puck Stops Here defensive heroics of Vezina Trophy co-winner, Parent. During the regular season, the Bruins had scored 349 goals as Esposito, Orr, Hodge, and Cashman finished 1–4 in the scoring race.

The Flyers had scored only 273 goals, fifth in the league, but tied Chicago for fewest allowed, 164, and finished only one point behind Boston in the overall standings with 112 points. They won the final 4–2 and, fittingly, the Cup-winning game was a 1–0 victory.

Buffalo did us in in 1975, beating us four out of six games in the strangest series you'd ever want to see. We went into Buffalo for Game One and seemed to suffer from a case of collective amnesia. Two years before, the Sabres had let us know they weren't going to be pushovers. They were a character team, built on good balanced offence and defence, all rooted in a Punch Imlach work ethic. They had given us all we wanted during regular season play as three teams – ourselves, the Sabres, and the Flyers, ended the '74–'75 calendar with 113 points each. Philadelphia had the most wins, 51, but we had the fewest losses, 14. Buffalo was right in the middle with 49 wins and 16 losses.

The Sabres quickly jumped us 3–1 in the first and, after a few angry words in the dressingroom between periods, we went back out and scored three straight to go ahead 4–3 before Gilbert Perreault tied it. Jim Lorentz gave them the lead early in the third period but we caught a lucky break in the last minute of regulation. We had pulled Ken Dryden and were storming their end furiously when King Kong Korab slid into his own net and got a skate caught in the mesh. That gave us a two-man edge in their zone and Jacques Lemaire fired one from in close that Danny Gare deflected into his own net.

In overtime, we survived a penalty to Bob Gainey and were feeling confident when we faced off in their zone. You could sense the negative vibes in the Aud, a fine family arena and one of the nicest crowds to play before. The Sabres were a great team but the Canadiens were tradition and history, and everybody sensed a kill. Jacques Lemaire moved in for the faceoff with Don Luce and after several false starts, Luce was waved out of the circle. He was replaced by Craig Ramsay, soon to become our nemesis in blue-and-gold, and Rammer did something strange.

He let Lemaire win the faceoff uncontested, but reached around Coco with his stick and got the puck. He one-handed it to his winger and broke for the open where he got the puck back on a 2-on-1. He came in on me with Danny Gare struggling to catch up and I got a hip on him and knocked him off balance. But he still managed to get a hand on his stick and passed over to Gare. 6–5.

We lost the second game 4–2 and returned to Montreal with our tails between our legs.

Then both teams played Dr. Jekyll and Mr. Hyde in one of the most astonishing turnabouts you could ever witness. We annihilated them, 7–0 and 8–2 to even the series, handling them as disdainfully as we would the Oakland Seals, and returned to the Jewel on Lake Erie brimming with overconfidence. How badly did we beat them at the Forum? We were so determined; Pete Mahovlich and Guy Lapointe combined on a short-handed goal while we were down two men. And then we scored another shorthanded tally right afterwards, while down only one man!

So both teams returned to Buffalo fully expecting us to win. It didn't happen. We had them 4–3 late in the game when they tied it and went on to win in overtime. In Game Six, Gerry Desjardins made 16 stops in the first period; they built up a lead and then held us off on three last-minute faceoffs in their zone.

We were out and we were frustrated. I'll never forget Steve Shutt's face the night of the season-ending party. Steve was quietly nursing a beer in a corner, his face a mask of barely-concealed pain and determination.

"I hate losing. I *HATE* losing," he said.

"I never want to feel this way again."

He almost didn't. And it would be a very long time before Steve cried in his beer after the Canadiens were knocked out of a playoff.

Guy Lafleur didn't have to say anything; he just sat there quietly puffing on a cigarette with a faraway look in his eyes. Almost as if he were visualizing future Stanley Cup wins.

Buffalo went on to lose to the Flyers in what can only be termed a colourful series, what with Jim Lorentz killing a bat on live TV and the Aud steaming up like a Turkish bath. And we would go on to win four straight Cups, starting the next season.

We would also go on to renew our rivalry with Beantown's finest, even though they would take on an entirely different look in the coming years.

When you focus on the post-Orr and post-Espo Bruins, the face you put on the uniform is that of Terry O'Reilly. He was their heart and soul as long as he played, and the Unluckiest

Bruin. His predecessors on the Big Bad Bruins won two Stanley Cups. Terry played for a lot of contenders, in fact, made them contenders with his presence and contribution. But he never got the big one, thanks to the Montreal Canadiens.

You don't pity your opponent in professional sports. Sympathy isn't the right word either. But if you fail to acknowledge that nobody ever gave more to his team than Terry did, then you're not the man you think you are. And he did it with class, even though he was a player who had to get into a lot of fights.

The thing I remember most about Terry is the night I got knocked out in the Garden . . . the only one who came in to find out how I was was Terry. That's the type of guy he was. He'd play tough, as tough as it took, but nothing dirty. In my mind, Terry and Mike McPhee personify the Canadiens-Bruins rivalry.

O'Reilly and Chris Nilan were trying to go at it and Chris Chelios tried to stick his nose in there too . . . and out of the corner of my eye I saw Brian Curran trying to get at Nilan from behind. I turned to intercept him just as he was jumping and he slammed on top of me. I fell straight back and hit my head on the ice. The next thing I remember was getting stitched up in the room.

I think what you can say about Terry as a coach is that he is doing a very good job; he's trying to get them to play the way he played and that will make a winner. He didn't get the Stanley Cup as a player but just might do it as a coach and that would be the most eloquent testimony to the man.

One reason why Terry never got the Stanley Cup from us as a player was Boston's futile game plan during his playing days: outmuscle Montreal. For a short period in the early 1960s, Montreal did have a problem with size. But an airlift of players like Terry Harper, Claude Larose, John Ferguson, and Ted Harris fixed that in a hurry and coincided with the beginning of two dynasties, the team of the late '60s that won five cups in seven years, and the team of the '70s that won five Cups in seven years. From 1964 to 1979, Montrel won ten Cups and was never intimidated because we were one of the biggest teams in the league.

And yet, there was Harry Sinden forever beating the bushes

for bigger, tougher guys who were going to run us out of the rink. It never worked; he never won. You'd think he would have learned. We had guys like Lpointe, Langway, Savard, Chartraw, Lambert, Tremblay, Risebrough, Lupien, and Bouchard. Nobody was ever going to intimidate us.

On the contrary, we intimidated Boston with talents like Shutt, Lafleur, Mahovlich, Larouche, Lemaire, and Savard.

And we intimidated Boston the only way you can truly intimidate a franchise; we beat them every time we met in the playoffs. We beat them when *THEY* were favoured to win; we beat them *WE* were favoured to win. We made them see the dreaded CH in their sleep. We made Harry toss and turn because every September he could foresee that season or playoff-ending press conference the following April or May where he'd be called upon to answer the Age-Old Question.

"Harry, how come you can't beat the Canadiens?"

Maybe, in fact, the players weren't intimidated. Maybe it was only Harry Sinden was so psyched out it got to the point that he talked about the "Ghosts of the Forum" to anyone in the media, Boston, and Montreal. Once he had convinced himself that he could never get a fair shake in Montreal, it was an easy task to pass on this negative message to his coaches and players. The refcrees are going to get you in the Forum: say it fften enough and even the hardiest soul wearing black-and-gold with the big B on the front will begin to feel some self-doubt. Say it loud enough, and some referees might be upset to the point of making it a sclf-fulfilling prophecy.

It would show up in games: we would score a big goal and Boston would sag unbelievably. And they were a character team, too.

We got the impression on our side of the rink that when Harry opened his mouth to his players, it was to build a neg-ative image or deliver a negative message about playing the Canadiens. What happens to the young player who has to go into a rink where your coach or general-manager has said, "Sooner or later, the ref is going to do it to us"? Sooner or later, you're going to make it come true by taking a dumb penalty, like Kraig Nienhuis did in the 1985–86 playoffs at the Forum. Right?

So when the Canadiens hooked up with the Bruins in a playoff hockey game, the frustration factor for them was huge. If I was on the receiving end, I know I would have a difficult time accepting it. It seems that in every series, we get the lucky bounce or that something happens and we end up beating them in the playoffs. That has to weigh heavy on players as individuals and a group.

It must be a heavy mental weight, especially overbearing in a town where the baseball team seems to exist only to be humiliated by the Damn Yankees in the Big Game. It can't be more frustrating for Boston baseball and hockey fans to know that at the onset of the season, the Yankees and the Canadiens, the most-storied teams in their sport, exist only to pound on their local heroes, even if they don't deserve to get pounded on. You can sense the resignation in the fans and the media.

Before every playoff series, the media trot out the Canadiens-Bruins streak and ask 20-year-old hockey players about a line of wins or losses that goes back to 1942. The easy or glib answer on both sides is that none of these players was even born in 1942 so the true length of the streak has nothing to do with them. That having been said, you know that this works on the psyches of the players on both sides.

It makes us play stronger. Because the streak has gone on so long, we say to ourselves, "Oh-oh, will this be the year? I don't want to be a part of the team that loses the first ever (in recent memory) to the Bruins."

A prime example has to be one of the most exciting games I've ever played . . . Game Seven of the Montreal-Boston semi-final, May 10, 1979.

This might sound a bit like a script for a beer commercial, but that was as close as it gets . . . I can't remember a more physical and emotional game in all the playoffs I've been in.

More than anything, too, this game illustrates the frustration of the Bruins versus the Canadiens.

We'd finished the regular season with 115 points, 15 ahead of the Bruins, who were rebuilding. They had long ago traded Phil Esposito and Ken Hodge to the New York Rangers for Jean Ratelle, Brad Park, and Rick Middleton; Bobby Orr was the property of the Chicago Black Hawks even though he hadn't laced up his skates in a year. And Don "Grapes" Cherry was the Bruins coach.

Our real rivals that year were the New York Islanders but they were ambushed by Phil Esposito and the Rangers, so the winner of our series would have an excellent opportunity to win the Cup. The Rangers were a good team but not one that figured to give either Boston or Montreal any difficulty.

Boston wanted revenge, pure and simple. We had handled them in the last two Stanley Cup finals, four straight in 1977 and in six games in 1978, and they were hungry. Both teams were battered after the first six games, all home ice wins. Doug Risebrough was wearing a speciall football faceguard on his helmet after Terry O'Reilly broke his nose in a fight two games earlier. Reggie Houle was back from a groin pull, Serge Savard was limping. They weren't saying who was injured but we knew they had their walking wounded, too.

We were determined that they wouldn't take it away from us at the Forum, and from the opening faceoff, we took the game to them. And to them. And to them. And Gilles Gilbert, *un bon Quebecois pure laine* was stoning us mercilessly. When we skated off for the second intermission, they led 3–1 on a pair of goals by Wayne Cashman and another by Rick Middleton.

This was becoming what Ken Dryden would call an exercise in absorption.

"We win because we absorb more punishment willingly than any other team I've every seen," he would say.

"We have a way about us of going through pain and adversity once the goal has been defined. That is what makes us so tough in a single, deciding game. We are basically going to absorb more pain, and file it away for future reference, as we get on with the task of winning."

Sitting in the dressingroom, facing 20 minutes and oblivion, I wondered if the sponge wasn't saturated.

For most of this game, it appeared that Guy Lafleur was going to have to absorb Don Marcotte. He wore Marcotte like a Siamese twin joined at the hip. Everywhere Guy went, Don went. Don Marcotte was a quality checking forward, never dirty, clean and physical in the style of Bob Gainey. But he didn't have Gainey's speed and by the start of the third period, he had just about run out of gas because Scotty Bowman was triple-shifting the Flower.

Marcotte was still gamely dogging Guy's heels when Lafleur smartly set up Mark Napier at 6:10. Three minutes later, Guy Lapointe tied it on a powerplay and the frenzied Forum smelled blood.

It turned out to be our own because one shift after Lapointe's goal, he was carried off the ice on a stretcher, with ligament damage to a knee. We pressed and pressed but Gilbert was unbeatable and when Rick Middleton snuck around the net and stuffed one in behind Ken at 16:01, you could see the writing on the wall: R.I.P. Montreal Canadiens 1978–79.

What happened next defies logical explanation. Perhaps the man best able to tell the story is Don Cherry himself, as he explains in his book *Grapes*.

". . . There were exactly 3 minutes and 59 seconds separating us from the biggest victory in our lives.

Could we do it? Everybody had his assignment, but I could tell that they were tight. Too tight. I would have liked to call a three day time-out and review all assignments, remind the players that the best defense is a good offense, and return Donny Marcotte to the fray, reasonably well-rested. Under the circumstances, I felt as helpless as a guy trying to catch the gold ring on a merry-go-round while sitting on an inside horse. The game had somehow gotten out of my grasp. It was up and down, fast, faster, fastest. Next thing I knew, Lafleur was going off the ice for the Canadiens and Marcotte had come back to our bench, while the play was still on. I walked over to Donny and gave him a pat on the back. He looked up at me, exhausted, and then looked back out onto the ice, Marcotte turned white. I heard him moan, "oh no!" Those deathless words will remain with me into my fourth reincarnation.

I looked out onto the field of battle and got that sinking sensation. I didn't have to count the players, I knew. *We had too many men on the ice*. My heart actually hurt then, and remembering now makes it hurt again.

I needed a large – about 40 foot long – hook to instantly

haul in my wandering minstrel. (Who will never be mentioned, we made a silent pact never to reveal his name.) If the referee and linesmen wore blindfolds for about a minute, I might be able to get somebody's attention and get him the hell back to the bench before we were slapped with a two-minute penalty.

No such luck. Linesman John D'Amico, a hell of a nice guy, noticed that we had six skaters instead of the legal five. I could tell in his heart of hearts that he didn't want to blow the whistle on us and that even he was hoping that a Bruin would have the good sense to get back to the bench. I could see in his eyes that he was saying to himself, "Don, I hate to do this to you but I have to!"

D'Amico's arm went up and the sound of his whistle cut right through to my bone marrow."

On our team bench, that same whistle sounded "over the top" and we stormed out of the trenches.

Here we were down 4–3 and the Bruins take a penalty for too many men at 17:26 of the final period of the final game. There is a God.

Halfway through the powerplay opportunity, Jacques Lemaire took the puck up ice and, crossing the Bruins blue line, dropped a pass to The Flower, who was steaming up the boards on the right wing. Guy didn't even hesitate; hammering a slapshot that was bouncing out of the Boston net behind Gilles Gilbert before anyone could react. It was since been called a howitzer, a cannon shot, a laster blast – all I knew is in all the years I played with Guy, I never saw him fire harder or truer. There wasn't a goalie in the world who would have stopped it.

The rest was anti-climax.

Nine minutes into overtime, Mario Tremblay and Yvon Lambert broke up ice 2-on-1 with Boston's Al Sims trying to stay between them and Brad Park struggling desperately to catch up with the play. He, too, had never won a Stanley Cup and sensed that this was his last kick at the can. Knowing that, he played a magnificent series.

Inside the Bruins zone, Lambert dashed for the next, getting ahead of Sims by about three feet just as Mario passed it across. Sprawled full length, Lambert put it behind Gilbert and we were on our way to the final.

In the first game of the New York series, the Rangers handled us easily 4–1. But we were running on empty, compliments of the Bruins.

You should have seen us at practice the day after the Boston win, the guys could hardly move. It wasn't that the Rangers beat us; we just didn't have anything left. And then the next day we saw Wayne Thomas and a few of the other Rangers making a typical Rangers mistake, smoking their big cigars and saying how they were going to beat us in playoffs. It was as if they'd already won the Stanley Cup. That woke us up and they didn't win another game.

We all knew that we had won the real Stanley Cup final before we played the Rangers. Man, we had *beaten Boston*, and around here that means something. Honour thy opponent because he honours you with his ability.

Soon afterwards, Don Cherry, Wayne Cashman, Brad Park, Stan Jonathan, Don Marcotte, Bobby Schmautz, Gary Doak, Gilles Gilbert, and Gerry Cheevers would be gone. And believe it or not, it wouldn't make much of a difference because the guys in the black-and-gold would replace them more than adequately.

The myth of the Canadiens invincibility over the Bruins has really taken hold in this decade, one in which the Canadiens have only one Stanley Cup, so far. It has attained folkloric stature mainly because we reversed our roles in the early '80s; Montreal was the underdog and Boston finally was ready to break the playoff stranglehold we had held since the earliest days of Maurice Richard, Ken Reardon, Butch Bouchard, and Bill Durnan.

The 1983–84 season and the ensuing playoffs were a classic case in point. Led by the superstar trio of Barry Pederson, Rick Middleton, and Raymond Bourque, the Bruins finished first in the Adams Division with 104 points, edging out the Buffalo Sabres by one point on the last Sunday night of the season. Quebec finished nine back with 94 points in third, and we floundered to Montreal's first sub-.500 season since

1942–243. Our 35–40–5 record for 75 points would have finished second in the Norris, third in the Smythe, and out of the playoffs in the Patrick. Boston's first-place finish gave up hope; we had played them even during the season while Buffalo had wiped us out. Up until that last night of the season, we'd anticipated an opening series with the Sabres.

That late-season surge by Boston proved their undoing. With 11 games to go in the season, managing director Serge Savard replaced Bob Berry with Jacques Lemaire and although Lemaire's stretch record was 4–7, we finally started to put our game back into place.

We didn't coast through the last weeks of the season but we didn't overdo it either. The Bruins did. We faced a tired team when the playoffs opened at the Garden, stole two quick games on strong goaltending from Steve Penney, and wrapped it up in three straight back home at the Forum. The look of absolute disbelief on the faces of Boston players as we shook hands after Game Three is something I'll never forget. If we began to forge the myth with the 1979 semi-final, we delivered the finished product with the 1984 sweep.

A year later, we went to a fifth game and a last-minute goal by Mats Naslund for a 1–0 victory, saved only by a last-second toe save on a labelled blast from Ray Bourque. In 1986, we swept the Bruins in a five-game series and did it one better in 1987, winning four straight in the newly expanded best-of-seven opening round. Go figure.

The Bruins of the 1980s certainly have been no patsies:

1980	46	21	13	105	(second, Adams Division)
1981	37	30	13	87	(second, Adams Division)
1982	43	27	10	96	(second, Adams Division)
1983	50	20	10	110	(first, Adams Division)
1984	49	25	6	100	(first, Adams Division)
1985	36	34	10	82	(fourth, Adams Division)
1986	37	31	12	86	(third, Adams Division)
1987	39	34	7	85	(third, Adams Division)
1988	44	30	6	95	(second, Adams Division)

In those eight seasons, they totalled 751 points, or an

average of 93.8 a year. We totalled 763 points over the same period, or 95.3 a year. Other top team totals in the same decade are Philadelphia 827 (103.3); Edmonton Oilers 813 (101.6); and New York Islanders 777 (97.1). So Boston has always been up there.

I think the 1986–87 and the 1987–88 Bruins were the best teams they've had in a long time. In the first of those two years, they stayed very competitive, even without Gord Kluzak who missed the entire season, and with injuries to guys like Ken Linseman and Charlie Simmer. What has hurt Boston the most in recent times is goaltending.

Harry Sinden and coaches Gerry Cheevers, Butch Goring, and Terry O'Reilly tried everything and everyone – U.S. Olympics hero Jim Craig, Cleon Daskalaskis, Doug Keans, Bill Ranford, Pat Riggin, Pete Peeters, Marco Baron, and Roberto Romano before they finally acuired Rejean Lemelin as a free agent. And then, late last year, they picked up Andy Moog from Edmonton, and their goaltending finally was set.

Before Lemelin and Moog, kids like Ranford or veterans like Peeters would play well in streaks and then slack off. I blame a lot of that on Boston Garden, where the shooters can be on a goalie so fast he doesn't have time to blink. Another factor that contributes to the wild mood and performance swings by goalies is the intensity of the Adams Division. With the Sabres, Nordiques, and Whalers sharing the division, there are few easy games.

At the blueline, the Bruins were notoriously weak before Kluzak returned and rookie Glen Wesley was drafted. Until then, Ray Bourque and a cast of thousands tried to stop the bleeding but with little luck. Other teams had a very simple game plan: Key on Bourque and hit him any chance you get to tire him out. With a soft defence, there was little Boston coaches could do to rest or protect their legitimate superstar. Bourque had to play and take his lumps.

Ray is a great hockey player in the mold of the flying modern defenceman that was cast originally by Bobby Orr. Although he doesn't have all of Orr's skills, (who does?) he is a dominating offensive defenceman who can play it very physical in heavy traffic. But no matter how good you are, when you end up playing 1-on-5, you're bound to become frustrated.

I enjoy the challenge of playing against the Bruins because Bourque is there, just like I could always get up for games against the Islanders with Denis Potvin, the Oilers with Paul Coffey, and the Maple Leafs with Borje Salming in his prime.

The best thing about Raymond is his ability to control the game; he has a very good head for hockey, although I think he shoots too much. I also think the Bruins make him carry and handle the puck too often. He's a terrific puckhandler, but he becomes a much more vulnerable target when he's always carrying the puck, especially in those 40 games he plays in Boston. Bourque is strong and can take a lot, but like anybody else, he'll slow down if they're always pounding him.

In Boston, they like to make Bourque-Orr comparisons but I think this does Ray a disservice. Bourque has a major advantage in that he is much physically stronger than Bobby was, and Bobby was no weakling. Ray has worked on two good legs throughout his career; Bobby didn't even have one good one. As for straight-up talent, he doesn't have all of Bobby's gifts. I played with both on Canada Cup teams and Bobby sparkled in 1976, despite being hobbled. Raymond became just one of the rest at the Canada Cup; he was surrounded by superior talent on that team and like the rest of us, the diamond lost its sparkle when it was thrown in with many others. When the rest are Coffey, Robinson, Potvin, Hartsburg, Ramage, Stevens, et al, that is no insult.

Before and after Ray won the 1987 Norris Trophy for top defenceman, it seemed everyone was comparing Paul Coffey and Ray Bourque. On the surface, they have similar styles, but Ray is much more physical than Paul and will be more effective in rough games, especially in the small rink. He is also better defensively in his own zone.

Offensively, Coffey is the closest to Bobby Orr that I've seen. His passing, skating, and shooting ability, and his pure speed coming up behind the play, make him a very dangerous adversary. Ray Bourque has very good skating ability and mobility but Coffey is on a higher level.

The Bruins of the 1980s have been Bourque and several other major contributors. Rick Middleton is not called Shifty for nothing; he is now, and always has been, a quality forward with tremendous skills – poison in the opposition zone.

A very quiet guy, he also has seemed to me to be a leader on that team, one who doesn't have to say much. There was talk a couple of seasons back that he'd lost a step, deadly for a smaller forward, but it didn't destroy his game; he adjusted. I knew he suffered for a while from the Barry Pederson trade because Middleton and Pederson read each other as well as any two teammates ever could. When they played together, it was like the same player in two bodies.

Another leader with the Bruins in recent years, and the man Chris Nilan loves to hate, is Ken Linseman. The Rat has been his nickname ever since his first days in Philadelphia and it followed him to Edmonton and Boston. "Why the Rat?" you might ask. Because Ken Linseman is a dirty hockey player and makes no bones about it. He'll slash you, give you the butt end, kick you, hit you behind the knee with the stick when your back is turned, you name it.

What strikes me the most about Linseman is that he's the type of guy you hate to play against but you'd love to have on your team. I think if he stuck to his game, which is built on his superior speed, rather than always taking the cheap shot, he'd be a perfect hockey player – probably all-star quality. He's good at faceoffs, he passes as well as anybody in the league, and he's certainly one of the quickest players there is. But he's been sticking people for so long I don't think he could get away from that style.

He played with my brother Moe in Kingston in junior and was a leader on their very good team. But he ended up in a big fight and got suspended for kicking an opponent in the head with his skate; as a result, Kingston was eliminated early in the playoffs.

One of the reasons he was traded from Philadelphia was that management figured he was running two Flyers into premature retirement with his antics: himself and Paul Holmgren. The Rat would start lots of fights and Holmgren would have to finish them, and big Paul was being worn out well ahead of his time.

Why the Rat? Ask former defenceman and teammate Lee Fogolin, whom Linseman bit on the cheek during one scrap.

Other Bruins who have impressed during the 1980s include Charlie Simmer, Cam Neely, Reed Larson, and even little Nevin Markwart. Simmer was not built in the original Bruins mold. A big man, he never played the big man's game or the physical game that the Garden demanded. The Bruins had no complaints, though. Although he slowed down somewhat after suffering a near-career ending injury with the Kings, Charlie was superb scorer with a nice touch around the net. For his size, he would seem almost invisible in our zone, able to position himself just outside a defenceman's line of sight, moving silently to the puck and burying it as it reached him. He had terrific soft hands and when the opportunity was there, he made the most of it.

Trading Cam Neely, plain and simple, was a huge mistake by the Vancouver Canucks. Yes, they got a terrific player in Barry Pederson, even after he'd missed most of 1985 with a shoulder problem. But Boston got Neely, and then Glen Wesley with the first-round draft choice that accompanied Neely to Beantown in what qualifies as the Steal of the Decade. Wesley will be a good one for a long, long time and Neely is a special player now. Neely can play in traffic and I'd always thought he was underrated with the Canucks. He's the perfect Bruin and will be one of the biggest stars they've ever had before his career ends.

Reed Larson played for many years in semi-obscurity in Detroit before coming to Boston in a trade for Mike O'Connell. Semi-obscurity in Detroit? Where 20,000 show up at Joe Louis Arena?

Yeah. Semi-obscurity, the kind you get when you're a superior player on a below-average team. For all his Red Wings days, Larson laboured on a perennial loser but he handled it like a gentleman throughout. He did everything they asked of him and when he came over to Boston, he took a bit of the pressure off Bourque. Reed's problem in the smaller rink is his style – while he still has the booming shot, he's a gambling-type defenceman and when he makes a booboo, it's usually a big one. If you miss a guy in Boston, he's on your goalie in a flash; there's no way that the other defenceman can get an angle on him and bail you out.

Little Nevin Markwart, it seems to me, personifies the pride in the B on the crest. He's about 170 pounds, takes a pounding, and always keeps coming back. He'll scrap with anyone and anything; he won't win too many, but he has a lot of heart. He's a bit like a small Claude Lemieux; he has a way of getting under your skin.

The makeup of the 1986–87 and 1987–88 Bruins teams shows that Harry Sinden has finally headed in another direction. While he has acquired some big bruisers – Neely, Bob Sweeney, Lyndon Byers, Jay Miller, and Willi Plett, he has begun to lean toward skilled players of all sizes like Randy Burridge, Steve Kasper, Craig Janney, and Bob Joyce. The Bruins will continue to be the Big Bad Bruins in that they will play a robust, physical game. But it will be rough, and not particularly dirty.

And now with the skilled players they are accumulating, Boston's game will finally travel well, especially on those big, inhospitable rinks where they used to flounder in the past. It is not a bad idea to try to tailor your team to your rink, in that you'll play 40 games there each season. But don't forget that you have to play the other 40 games on 200' by 85' rinks. If you build your rink, and your rink is an oddity, that puts you at a disadvantage out there in the real world.

Those numbers strangely mirror ours, 232–83–45 for 509 points at home and 150–151–59 for 359 points on the road. But we underwent two major transitions in that time, and apart from 1980–81, were not expected to challenge for the Cup. Boston, on the other hand, was considered a serious contender throughout the decade.

Frankly, they should have been a much better team than we were in that period.

Boston home and away—1980

	HOME				AWAY			
1980	27	9	4	58	19	12	9	47
1981	26	10	4	56	11	20	9	31
1982	24	12	4	52	19	15	6	44
1983	28	6	6	62	22	14	4	48
1984	25	12	3	53	24	13	3	51
1985	21	15	4	46	15	19	6	36
1986	24	9	7	55	13	22	5	31
1987	25	11	4	54	14	23	3	31
1988	24	13	3	51	20	17	3	43
Total	224	97	39	487	157	153	48	362

One thing everybody noticed about the Bruins this past season was that it was the least physical and best skating team Harry Sinden has put together in a long time. That doesn't mean that they can play on the big rinks. Their away record of '87–'88 shows that clearly. But with Burridge, Joyce, Janney, Bourque, Kluzak, Linseman, Wesley, Neely, and Kasper, their road record in coming years should be very good.

As this chapter is being written, the Canadiens and the Bruins are fighting to the wire in the Adams Division. Buffalo, Hartford, and Quebec are far behind and long forgotten.

Will the Canadiens finish first? Will Boston surge forward in the last weeks and edge ahead?

Will we meet Boston again in the playoffs?

Will they finally beat us?

NINE

A Gathering of Solitary Men

IT WOULD sound like far-off thunder, that rumbling just below the horizon that tells your ears that the beautiful sunny day your senses are still enjoying isn't going to last. It's the noise that parents delight in describing to young children as "the angels are bowling."

At the Forum, the players enter either at the garage door on de Maisonneuve (north side) or at the pass gate and press entrance on Atwater (northwest corner). It could be a couple of hours before a practice or even a game, and we'd hear it, the sound coming from the rink as we walked in the corridor to the dressingroom.

"Boom."

A few seconds pause.

"Boom."

Nearing the dressingroom, dead centre on the west side, you could hear another sound, that curious "shuuussh" scraping sound made by a skate blade cleaving fresh ice.

"Shuush, shuush, shuush . . . boom."

All was right with the world.

The Flower was communing with the gods of hockey.

A Solitary Man.

Perhaps the strangest thing about the Canadiens of the late 1970s, the best team that I ever played on, was that this group was dominated by some very private, almost solitary men.

Guy Lafleur. Ken Dryden. Jacques Lemaire. Serge Savard.

Bob Gainey. Scotty Bowman. All intensely private individuals, who preferred to keep their own counsel. Solitary men all. Yet, ironically, all consummate team players. I'll talk about all but Gainey in this chapter; Bob deserves special attention elsewhere.

After many years in hockey, in the professional ranks and out, it has become evident to me that it takes all kinds of individuals to form a group, or team, that strives toward a common goal.

In the middle 1970s, the Montreal Canadiens were being molded into a group that would win four straight Stanley Cups. We knew we were good; actually we knew we were much better than good. We knew that we could harness our collective energies and win several Stanley Cups. Most importantly, we trusted each other. We trusted the contribution that each player could and would make: Steve Shutt's garbage goals by the dumper load, the Flower's spectacular free-form cavalry charges, Jacques Lemaire's devastating shot and pinpoint passes, Ken Dryden's big saves, Serge Savard's coolness and leadership in our defensive zone, Bob Gainey's dive-bombing runs in theirs, and Scotty Bowman's Patton-like preparations for a big game.

We trusted Doug Risebrough, Mario Tremblay, and Yvon Lambert to leave a wake-up call when we were sleepwalking against lesser opponents; Yvan Cournoyer to fire in on the off-wing on all afterburners and terrorize their goalie; and Jim Roberts and Doug Jarvis to pin their forwards in their own zone while some venturesome defencemen quickly got back into position.

We trusted Pierre Bouchard, Gilles Lupien, and Rick Chartraw to quickly douse the flames of opposition belligerence and Guy Lapointe and myself to deliver big hits in our zone and move the puck quickly up-ice into theirs.

And, in those moments when our backs were against the wall, we trusted Don Awrey, Bill Nyrop, Brian Engblom, and Rod Langway to throw their bodies into the breach; blocking shots and banging bodies in the crease and corners until we could regroup and press to the counterattack. All of the players on this team knew their roles; strangely enough, though, few were role players in the modern definition. We had a roomful of leaders.

Thus, we were a team.

For me, these are the elements of a team; the unspoken communication, the feeling of unity and oneness, of everyone being on a wavelength or frequency that no one else can tap. We could say more to each other sitting in silence between periods than most other teams could in a week full of loud meetings.

On those occasions when the machinery hummed beautifully, everthing meshing as planned and with the other team in total disarray, we would sit in the room shaking our heads in wonder, the silence only broken by Steve Shutt's highpitched giggle and a "scary, ain't it?"

Which is not say our room was quiet; far from it. With the Happy gang of Peter Mahovlich, Jim Roberts, Guy Lapointe, Rejean Houle, Steve Shutt, and Rick Chartraw on the same team, Led Zeppelin could be playing full blast on the boom box and you might not hear it.

Our acknowledged leaders were men of character. I should start with Guy Lafleur, the "blond kid from Thurso" who had beaten me and the Russell Lions in the Cornwall peewee tournament when we were 12 years old.

In the early years, our lives ran along several parallels. Both of us came from rural or small towns, just outside Ottawa, mine in Ontario, his in Quebec. We came from large families – Guy had a bunch of sisters – who supported us and our hockey aspirations from our earliest days.

Guy started playing hockey when he was about five, on a rink his Dad built behind their house. By age seven, he was as good as most of the bigger boys, some aged 10 and 11. By age nine, he knew he wanted to be a serious hockey player. He would sneak into the local arena in the early morning hours, through a hole in the wall, and skate by himself while the caretaker slept. When he was finally found out, the caretaker showed Guy the main door and said, sternly, "use it . . . the next time you come." He was also Guy's hockey coach.

That solitary skate bacame a habit Guy carried through his entire hockey career.

"I started training in my own way then," he said.

"I worked at a friend's dairy farm (sound familiar?) and I would do my own version of cross-country running, sometimes going up to ten miles. Everybody thought I was nuts."

But it worked. The skinny nine-year-old was deceptively fast and strong and won the scoring championship in his class the next February at the Quebec Peewee Hockey Tournament. Two more Quebec tournament appearances later, and hockey people in the provincial capital began calling Rejean Lafleur in Thurso.

"Send the boy down. We'll board him with a nice family, send him to a good school, and he'll develop into a top hockey talent."

For a year it was: "No, the boy's too young."

Then, it was: "Yes, he's coming."

With that, our paths parted. I left home to play Junior A for Kitchener when I was 19, married and father of one. Guy Left Thurso, Quebec to play Junior B in Quebec City when he was barely into puberty at age 14. That took a very special kind of courage.

"I was scared out of my mind," he once told me. "After begging my Dad to let me go the year before, I spent a lot of my first months there on the phone, begging him to let me come home."

Guy played a year of Junior B and then moved on up to Junior A. In his last year of Junior with Quebec Remparts, he scored an unheard of 130 goals and 79 assists for 209 points, and added 22 goals and 21 assists in 14 playoff games as the Remparts won the Memorial Cup.

On June 10, 1971, Guy Damien Lafleur was the Montreal Canadiens' and the NHL's first draft choice . . . exactly 19 spots ahead of Larry Clark Robinson.

I wouldn't have traded places with him for the world.

For me, there was no question of an automatic berth with the big club. I was going to training camp hoping to play well, refine my skills, and then get called up in a year or two.

With Jean Beliveau retiring the day before, and with Guy's Quebec City career closely paralleling Jean's, the word was out. The kid was going to be the next great French-Canadian superstar, holding high the torch passed from Richard to Beliveau to himself.

Jean offered to let Guy wear his illustrious Number 4, the same number Lafleur had worn with Quebec. "Non merci," said the Flower. "The pressure is going to be bad enough." He was right. The Third Coming was a test of his character and ability. Montreal fans, perenially starved for a Stanley cup parade in May, were willing to allow that Guy wouldn't score 130 goals a year in the NHL. Not right away, anyway. But half that number would do just nicely.

While I was serving my apprenticeship in Nova Scotia, alongside many other Montreal futures, Guy was slugging away on the third and fourth lines with the big club, learning Scotty Bowman's "everybody plays two ways" system. He finished his rookie season with a very respectable 29 goals and 35 assists. Unfortunately, number two pick Marcel Dionne had 77 points that year and a third rookie, Rick Martin, had 44 goals and 74 points.

For the next two seasons, both Martin and Dionne would have higher point totals that the Flower. They would also each have about twice the ice time enjoyed by Guy, something few of Montreal's so called knowledgeable fans would admit to in their backhanded comparisons. That kind of talk put undue pressure on Lafleur; he didn't control his icetime or the Canadien's strategy in allowing him to mature at a steady, if slower, pace than some fans might want. He was following the Canadiens' age-old maturation process, as Yvan Cournoyer, Jacques Lemaire, and other young stars had before him.

I remember those TV commercials for Paul Masson California wines that featured Orson "no wine before its time" Welles. Sam Pollock might have done the commercial with more conviction because it described perfectly Montreal's approach to young vintages.

To continue the wine analogy, when Guy finally matured in 1975–76, it was a very good year. He would not only win his first scoring championship, he'd take the Montreal Canadiens with him on a ride that wouldn't end until four more Stanley Cup banners hung high in the Forum rafters. Neither Dionne nor Martin ever won the Cup.

What few fans remember today is that Lafleur played out of position for most of those first three years. With a flock of right and left wingers available to the club, and the retirement of Jean Beliveau, and trade of Ralph Backstrom (used to ensure the acquisition of Lafleur), there was a shortage down the middle and Guy often played centre. He never complained where other so-called superstars would have been burning up the telephone lines with their agents.

Which is why when his teammates would hear the thunder in the rink as they came to practice at the Forum, they knew it was money in the bank. It was a solitary skate Guy had begun in Thurso, and later continued with the Remparts when he would be on the ice at Le Colisee an hour before their scheduled late afternoon workouts.

It was a time when a very special hockey player could be alone, and not so much think about his sport but let the organism take over, the machine running on automatic: his skates the normal extension of his legs and feet; his stick the continuation of his arms and hands. Guy would skate in a variety of patterns on the ice, wherever his body took him, feeling the boards, sensing rather than seeing the peculiar bounce you would get if a shot hit a certain spot just so, feeling where the net was with his back to it, and then wheeling and firing the puck just inside a post or just under the crossbar. None of this dead-centre shooting for the Flower; in a real game, that spot was occupied by a goalie. And when Lafleur would make the same miraculous shot in a real game, the fans, the media, the opposition would roll their eyes skyward in disbelief, never once thinking that a movement so natural could have been practised. Having watched the Flower, I felt he could probably do the same thing while blindfolded, so good was his on-ice gyroscope.

Occasionally, teammates still in civies would watch quietly, saying nothing, feeling the electricity and sharing in the spirit. More than once in the 11 years we shared, I'd seen some teammates come out early, dressed for practice, watch Lafleur for a few minutes, and return to the dressingroom for "another piece of equipment," anything to avoid an intrusion on the ice. That solitary skate developed the kind of moves on the ice that left fellow hockey players, teammates and opponents, shaking their heads.

On the bench, either bench, during a game, players would watch his every move. The supreme compliment was "he's a player" – sports world shorthand for "he is a supreme talent who makes the rest of us look like the mere mortals we really are."

Guy Damien Lafleur was a player, and a very special cog in the Canadiens' Stanley Cup wheel: he was the artist who inspired us all.

Simply, he was the most exciting hockey player I've ever played with. And possibly, the most exciting hockey player I've seen to this day, with the minor exception of Mario Lemieux. The exception I make with Mario is that he's a lot taller and a lot smoother than Guy was, more of a battleship or heavy cruiser to Guy's destroyer. His moves are predicated on his size and almost a freeze-frame smoothness. Guy, on the other hand, was strictly fast-forward. You'd only really see the moves when you replayed it all in slow motion.

Guy was the only player I've ever seen routinely bring people out of their seats when he carried the puck. From what observers of the game in the 1950s tell me, Lafleur-Gretzky is the same thing as Richard-Howe. Lafleur and Richard were excitement personified, controlled bursts of offensive creativity that would demand an emotional response from a crowd. Howe and Gretzky played a much more intellectual game, less exciting for the fans, perhaps, but certainly no less effective.

I can remember no other player who would lace on his skates the day before training camp and go out there looking like he'd never been off skates. He was such a tremendous athlete and had reserves others didn't; but in the end this probably was his downfall.

He made such strong demands on himself that he couldn't face being only a good player. Being such a natural athlete, however, had its drawbacks. If anybody could screw up a drill in practice it was Lafleur. Scotty Bowman would gather the players at centre ice, all of us in our different-coloured practice sweaters to distinguish the various forward lines and defensive pairings.

"I want the forwards to skate to centre ice, turn behind a defenceman, look for the puck and then make a pass up the left wing."

Guy would be the first to screw it up. And not only once. You just couldn't limit that natural ability to the strict confines of diagrammed drills and pass patterns. Guy was a natural, self-taught dancer who worked on exquisite, split-second muscle memory; he could never follow the foot chart on the floor. Serge Savard and I played much of the time with Guy and Steve Shutt and either Peter Mahovlich or Jacques Lemaire at centre. When coming out of our zone, our breakouts almost always went up the left side; if we did go up the right side Serge or I usually carried it.

Why? Because the moment one of us picked up the puck in our zone, Lafleur was gone, doing his own thing . . . drawing the defencemen out or getting into an opening. That made it tough on Shutty; the onus on him was to stay in his own end or in position on the left side so we could get the puck up to him and out of the zone. He had to do a lot of mucking along the boards and get the puck up to Flower. Once his homework was done, Steve was quite free to get into position in front of the opposition net and score his 60 goals or so.

When Guy was no longer able to do the things he thought he should be able to do, he thought he didn't have it anymore. Ironically, in the end when he wasn't scoring, he had probably become the most complete hockey player he'd ever been, even compared against the time when he was scoring all the goals.

Just before he retired, the only fault in his game was that the puck wasn't going into the net. Guy was still a tremendous hockey player who could have played several more seasons in the league, had he been able to accept that he would score less. But he couldn't accept that; he felt he was put on this earth to be a goal scorer and if he couldn't be one, there was no reason to prolong his NHL career.

He had his own definition of perfection and lived by it.

I played 11 years with the Flower and had my share of conversations with him during that time. We staged a common hold-out against the club in 1982 to back salary claims and during that time we spoke a lot to each other on the telephone; comparing strategy and results. Yet, when it was all over, what frustrated me the most was realizing that I never really got to know Guy; nobody did. He was an integral member of an extremely close-knit group, but he had a private place with no access to anyone else.

I think it was protection, like armour. He had lived with all of these heightened expectations from a very young age, and when he was drafted he was expected to be the next Beliveau. I wouldn't have lived his life for all the tea in China. There wasn't a place he could go, there wasn't a thing he could do in public. His summers were taken up with commercials, people wanting his time, all the time. Since he could not physically escape, I think he found a way to mentally escape, a quiet little place inside where he could be at peace with himself. As if he was saying to everyone, "you have a piece of me, but not all of me."

I often wonder what it would have been like for Stephane Richer if Guy had been able to stay on for a few more years, to help the transition between the two; if Guy had been able, as a teammate, to explain the Forum pressure-cooker to Stephane, to ease him through or around some of the early crises.

The again, he might have been the worst choice to initiate a potential young superstar into the bosom of the Montreal Canadiens hockey club. We'll never know.

If Guy Lafleur was the acknowledged superstar from the very beginning, Serge Savard was the everday guy elevated to exalted status. Nicknamed The Senator at an early stage in his career, he was quiet, conservative, and a pure leader; a player who could communicate extremely well with a few words. He was one of the few teammates I knew who belonged in a three-piece suit.

With no hockey to move himself into the spotlight, he would have been a successful small-town lawyer, before moving into politics and eventually, the highest levels of government. Serge always gave me the impression that he listened, actually listened to what other people were saying, absorbing their words and opinions before responding with his own. On the ice, he was a leader. I played and roomed with Serge for seven years and, on the ice, I could always count on him to cover for my mistakes. No matter what kind of bonehead mistake you could make in the other team's zone, you instinctively knew that when you turned to look up ice, Serge would be back there, policing the area.

Serge, like Guy, was an intensely private individual, but did not exhibit the shyness of Lafleur, Jacques Lemaire, or Scotty Bowman. He pondered before he spoke; he weighed all the options before he committed himself. In a game, that was a great reassurance to me and to Ken Dryden. The Senator just never, ever, found himself out of position.

Serge was our E. F. Hutton; he didn't talk much, but when he did, everyone listened. He always seemed older, more mature, than the rest of us and that was partly due to the types of people he hung around with outside hockey. His crowd was an older one, and comprised almost totally of people outside the game. Serge was involved in many business dealings and always seemed to have something going so it was pretty normal to see him either in a three-piece suit, or surrounded by them.

Off the ice, he was never without his foot-long cigar, a folded Racing Form tucked under an arm, and a phone in his ear connecting him with Blue Bonnets, checking out his own stable of horses, or other business interests.

As with Guy, there was little conversation. We were roommates on the road for the better part of a decade, but we hardly ever sat down and talked one-on-one. I respected his judgement a lot, however, and he would be the one I went to if I wanted advice on legal or contract matters.

When it came to the game, we didn't have to communicate a great deal. It got so that we knew where the other was in certain situations, instinctively trusting that person to be there.

Serge had a patented move that broadcaster Danny Gallivan christened the "spinnerama." He would skate up the right wing boards out of our zone, usually right at an oncoming winger. Just as both reached the vicinity of the blue line, Serge would spin around 360 degrees, and away from the checker. He'd perfected the move in both directions, clockwise and counter-clockwise, and teams that sent in one or two forecheckers were reluctant to get too close to Serge because he'd burn them. We'd work variations of the play, as well. When he'd pull that move, I'd cut towards him at full speed and he'd give me a quick, short pass. That usually eliminated not one, but two checkers, and we would have a 4-on-3 going into their zone.

We scored a lot off that play, but Serge was usually the fourth man so he didn't get the assists or the recognition that was his due. After being burned so many times, other coaches dropped their checkers back into the neutral zone, enabling us to come out of our zone more easily and even faster.

That's what we call Inside Hockey and it's one of the reasons why Serge was such a contributor to the Montreal Canadiens during his career, which included seven Stanley Cups.

Our connections were not always the smoothest, however. I remember one night against the Flames, one of their wingers was skating in on net and Serge was chasing him. I angled to-wards the player and, haunches high, knees bent and driving, threw a famous Larry Robinson number one special hip check at the guy.

And missed completely. Well not so completely. I got Serge right in the stomach and he went down like he had been hit by a truck. He was winded and stayed down for a good five minutes.

I was beside myself. "Serge, are you okay?"

"I'll live," he gasped as other "concerned" teammates gathered round started laughing.

"Tomorrow morning, your tests for colour blindness start!"

Serge Savard was the ultimate defensive defenceman. Two broken legs in the late 1960s had slowed his rushing, changed his style a bit, and that, of course, cost him a lot of recognition in the eyes of the Norris Trophy voters, especially south of the border.

"That's for you and Pointu to do," he said when we talked about it.

"I prefer to stay back." Serge's highest points season was 1974–75, with 20 goals and 40 assists, so he wasn't going to get much consideration for the best defenceman award. But, Bobby Orr aside, and in some of those seasons Bobby didn't play much because of injury. Serge didn't get many votes. Serge Savard was a dominating presence on the ice, especially in games against the Orrs, Parks, Potvins, Langways, and friends. Somehow, some way, Serge Savard, Brad Park, Borje Salming, and Guy Lapointe never won a Norris. And Randy Carlyle did. Go figure.

Still, he did make it to the Hall of Fame. I wonder if he'll make it again, this time in the builders' category, for the work he's done and will do in the Canadiens front office.

If I said that Serge Savard might have been a lawyer had he not embarked on a career as a hockey player, Ken Dryden was both.

How does one describe Ken Dryden? How do I remember him? For starters you have to say he was a very deep individual, very analytical, very smart. You got the impression he had to work at being a teammate, not because he thought he was above it all or above us, but more because he was in constant analysis mode. He had his quirks and idiosyncrasies like the rest of us, but he also was a very private person who really seemed to look out at the world. Ken was an observer, interested in everything. On the bus or the plane, most of us would fight for our chance to rifle through the sports section of the newspaper, peeling away other sections like an orange. Four or five of us would be tugging and pulling at the Sports or maybe the Stock Exchange listings; Ken would be quietly reading the front section, cover to cover.

In my mind, Ken was just a reserved person, one who preferred not to make a big show of anything. He'd certainly merit and share in our triumphs and victories as the best goalie of our day, and he'd share in the locker room kidding and pranks to a certain degree. But he never initiated it; it just wasn't his style.

The problem with the quiet person, of course, is that other, noisier or more outgoing people tend to view him or her with suspicion. Like the wallflower at a party makes the revellers uncomfortable or guilty. Or both.

What's he hiding? Doesn't he like us? Is he looking down his nose at us? Those suspicions feed on themselves, magnify, and sometimes can get a genuine, but shy person in trouble with the group. Did those doubts assail us? No. We all knew why Ken was there, and it was for the same reason we were there: Hockey. A special talent in a special sport brought us together in the same room. Outside interests, other talents were laudable as long as they didn't intrude on the team.

After reading, and re-reading Ken's *The Game*, I understand him now better than I ever did. The real Dryden emerged to express those thoughts that had stayed beneath the surface for a long time. And he admitted that his personality could foster misgivings or suspicions.

> I feel comfortable on this bus, with this team. I'm not sure anyone else knows that. I'm not sure even my teammates know it. I don't say much. I often like to be alone. My background and interests are different enough to make me seem different (being a goalie forgives a lot; being a good goalie, a lot more). Still, by now I think most understand. I have changed in eight years. Before my sabbatical season, 1973–74, I had little time for the team. It was due in part to my dual life as a law student, but only in part. I was young, and in pre-dynasty times, better than the team. I had standards no one could meet. Those who didn't backcheck as often as I thought they should, those who

drank too much, let me down. They had seemed more like
opponents than teammates, lined up against me, keeping me
from being what I wanted to be. And, silently, I raged at them.
Early in the 1973 playoffs, Bowman took me aside. He wondered if I felt myself "too big" for the team. I don't remember
what had prompted it. It didn't matter. I was hurt, and furious.
For the rest of the playoffs, I sulked, desperately sure he was
wrong, afraid he wasn't. At the end, I got my revenge. It was
Bowman's first Stanley Cup. When the team celebrated on the
ice, he hugged me as did the others. I hung from him like a rag.

Which other player who sat out a full NHL season in a
contract squabble could call it "a sabbatical"? Name one other
player who actually defeated, yes defeated, Sam Pollock.
That was Ken Dryden.

Ken Dryden was a very special person, and an even more
special athlete; we all knew that in the room and, yes Ken, we
accepted you for what you were, and are. Every newcomer to
the team was quietly given a course in Ken Dryden 101 by
Professors Shutt, Tremblay, and Lapointe. The course
material will never be made public because some of your
former teammates feel it might prove actionable and, after all,
you are a lawyer . . .

Shutty was our Ken Dryden expert. In Dryden's last couple
of seasons, when he knew he would be writing a book after his
career was over, Dryden recorded every word, every utterance
by Shutt. Steve would be tossing off lines a mile a minute and
Ken would be furiously scribbling. "Hey Shutty, I missed that
last bit. Do you want to repeat it just so I get it right."

"Come on Kenny, get a stenographer. I'm six lines past
that." And with a hearty "beep, beep," the Roadrunner of the
Mouth would be off again.

Shutty made it into Ken's book. We all knew he would. This
scene in *The Game* is taken from a team bus ride.

The overcast has burned away. I try to sleep, then read. I
look out the windows, at turnpike countryside, mile after
mile. It's a day to look out windows, to let energy run

down, and feel it trickle back. Then feel it build again. It happens each year at this time. When I feel spring, or the playoffs, I never know which it is. It's an instinct, as sure as the seasons, something that happens, that cannot be rushed. When it's time, I will know.

I lean back in my seat, and close my eyes.

"Ya weren't sleepin', were ya?" It's Shutt.

"Huh? Oh no, Shutty."

"I was brilliant last night, eh?"

"Huh? Oh yeah, Shutty, yeah, you were brilliant."

"I was, wasn't I? Happens every time I drink. Can't understand it. Wish I could remember what I said. I oughta drink more often, hee hee hee." It comes in a dizzying burst. I can't keep up. He sees a pad of paper on my lap. "Hey whatcha doin'?"

"Huh? Oh, I was just writing down some things. May use 'em sometime."

"Ya writin' a book? Hey great. Need some help? Want some of my quips? Hey, we could do it together. We'd quip 'em to death. Give 'em quiplash hee hee hee." And he's gone.

As trite as it sounds, Kenny was Kenny. Cool, intelligent, intellectual, reserved.

Most of the time.

Like all of us, he had his little quirks. Several players, he felt, had his number. Guys like Larry Romanchych and Eric Vail of the Atlanta Flames and Reggie Leach of Philadelphia. All three had made careers of scoring goals from an embarrassing distance on Ken and had him psyched out entirely. Before a game against those teams, Ken would give us a pep talk… "Keep 'em to the outside" he'd rail. Translation: "If any of those guys touch the puck, get a gun and shoot 'em."

Sure enough, Larry Romanchych, author of 68 goals in five NHL seasons with Chicago and Atlanta, would come towards our zone with the puck and above the crowd you'd hear a frenzied Kenny: "Get 'im, get 'im, get 'im! Stand 'im up, stand 'im up!" Romanchych, of course, could hear this and would occasionally give Dryden a weird look during a stop in the play, as if to say: "Why're you always yelling at me? What did I do?"

Guy Lapointe, class clown, would occasionally be heard to

speculate on the bench: "What if Romanchych just happened to be coming over the blueline, nah, better yet make it Vail, he's got a harder shot: what if Vail just happened to be coming in over the blueline and my skate just happened to get caught in a rut and I just happened to fall down and Vail would go in all alone. Would Ken throw his stick at Vail? Or at me?"

Like Guy Lafleur, Ken had a great deal of pressure to deal with. He was so good a goalie, an all-star performance was just expected of him, game in and game out. When we won the Stanley Cup, the media would say Lafleur did this, Lemaire did that. And when you looked at the replays, there was Dryden making huge stops throughout the game. Don Cherry and Phil Esposito have said the Bruins were always prepared to contain our offence, especially Lafleur, but the guy it seemed they could do nothing about was Dryden.

We were three levels deep. And Dryden was Level Three.

If you got past some of the best offensive and defensive forwards in the league, you ran into what Cherry called "the trees" on defence. And if you defied the odds and got this far, there was Dryden. It was like climbing a mountain without ropes, everywhere you turned was another obstacle and no place for a hand hold or a foot hold.

The last in our group of Solitary Men as leaders on the ice was Jacques (Coco) Lemaire. When Jacques first entered the NHL in 1967–68, one Montreal columnist had written that "Lemaire could go into the corners with raw eggs in his pockets and they would be intact when he emerged." In other words, Jacques was something less of a solid checking player. Just a flashy rookie with a big shot.

Today, that statement would be greeted with amazement, especially by those young fans who grew up watching Lemaire's exploits during the late 1970s with the Canadiens team that won four straight. In that period, Jacques Lemaire was simply the most complete player we had. He was a superior checking centre, a tremendous passer to both sides, an important offensive threat with both his speed and incredible shot, and a quiet leader on the ice, first with Yvan Cournoyer and later with Guy Lafleur and Steve Shutt.

Of the group of quiet players I have mentioned, Coco was the one I got closest to. We spent a lot of time together in the summers up at his place in Lac Labelle, our kids were around the same ages and Jeannette got along very well with Michelle Lemaire.

Jacques was a painfully shy man when it came to all of the media attention and adulation that surrounds a team like the Montreal Canadiens. In his Utopia, he would be able to play his terrific game on the ice and then turn invisible in the dressingroom when the media came in for the post-game interviews. He didn't particularly dislike individual writers and TV/radio reporters, he just preferred to blend into the background, avoiding the media circus altogether.

I still believe to this day that he could have won a scoring championship or two had he not been so uncomfortable with the limelight. As a result, he seemed happy to go out there and score his 35 or 40 goals, but not more in case it would attract undue attention.

Jacques Lemaire was the total professional, capable in all areas of the game. I can't remember a teammate who was in better shape than Jacques, past and present. He could skate, shoot, pass, and skate some more. He was also one of the smartest players I've ever played with, a real student of the game. A lot of people didn't realize it, but while he was playing, he really studied the game. When he left us to go to Switzerland after the 1979 Stanley Cup, he was ready to make the transition into a coach, mentally and physically.

He'd learned a lot about the game after time spent with two of the best who ever patrolled the runway behind the Montreal bench – Hector (Toe) Blake and William Scott Bowman.

As I mentioned before, Guy Lafleur and I became the property of the Montreal Canadiens on the same day, the day after Jean Beliveau retired. Joining us in the organization June 10, 1971, was Scotty Bowman, replacing Al MacNeil who himself had replaced Claude Ruel.

Scotty Bowman was my first and probably my best coach with Montreal. There's no question he was the best coach in that era. I don't know if he could coach today or not. The kids are different now too. He was the type of coach who could get the most from his players and would use anything at his disposal to do just that.

I know there were nights when I would wake up dreaming that I was strangling him. But I think that's a general rule about all good coaches and their players. At one time or another, you're going to hate him. I don't think that it's hatred in the most emotional sense of the word; but the kind of reaction you have because he'll do something to irritate you and get you to play better.

Scotty was the best in the world at getting to his players. There was simply none finer. I've heard the word motivation thrown around loosely for years and there are fewer good motivators in coaching than the media would have us believe. A superb example, today, is Jacques Demers of Detroit. He, in many ways, reminds me of Scotty Bowman, a true leader and boss who would not hesitate to sit down a so-called star if the latter deserved it.

Scotty would motivate us, all right. Either through negative or positive input, he would deliver his message. Right in the middle of a hockey game, you might find yourself growing cold on the bench and wondering why, examining your conscience while trying not to blow your top. And, usually, you'd get the message. Scotty had the simplest motto: "My way or the highway." You produced his way, or you didn't play.

For instance, if I made some bad passes, which I have a habit of doing, he would count the giveaways or unforced errors, bad passes that resulted in turnovers. Between periods, he would pinpoint all the things that we did wrong and giveaways were always at the top of the list.

I might have committed four or five giveaways, playing more sloppily than usual, and without really being aware of it. The sudden anxiety attack brought about by cold contact with the team bench for a prolonged period of time would bring the message home, straight and true. As a prescription, it generally worked wonders. The next game I'd concentrate a lot more and play great and Scotty would put me on the ice all the time; and all of that emotion was forgotten.

As for preparing a team psychologically, Scotty was one of

the best. He was a master of tweaking our team ego and one of his favourite means was to build up the opposition. He loved to make comparisons with other teams that were positive for them, knowing that this really hurt our feelings.

He loved to compare us with Philadelphia. We'd be talking about our powerplay, preparing to play Colorado or Oakland that night, and he'd say: "You've got to move the puck around like Philadelphia does." Or "If you're going to forecheck you have to do it a lot like Philadelphia does." After the pre-game meeting, Scotty would go to his office, and somebody like Guy Lapointe would get up and mimic the coach with a bit of a swish and a flourish: "Remember boys, you have to play like Philadelphia does, because they are so good and we suck. Even though we're only 15 points ahead of them in the standings and they couldn't catch us if the season lasted until August."

We weren't even playing the Flyers that night, but that was also part of the Master Motivator's plan, his way of reminding us never to forget who would be waiting for us somewhere down the road. You got the feeling that Scotty might have paused by the door after leaving the room, enjoying Lapointe's performance even more than we did.

Scotty's personal motivational messages, either delivered directly to the player in question or through a media "wake-up call" – phrases like "so-and-so has been dogging it says a club source" in the morning paper woke you up quicker than thick, black coffee – were highly effective. But combined with his obsessive need to know everything, but everything, that was going on with the team, inevitably they led to conflicts.

Inevitably meant, with Pete Mahovlich.

Who said that opposites attract? These two were opposites and all they attracted was bitterness. They were always at each other. No two individuals could possibly look at life more differently than Big Pete and Scotty. William Scott Bowman was Verdun blue collar; from the large working-class suburb of Montreal just west of downtown. He was taught the "pull yourself up by your own bootstraps" work ethic at a very young age and firmly believed in its values.

Peter Joseph Mahovlich was the original Party Animal. The

younger brother of Frank, Peter had grown up idolizing his
famous brother and the lifestyle of the professional hockey
player. He had seen the fairy tale life at an early age and liked it.
His favourite saying was: "Who has more fun than people?"
Big Pete had friends everywhere he went and did his darnedest
to make sure none was left out when the Canadiens passed
through. Peter was our official Social Director because his
social calendar was always full and "there's lots left over for
everybody!" I remember trying to keep up with Peter for a
couple of days and quickly discovered that partying with the
boss was a thing for professionals only, no amateurs allowed. I
was wrecked after only two days.

Having fun with Peter was hard work!

Yet, when he hung them up, Peter had four Stanley Cup
rings, all richly deserved and richly earned. When it came time
to play hockey, he was as serious as the most serious NHL
player who ever played. Would you like to win a trivia question? Q: Which, of the two Mahovlich brothers, scored his
200th goal earlier in his career; Frank or Peter? A: If you
answered Peter, go to the head of the class. Frank was in his
seventh season, Peter was in his sixth, when they each reached
that plateau. Big Peter had five 30-plus goals seasons for the
Montreal Canadiens; he wasn't a passenger.

Peter was Scotty Bowman's personal brand of itching pow-
der; he was always under the coach's skin.

Like the time Peter came back to the hotel, late for a curfew
one night, or I should say one morning, in Detroit. Peter was in
another time zone and he boasted of his problems with moving
the clock backwards and forwards. "I don't change my
watch," he said. "Eventually we'll get somewhere where I'll
be back on track." He was right, eventually his watch would
say the same ours did but it was hard to tell exactly when this
would happen. Peter never looked at his.

Having played in Motown, Big Pete had quite a few friends
in the area and it would have been downright rude if he didn't
spend a little time with all of them. This time in particular,
Scotty was waiting for him when he breezed into the lobby
well past 2 A.M.

"You're late for curfew," Scotty railed, his voice taking that curious, whining tone we knew so well when he was exercised.

"You know how long I've been waiting? I've been here for two hours and that'll cost you $200."

With his best "no problem" shrug, Peter reached into his pocket for the money. Then, he went to the pocket again for another handful of cash, and slapped this into Scotty's outstretched palm.

"I'm gonna help you get your beauty sleep tomorrow night, Scotty. Here's the money for tomorrow, too. Don't bother waiting up for me because I'm coming in at four."

It was good thing Scotty didn't take credit cards. Peter's motto was "Don't leave home without it."

On another occasion, in Denver, Big Pete slept in and was late for the bus. Not by a whole lot, a few minutes at most. Scotty always sat at the back of the bus. This is highly unusual, by the way. Every other coach I've had always sat up front on the bus or the plane, leaving the back for the players. But Scotty was paranoid about knowing everything that went on with the team so he sat in the back so all the action would be in front of him, not behind his back. It was the best way to check who was bringing beer onto the bus, too.

So Peter, a natural back-of-the-class joker if there ever was one, did the coach one better by sitting right at the front. He sat on one side and Yvan Cournoyer sat on the other, right behind the bus driver. And way at the back, Scotty could never know what Peter was doing way up at the front. It was guerrilla war practised by a master.

Anyway, on this occasion Peter came leisurely strolling in a minute late with his coffee and swung casually into his seat. Peter said something that I couldn't quite catch, something to the effect that the driver could now leave because all were present and accounted for. Even way back at the end of the bus, the coach had rabbit ears. From Scotty came a distinct: "Fuck you, Mahovlich."

"Fuck me?" queried an incredulous Peter, turning towards his audience and warming to the debate.

"Well, fuck *YOU*." Those tiny four-letter words on paper

Larry Robinson

Moe and me (with calf) on the farm in Marvelville, many, many years ago.

I'm about 12 here.

My Dad, Leslie Robinson, poses with my older brother Brian, big sister Carol, and you-know-who on the calf.

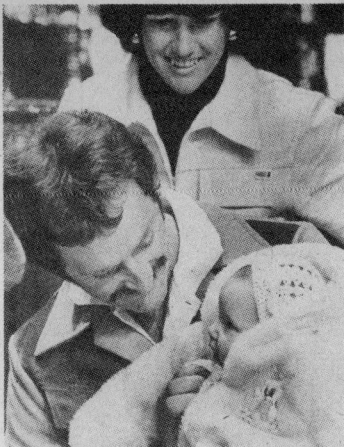

Rachelle Robinson makes her debut
at the Forum while Mom makes sure
Dad doesn't drop her.

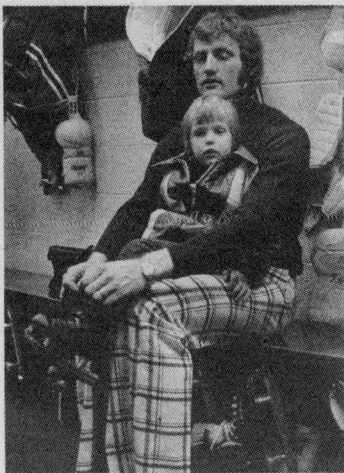

With my son Jeffery at a family skate at
the Forum in the 1970s.

Yours truly as a rather hirsute defenceman in the 1974-75 season.

Bobby Clarke never quit, but neither did the firm of Robinson & Dryden. We surprised everyone but ourselves by sweeping the Flyers in four to win the 1976 Stanley Cup final. (*Canapress*)

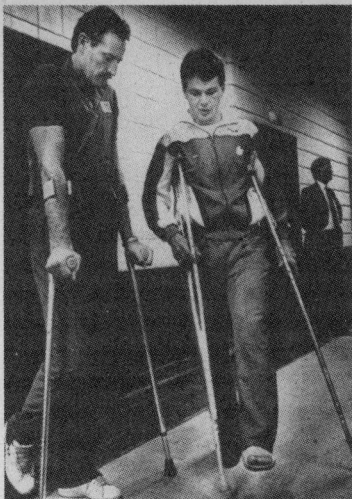

We can't kick! I broke my leg playing
polo and Claude Lemieux injured his
ankle during the 1987 Canada Cup.
The Rockettes, we ain't. (*Canapress*)

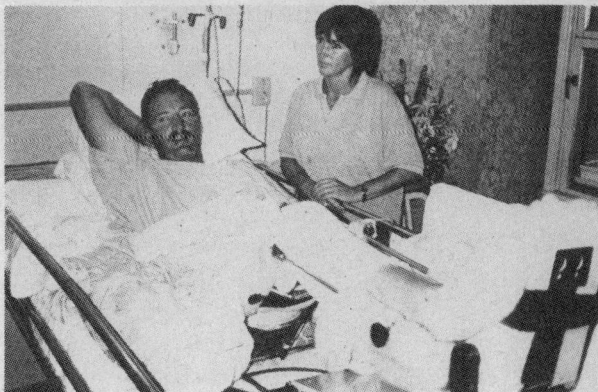

What, me worry? Jeannette looked a lot more worried than I did
after my leg surgery August 10, 1987. I'd have my anxious
moments a little later when it came time to walk again. (*Canapress*)

Montreal-Boston games are always played against the boards, as Greg Johnson and I demonstrate. (*Allen McInnis/Canapress*)

The Prime Minister of the country and he has to ask hockey players for the time? . . . actually, the government held a special luncheon for Team Canada in 1981 and Wayne Gretzky and I were the only ones to show up. Prime Minister Trudeau took it in stride. (*Canapress*)

The Boys on the Bus; just because Ron Duguay, Guy Lafleur and I were members of Team Canada 1981 didn't mean limousines and caviar. In fact, we were travelling to practice in suburban Verdun because the Forum was booked for a rock show. (*Canapress*)

The Canadiens' all-time dream team: In 1984, to commemorate the 60th anniversary of the Forum and the 75th anniversary of the Canadiens, a fan vote was held to select the all-time Canadiens team. The winners included the late Jacques Plante (goal); myself and Doug Harvey (third from right) on defence; Toe Blake (coach); Jean Beliveau (centre); Dickie Moore (left wing); and Maurice Richard (right wing). Joining us in this group photo at the Forum Jan. 12, 1985, are the late Aurel Joliat (centre with cap) and the current Canadiens' captain Bob Gainey (far right). Even though I now wear a Los Angeles uniform, I'll never forget *this* honour. (*Denis Brodeur*)

The old and the new: Rangers rookie Tony Granato and myself in action at the Forum last season. (*David Bier*)

The electronic porcupine or the media scrum,
a fact of life in all those years in Montreal.
(*David Bier*)

I don't care how small Theoren Fleury is, he stays out of the crease. Then again, if I had known Brian MacLellan was behind me . . . Little *did* I know this would be my last Stanley Cup final as a Canadien. (*Canapress*)

My old coach Scotty Bowman was on the receiving end of playoff elimination with his new team, Buffalo Sabres, when this photo was taken in 1986. (*Canapress*)

It was a bit of an anti-climax, but Wayne Gretzky and I enjoyed it nonetheless after beating Sweden in the final of the 1984 Canada Cup. The Big Game was our 3-2 overtime win over the Russians in the semi-final. (*Canapress*)

Sean Burke and I discuss a few (late) defensive ideas as Luc
Robitaille and Wayne Gretzky celebrate a Campbell Conference
goal during the 1989 All-Star game. And to think Wayne, Luc and
I are now teammates! (*Bruce Bennett*)

Two heads are better than one, Patrick Roy and I seem to be saying, after beating Philadelphia 3-0 during the 1989 Wales Conference final. (*Canapress*)

The King-maker and I: Bruce McNall and yours truly pay a visit to
The Pat Sajak Show the week I become a Los Angeles King, July 1989.
(*Bob Burton*)

I'm actually biting the Stanley Cup to see if it's real silver . . . a happy moment after our third straight Stanley Cup win, and second straight in Boston Garden. This came May 25, 1978. In my other arm is the Conn Smythe Trophy. (*Canapress*)

pale to insignificance because I could not possibly do justice to the tone and delivery of the two combatants. Suffice to say the joust went on like that for several minutes, from one end of the bus to the other. The guys were in tears they were laughing so hard.

I sometimes wondered if he and Scotty didn't rehearse these incidents. We could laugh because we knew that Peter would always be there when it mattered, that he would never let his flamboyant lifestyle hurt his game. He had a major contribution to make to our success as a team and he knew it. And he knew we knew it.

Scotty was dumb like a fox about things like that. He knew who his safe targets were, guys like Peter who would forget a situation minutes after it occurred. He knew when he could let off a little steam at the team, and when to give the team a chance, through a third party or safe bypass, to vent a little anti-Scotty steam itself. When Peter was engaging Scotty in a battle of four-letter words, you felt that Scotty had started it on purpose because he felt a little directed insubordination would help the team mood. Maybe he'd seen us starting to tighten up as a group and he wanted a little levity.

He'd take a few public shots if it kept us winning. And it did. Other coaches have a hard time understanding that rebellion to authority, in nearly all cases represented by the coach, is an integral part of a team's makeup. When you operate as a group under intense pressure for periods of eight to ten months a year, and under conduct rules designed for a boy's school, there are going to be blow-ups. The mature team will recognize them for what they are, a safety valve.

Psychology aside, Scotty's main strength was his game generalship. Scotty could prepare a gameboard attack with the best of them. He would come in for our 6:30 P.M. meeting before an eight o'clock game and dissect the other team and our assignments so that we were all clear on jobs out there. We had a regular menu to peruse; different plays at even strength, powerplays, penalty-killing, and basic stuff of that nature.

Scotty would have His Look. I can see him still; his nose and chin pointed straight up in the air, as he started in on how we'd been playing, and who we were playing against. He'd go over their best players – how they were playing and who we had to watch. In this, he wasn't really different than anyone else. It was really well-researched, though. He always did his homework. He prepared a Game Plan for every game. We'd skate out into battle ready to follow the Game Plan.

Of course it'd all last about five minutes.

Scotty's biggest asset was his ability to handle different stiuations behind the bench, on the fly. I've never seen a better coach at marshalling his resources in the heat of action; he knew when to use Chartraw and when he had to play Bouchard. He mixed lines like a master chemist and the new potion never seemed to blow up in his face. We rarely had off nights in 1976–77, the year we went 60–8–12, because Scotty was so good at heading them off. If the top line came up stale, Guy Lafleur might find himself paired with Doug Jarvis and Bob Gainey on the alleged checking line. Steve Shutt and Big Pete might suddenly find Mario Tremblay on their right side, or Jacques Lemaire might be centring Pierre Bouchard and Rick Chartraw.

Don't ask how he did it; all I know is it worked.

If Scotty was a master at mixing us up physically, he did even a better job emotionally. I think you have the impression by now that Scotty wasn't real easy to get along with. His quirks kept us off-balance and he made this work for us too. We'd come in after playing a brutal game, just brutal, and he'd be waiting for us.

"Ya didn't want to skate tonight? Tomorrow at practice, you're gonna work!" And he'd stalk out of the room.

At practice the next day, he'd be chipper; smiling and joking around. The veterans would put in about 30 minutes and he would send us off the ice. Then, Mr. Hyde would rear his ugly head; we might come off another road trip where we went out and played terrific, and he'd just bang the hell out of us. He was very contrary. You never knew what to expect from him.

That's what made him strong. The best thing he could do with a team like ours was to stop us from getting complacent, keep us totally off-guard and always guessing.

Coaching leadership isn't just game generalship, group contact, and one-to-one contact with players. It's total organization, and the ability to convey this feeling to the team.

Scotty was very well organized. When you went on the ice for a practice, you knew what you were going to do. Our practices with Scotty weren't more than 45 minutes to an hour. But we never stood around. There were never little huddles or mini-meetings all over the ice. We ran from one drill to the next. There was always a lot of movement in the practices and everybody knew what they were doing.

Scotty the general would take an overview of the practice run by his Regimental Sergeant Major, Claude Ruel. Their system reminded me of a lot of the old British war movies; with the cold, unreachable general being made human by his right-hand man, the sergeant-major. Scotty would be out on the ice but Claude would be running the drills.

The coach was the hard-nosed guy who gave everybody crap and Claude was there essentially to smooth things over and take all the young kids under his wing. The veterans who played a lot would practise for 45 minutes, maybe an hour and off they'd go. The kids would stay on for extra work. With Claude, again, you were always on the move. He'd be sitting in the corner watching everything. He was special; he had only one eye and he was 60 pounds overweight but he could skate and pass the puck like nobody else I've ever seen. And standing still. It's a lot easier to make a pass when you're on the move. He wouldn't miss too many passes standing still.

Just as it suited Scotty to play the hard guy, it suited him to have Claude around to soften the edges. If Peter was Scotty's favourite target on the road and during games, his practice foil was the irrepressible Steve Shutt. Bowman delighted in getting on Shutty's case in workouts. Shutty couldn't pass, he couldn't shoot, he couldn't skate. He'd get all over him when he was in that mood. I remember one time Steve made a long cross-ice pass and the puck skipped over Flower's stick and hit Scotty in the ankle. Limping noticeably and yet trying not to let it show, Scotty screamed across at Shutt: "It's a good thing it was your shot, it might have hurt me."

Of course, being the great field general he was, Scotty wanted to be close to the action and always seemed to be in the road during our line rushes. There'd be several close calls a practice. We invented the first hockey pool but it didn't have anything to do with goals and assists; it was who could get closest to Scotty without actually ever hitting him.

Whatever would build team unity, an us-against-them mentality, he would use. He wanted to keep things on an even keel for the players and worked hard at protecting us from outside influences and pressures.

As a result, we always seemed to have a lot of fun in our practices; there always seemed to be a good pace to our workouts. A few guys would occasionally come in a little hung over and Scotty knew it. I remember Charty came out a few times on the ice with his skates just loosely done. Like most single guys, Charty just loved Montreal and its many beautiful opportunities. He was a character. A special kind of comic relief and also a player you could count on when the chips were down. Scotty recognized his value to the team and turned a blind eye.

In the end, that was Scotty's real strength. He'd treat us all as individuals, each with a specific role to play on the team, but come at us only as a team. It was a fine balancing act for a man who to this day has not received the credit he deserved for the job he did then.

This man was our leader, just as Guy Lafleur, Serge Savard, Ken Dryden, and Jacques Lemaire were leaders. And we were the best.

TEN

Doing It

A GREAT team doesn't just happen. It comes together over time, maturing slowly, overcoming early setbacks, adding the right parts until, suddenly, it's there.

That was the case with the Montreal Canadiens of the second half of the 1970s.

By the beginning of the 1975–76 season, the following players remained of the team that had won the Stanley Cup in 1971:

Forwards: Peter Mahovlich, Yvan Cournoyer, Jacques Lemaire, Jim Roberts.

Defence: Guy Lapointe, Serge Savard, Pierre Bouchard.

Goal: Ken Dryden.

You couldn't ask for a stronger nucleus than that in those days, especially considering that all of these players were coming into the primes of their careers, their late 20s and early 30s. The other part of the dynasty came together in the first five drafts of the 1970s.

1971 – Jean Beliveau and John Ferguson retire; Scotty Bowman hired; me, Guy Lafleur, Murray Wilson, drafted. Canadiens win Cup.

1972 – Steve Shutt, Bunny Larocque, Dave Gardner, John Van Boxmeer, Bill Nyrop drafted.

1973 – Bob Gainey, Glenn Goldup, drafted. Canadiens win Cup.

1974 – Cam Connor, Doug Risebrough, Rick Chartraw,

Mario Tremblay, Gilles Lupien drafted. Ken Dryden sits out season.

1975 – Pierre Mondou, Brian Engblom, Paul Woods, Pat Hughes drafted. Dryden returns.

Four other players came via trades: Yvon Lambert was acquired from Detroit, Don Awrey from St. Louis, Doug Jarvis from Toronto, and Jim Roberts, a member of Montreal Stanley Cup winners in the mid-'60s, was reacquired from St. Louis.

The team that reported for training camp in September, 1975 had all the elements necessary for a major assault on the championship. Up front, Guy Lafleur and Steve Shutt were potential 50-goal scorers, while Cournoyer, Lemaire, and Mahovlich could each be expected to score 30 or more. Yvon Lambert and Murray Wilson were potential 20–25 goal snipers and the kids, Mario Tremblay, Bob Gainey, Rick Chartraw, Doug Jarvis, and Doug Risebrough could be counted on to play a strong, physical defensive game in all three zones.

Back of the blueline, we counted on the combination of Serge Savard, Guy Lapointe, myself, and John Van Boxmeer to add 50 goals to the team total, while Don Awrey and Pierre Bouchard would concentrate on defence, giving little thought to the team attack.

To top it all off, we had Bunny Larocque and Ken Dryden in goal. Dryden was the best goalie in the league and Larocque was one of the best second goalies anywhere, especially since the Dryden sabbatical two seasons previous had allowed him to play over 30 games.

Our pre-season expectations turned out to be almost right on: The Flower and Shutty combined for 101 goals (56–45); Big Pete, Yvan Cournoyer, and Jacques Lemaire were just short of 90 with 86 (32–20–34), even though Coco missed 17 games due to injury: Lambert and Wilson added 43 (32–11), while Murray missed 19 games. The kids did their job, even scoring some important goals along the way (Mario 11, Doug Risebrough 16, Bob Gainey 15, Doug Jarvis 5.)

On defence, the four rearguards we'd counted on to add 50

goals came up five short with 45: myself 10 goals, 30 assists; Serge 8 goals, 39 assists; Van Boxmeer 6 goals, 11 assists in 46 games; and Guy Lapointe 21 goals, 47 assists.

We totalled 337 goals, and allowed 174, which is another way of saying we played 80 4–2 hockey games. We finished with 58 wins (a record), 11 losses (a record for an 80-game season), and 11 ties, for 127 points (also a record).

A year later, we were even better: 387 goals for (4.83 a game) and 171 against (2.13 a game). That per-game average added up to the best-ever winning percentage over an 80-game season, .794, on 60 wins, 8 losses, and 12 ties for 132 points. I cannot rightly say what was the more impressive feat, winning 60 games of 80, or losing only 8 of 80. I guess it depends if your orientation is offensive or defensive. The team to come closest to winning 60 games in the 12 years since? The Montreal Canadiens of 1977–78, with 59.

Enough dry statistics. They may be eloquent testimony to the success of a franchise, but they say little of the personality of a team or of the good times the Canadiens enjoyed while winning four straight Stanley Cups.

As the '75–'76 season began, we intended to spread the word to the other 16 teams in the league.

What do I remember about 1975–76?

Resolve and weirdness. New Year's Eve and the playoffs. My 1975–76 memories are made of these things. Resolve because Buffalo had defeated us in the playoffs the year before and we felt they'd been lucky. The games they'd won were close. The games we'd won were blowouts. But they won four games and we won two and it was the Canadiens on the golf course when the Flyers and Sabres met in the final. At training camp in September, 1975, we resolved to be playing in the 1976 final. We demonstrated that resolve in Philadelphia and carried it into the season, winning consistently throughout the year.

Weirdness because after many years and more than 1,000 games, incidents run together, like a collage. Was that hit against Anton Stastny in the '82 or '85 playoffs? Did Pierre

Bouchard and Stan Jonathan have their set-to in '77 or '78? Who did we play in the '76 playoffs before we played the Flyers in the final?

I could not answer any of these questions without consulting league record books, scrapbooks, and other documents. Yet I can remember weird little incidents, like the night Guy Lapointe mooned Kansas City. Accidentally.

The Scouts were on a rare attack toward our zone and Lapointe was skating backwards, making sure he kept the puck carrier in front of him. Nobody knows exactly how it happened, but he tripped over something on the ice, or got his skate caught in a rut, and over he went, in the beginning of a backward somersault.

And there he stayed, right in front of our team bench. His legs got so far over his torso, Guy was caught in that awkward position and couldn't get up. He couldn't get any leverage and stayed there, essentially pinning himself to the ice.

I had been concentrating on my man on this 2-on-2 attack when, suddenly, it became a 2-on-1. I looked frantically around for Pointu and spotted his predicament. The whole bench was laughing and guys were shouting gratuitous advice down to the stricken defenceman. Here I was with a 2-on-1 coming at me and also trying not to break up. I can't remember if they scored but I do recall that Guy had a lot of new nicknames for about a week.

Another time at the Forum, Syl Apps Jr. of the Pittsburgh Penguins was coming down the left wing. A very smart and smooth player, Apps was a right-handed shot and a good one so I tried to keep him off to the side. He realized that he didn't have a good angle, my stick was covering the middle, and instead of shooting, he decided to pass into the centre. The puck went right up my stick and bang, right in the face.

After recovering, I returned to the bench and the guys were all laughing. I didn't know why until after the game when I saw myself in the mirror. My nose was the size of my left arm. Or about a third of Tim Hunter's. Right after the game, I went to hospital and had it operated on. That summer, I was in hockey school with Denis Herron, a very close friend. He caught a shot and casually threw it with his catching glove; bang, right in the honker and back to square one. Denis is still a very close friend and occasionally asks me about my nose.

Two things I'll never forget about 1975–76 are New Year's Eve and the All-Star game six weeks later in Philadelphia.

New Year's Eve was something special: Montreal Canadiens' first game ever against a Soviet club team, Red Army, which means the Canadiens against the Soviet National team minus one or two individuals. I can't forget this game because thousands of hockey fans won't let me. It was simply one of the greatest games played in our era, at any level.

They called it the Super Series and the Soviets sent over two teams, Wings and Red Army, to play against an assortment of NHL squads. They got the jump on us right away; Red Army banging out the New York Rangers 7–3 at Madison Square Garden and the Wings dumping the Penguins 7–4 in Pittsburgh. The Soviets had skated away from the Rangers and Penguins, toying with them in the final period, and NHL fans were singing that old refrain: the NHL can't skate with them.

Not exactly. What they were saying was that if anybody could skate with the Soviets, it was Montreal. We'd been running away with our division and were prohibitive favourites to derail the Philadelphia Flyers in the Stanley Cup playoffs in five months time, so we had an enormous emotional stake in this game which would be televised from coast to coast.

And what a game it was! Pete Mahovlich, Serge Savard, Yvan Cournoyer, and Ken Dryden had been part of the team that beat the Russians in the memorable September Showdown of '72. Wearing the uniforms with UCKA (our CSKA) on the crest were '72 series veterans Vladimir Petrov, Valery Kharlamov, Boris Mikhailov, Vasily Vasiliev, and Vladislav Tretiak.

I still get goosebumps thinking about that game. We swamped them in the first period, showing the Soviets and North American fans that here was a team that could skate with the Russians in the Forum, in Moscow, or on Lake Champlain if we had to. Shutty got it going just after the three-minute mark when he unloaded a slapshot from his off-wing. Tretiak never saw it.

Four minutes later, Doug Risebrough moved through traffic, got a good shot off and Yvon Lambert was there for the rebound. 2–0. I'd never heard the Forum so noisy, even in Stanley Cup play. The noise never stopped; it went on for 60 minutes in a game that ended 3–3. We outshot the Soviets 39–13; Tretiak surpassed himself to keep it close. One of the most ridiculous comments I heard after the game was that the score reflected the play; that the shots on goal were a mirage because the Soviets only shot when a pure scoring chance arose. B.S. They had 13 shots on goal because they couldn't get any more. We shut them down in three zones. We should've won the game.

That having been said, I take nothing away from their effort either. I can't recall ever playing at such a high emotional level through an entire 60 minutes in any other game, before or since. It was a clean game punctuated by hard checks, pinpoint passing, and mile upon mile upon mile of skating. The Red Army challenged us and we rose to the challenge; I don't think I've ever seen the Canadiens skate, shoot, check, and pass like we did in that game. I never wanted it to end.

How good was that game?

It was so good I had flashbacks. I'd be in the middle of a league game a couple of weeks or a month later, and I'd suddenly tune out, clearly visualizing specific things that had happened on that New Year's Eve. Thirteen years later, I can still describe it from beginning to end.

Another sign that individual players on the Canadiens were gearing up to take it all came in the All-Star game in Philadelphia. Floyd Smith of Buffalo and Fred Shero of Philadelphia, the Stanley Cup finalists the year before, were the respective coaches of the Wales and Campbell conferences. It was supposed to be a Flyers' showcase; after all, they'd won the Stanley Cup for two years running. What it was, was essentially the Montreal Canadiens (six of us) and the Buffalo Sabres against the Philadelphia Flyers and the New York Islanders. We won 7–5.

But that score does little justice to the domination we exerted. Led by Peter Mahovlich, Guy Lafleur, and Guy Lapointe, we blasted Flyers' goalie Wayne Stephenson for a 3–1 lead in the first, then banged four more past Chico Resch in the second, to take a 7–1 lead after 40 minutes. Peter ended up winning the MVP award, on the strength of his goal and three assists; if he hadn't won it, the Flower would have got it for his goal and two assists. We were so overpowering, the staunch Flyers fans were abandoning the Spectrum in droves midway through the game.

And so it went. As the '75–'76 season wound down, all the signs were positive.

We were beating the good teams, 6–0 over Philadelphia, 5–1 over Boston, and 3–1 over Buffalo, and easily handling the league doormats, 6–1 over St. Louis, 7–1 over Oakland, and 4–2 over Los Angeles.

When you're hot, a curious dynamic takes over the game. You get away with a lot of things – referee's calls, hot dog passes, allowed and disallowed goals. The late-season game against the hapless Seals was a case in point. I scored a pair and barely missed a third, giving me five in the last seven games; Shutty added another two. Well, let's say one-and-a-half. In the first period, he steamed into the Oakland zone and really cranked one. It hit underneath the crossbar, bounced down and out of the net. It didn't go in but that didn't faze Shutt. He raised his arms high, turned and skated casually toward centre ice. That convinced the goal judge and the referee and he had the goal.

"Have I ever lied to you before?" he asked as a chorus of catcalls and raspberries greeted him at our bench.

On this night, he was outdone in the hotdog department by a master. Midway through the second period, Big Pete skated into the corner to the right of goalie Giles Meloche. Facing the boards, and with a defenceman all over his back, he casually passed the puck back through his legs . . . right onto The Flower's stick. It was in the net before Meloche could move.

Peter was straightfaced after the game as he explained the goal to reporters: "I knew the Flower was there and so was one of their guys. I had a 50 per cent chance of being right, didn't

I?" The writers actually wrote this down in their notebooks and later in their game stories, to the amazement of all of Mahovlich's teammates.

We wrapped up the season, and first place overall, with 127 points, nine up on Patrick Division winner Philadelphia and 14 ahead of Adams Division leader Boston. (Today's fans may have forgotten that at the time, Montreal was in the Norris Division with Los Angeles, Pittsburgh, Detroit, and Washington; the Adams consisted of Boston, Buffalo, Toronto, and California.)

Under the system in place at the time, and probably the best playoff system ever devised by the league, which of course is why the geniuses in the executive suite abandoned it, the first-place winners – Montreal 127 points, Philadelphia 118, Boston 113, and Chicago 83 – would get a bye in the first round of the playoffs. The remaining eight teams would play best-of-three series, 1 vs 8, 2 vs 7, etc., and when those were over, the quarter-finals would begin. That year, the eight first-round teams, in order, were:

1. Buffalo 105 points, 2. NY Islanders 101, 3. Los Angeles 85, 4. Toronto 83, 5. Pittsburgh 82, 6. Atlanta 82, 7. Vancouver 81, and 8. St. Louis 72. (Note that St. Louis was the only sub-.500 team to make the playoffs that year, a much better state of affairs than what we have now.)

Buffalo, Islanders, Toronto, and Los Angeles survived the first round. The remaining teams, and their season point totals, lined up like this:

1. Montreal 127 vs 8. Chicago 83
2. Philadelphia 118 vs 7. Toronto 83
3. Boston 113 vs 6. Los Angeles 85
4. Buffalo 105 vs 5. Islanders 101

So we were set up for what some local papers called the "Thanks for the Memories" or "Bob's USO North" series with the Hawks. It was so-named because Montreal was in the midst of final preparations for the 1976 summer Olympic Games that April and part of the cultural festivities was going to be a Forum spectacular featuring comedian Bob Hope, the late Freddie Prinz, the late Bing Crosby, and a cast of thousands. I scored our first goal; we went on to win 4–0 and I got to pose with Mr. Hope after the game when he visited our dressingroom to congratulate the team. We blitzed the Hawks, the best of the league's weakest (Smythe) division – they would have finished fifth in the Adams, Patrick, and Norris divisions – in four straight games and then waited for the other series to wrap up.

It took a while. We sat around for a week waiting to see if we'd be playing Toronto, Los Angeles, or the Islanders in the next round. While we waited, we amused ourselves with 90-minute practices and tours of the Olympic installations, anything to keep us from dwelling on the many playoff permutations. About the only worry for the winner in a blowout is that you might get rusty during the forced inactivity, while waiting for the others series to end.

As it worked out, the stubborn Kings took Boston to seven games before succumbing; so did the Maple Leafs with the defending champion Flyers. The series that figured to be the toughest of the lot, Buffalo and Islanders, was the shortest as the Isles clipped the Sabres in six.

That left Montreal against New York and Philadelphia versus Boston in the league semi-finals. Our between-series lay-off was 12 days.

The Islanders were still pretty new to the league, but under the inspired leadership of Bill Torrey and Al Arbour, they'd become a team to contend with in four short years. They'd joined the league, along with Atlanta Flames, in the expansion of 1972–73. You only had to look at the record of both teams to see that management knew what it was doing in both cases:

	Islanders					*Atlanta*				
	GP	W	L	T	Pts	GP	W	L	T	Pts
1972–73	78	12	60	6	30	78	25	38	15	65
1973–74	78	19	41	18	56	78	30	34	14	74
1974–75	80	33	25	22	88	80	34	31	15	83
1975–76	80	42	21	17	101	80	35	33	12	83

Bill Torrey and the Islanders went for youth, right from the beginning. The NHL and hockey were solidly implanted on Long Island and in the Greater New York area so they could afford to build their team through careful draft selections.

Down in Atlanta, Bernie Geoffrion and Cliff Fletcher had another problem: they had to become competitive right away and try to sell the sport in virgin territory, the Deep South. So they opted for trades and the quick fix; the accumulation of veteran players. It helped that the Flames were playing in the weaker West Division their first two years. But by 1974–75, when the Kansas City Scouts and Washington Capitals joined the league in its second expansion in three years, the Islanders and Flames both found themselves in the new Patrick Division, alongside the Rangers and the Flyers.

Bill Torrey did a masterful job with the entry draft in the Islanders' first three years–1972 Billy Harris, Lorne Henning; 1973 Denis Potvin; 1974 Clark Gillies and Bryan Trottier. Add players like Eddie Westfall, Bob Nystrom, Bob Bourne, Chico Resch and Billy Smith and you had the nucleus of the team that would win four straight in the early '80s.

The team we met in the semi-finals that year had a lot of character, but it was not yet mature as a group. Al Arbour had the Isles playing an extremely disciplined brand of hockey for their collective youth. And fortunately for us they didn't yet have the explosive scoring power of Mike Bossy; he'd be along in another two years.

Which is not to say that they didn't give us all we could handle. We got an indication of that right from the start. Early in the first period, Denis Potvin blasted a puck off the corner boards in our zone. Ken Dryden moved out of the net to intercept it but it bounced back at a funny angle, closer to Westfall. Eddie won the race and it was 1–0 Islanders. Shutty tied it a short while later, but Billy MacMillan gave New York the lead at 6:59 of the third and for a while it looked like it might hold up.

Arbour had his defence setting up a wall in front of Billy Smith; Denis Potvin, his brother Jean, Gerry Hart, Dave Lewis, and others flung their bodies in front of every shot we took. Everything seemed to hit some body part, skate, or stick. Whenever a shot *did* get through – we actually outshot them 20–17 on the game – the entire five skaters in blue would converge on the spot, smothering rebounds in a scrum. That tactic worked beautifully as the game wore on until Doug Jarvis, our superb rookie centreman and defensive forward got clear and went in on Smith. I was determined to follow him all the way so, when Smith made big on Jarvis, I was there with the puck – and an empty net.

Then Yvan Cournoyer took a lovely pass from Jacques Lemaire and put it in off Smith's pad and we escaped with a 3–2 victory. We won the second game of the series, another close contest, and headed for Nassau County Coliseum for Game Three. We had to play the game of our lives to escape: yet another 3–2 squeaker. Garry Howatt and Bryan Trottier got us back on our heels with goals at 11:29 and 12:44 of the first period and Chico Resch stopped everything we fired at him for two periods, especially Guy Lapointe on a perfect pass from behind the net from Guy Lafleur, then Jimmy Roberts, the trailer on a 3-on-2.

The Long Island crowd was chanting "Chico, Chico," at every stop in play in the second period as we fired 14 blanks. Resch stoning Yvon Lambert, Mario Tremblay, and Steve Shutt while Dryden kept us in the game with a big save off Clark Gillies. When Resch couldn't get to the puck, the Islanders' second goalie, Gerry Hart, was sliding out in front of every puck that moved. It was clean, hard-hitting game and the only penalties referee Ron Wicks called were three sets of coincidental minors in the first.

Finally, at 1:09 of the third, Bert Marshall was sent off for tripping and we had our first powerplay. So, of course, the Islanders had the best scoring chance: Billy Harris and Lorne Henning breaking in on a 2-on-1 and Harris dropping a pass to Henning who forced Dryden to make a game saver. Twenty seconds after the penalty ended, Steve Shutt scooped a puck out from under Denis Potvin, who was desperately trying to freeze it in the corner, fed it to Guy Lapointe who fired it into the net. That only served to arouse New York and Dryden again and again had to make big saves. We were on our heels when Serge Savard was sent off for tripping midway through the period.

Just as the Islanders had threatened in their short-handed situation, we threatened in ours. Jimmy Roberts picked up the puck at the red line and headed for the New York end. Both defencemen, Denis Potvin and Ralph Stewart, converged on him but both backed off at the same instant, each thinking the other was going to make the check. Jimmy found himself with the puck about 20 feet from Resch and tied the game with a slapshot to the top corner, just beyond Resch's outstretched arm. At 16:12, Yvon Lambert took a nice feed from Yvan Cournoyer to score the winner.

We beat the Islanders in five games, but they put the entire NHL on notice that they would be a force for many years to come.

Meanwhile, in a bit of a surprise, the Flyers handled the Bruins in five and we were in the final against the defending Stanley Cup champions. They had several things to prove. First and foremost, they remembered the September, 1975 exhibition game at the Spectrum where we literally beat them up. Then there'd been the Super Series, where we tied Red Army 3–3 and Philly defeated them 4–1 in a fiasco where the Russians stormed off the ice to protest what they called "biased refereeing and unfair play." The Russians had returned home praising the Canadiens to the skies and decrying the "goons" in Philadelphia. Many North American sports commentators had picked up on that and the Flyers were upset. Adding insult to injury, Montreal Canadiens players had dominated the All-Star Game held in Philadelphia.

Last and not least, the Canadiens had been the last team to beat the Flyers in the playoffs, in the semi-finals en route to our Cup in 1973.

The Flyers were wired.

So were we.

The first game was Message Central, the Big Switchboard on Ice. Ken Dryden and Wayne Stephenson, both former Team Canada goalies, declared that easy goals would be a thing of the past. Andre (Moose) DuPont and Mario Tremblay let it be known that they were in contention for the light heavy-weight crown of Quebec while Dave Schultz and Pierre Bouchard contested the heavyweight title of the NHL. On their side, Reggie Leach was beating goalies with bullets while we were getting big goals from all over our lineup.

(In all, we would play 13 games that playoff year, winning 12 and losing only one; and ten of our players would score three goals or more. As they say, that's teamwork.)

In Game One, the Flyers let us know that they intended to take the game to us, taking a quick 2–0 lead on goals by Leach and Ross Lonsberry in the first as we lurched and stumbled all over the Forum. Leach's goal was a laser, just 21 seconds into the game, and should have woken us up. I personally stank out the joint; I was on the ice for both Philadelphia goals. We all were thankful when the siren went to end the period. We weren't skating a bit and deserved to be in a deeper hole than that when the second period began.

When a team like the 1975–76 Montreal Canadiens was not skating like it should, you could depend on some burner like Lemaire, or Wilson, or Cournoyer, or Lafleur to sound the charge. All four could impose their speed on any opposition almost at will.

That's why it took Jimmy (Slow Boat to China) Roberts to get us going yet again, just as he had done against the Islanders. He scored early in the second period to halve the Flyers' lead and I managed to tie the game on a nice pass from Peter Mahovlich as the momentum shifted. We swarmed all over the Flyers and should have put them away then but anxiety did us in. We rushed shots and missed opportunities because we were tight. It had been a couple of years since we'd last been in a final and we were nervous, plain and simple.

We finally won the game, outscoring them 2–1 in the third period, but it took a Ken Dryden toe on a Jim Watson shot with four seconds left to ice it. It was a nailbiter all the way.

This is not something a player will admit at the time; you save these revelations for a book like this 10 or 15 years after the fact because you don't ever want to give the other side the edge of knowing you're as tight as they are. The Flyers were good but they were missing two key ingredients, goalie Bernie Parent and centre Rick MacLeish, perhaps the most underrated of all of their forwards during their two Stanley Cup seasons.

They still had the Watson brothers, Tom Bladon, Bobby Clarke, Leach, Lonsberry, Saleski, Mel Bridgman, Schultz, Bob Kelly, and a fierce will to win. And they had my favourite, Gary Dornhoefer.

Back in the 1973 semi-final, Dorny and I had hammered each other at will. It seemed as if we had an unspoken agreement; wherever we met on the ice, it would be a collision. There was no animosity, just two pros acknowledging that the other had a job to do. Gary's job was to play tough along the boards and stick his rear end in the face of our goalie every time his team was pressing in our zone. We had a Gary Dornhoefer on our team, too. His name was Yvon Lambert. These two were the very best in the league at standing just off the crease and absorbing punishment to give their teammates scoring opportunities.

You could knock Lambert and Dornhoefer down ten times in a game, and ten times they'd be up again and coming at you. They were hard-nosed players. They were irritators. They also were two players who had my fullest admiration because they took their shots and never complained.

Gary Dornhoefer and I became part of NHL and Montreal Forum folklore early in the third period of Game Two of the final, a 2–1 victory for us.

We were leading 2–1 midway through the third when Dorny led a rush up Philadelphia's right side, our left. I was playing left defence and I angled towards him, trying to get a hip into him. One reason Gary and I collided a lot was the fact that he was tall, 6'2", and skated pretty much upright when he carried the puck. Other players like Gil Perreault were about the same size but were low, almost in a crouch when they skated, and you could never get a solid hit on them. Gary presented a big target to opposition defencemen.

He was just inside our blueline when I got my hip into him.

Bang into the boards he went, and down he went. When he got up, he was looking at the boards curiously. I had just enough time to take that into view before I turned and went after the puck. I was corralling the puck when I heard the whistle blow.

"Jeez, he's gonna give me a penalty for that? It was a clean hit!" I was steamed and turned around, expecting to see the referee pointing at me and skating toward the penalty box. But that wasn't it. The referee and both linesmen were in consultation on the other side of the rink, near where Dornhoefer and I had collided. We had broken the boards, as it turned out, there was this big dent near the top. While workmen tried to repair the damage with hammer and crowbar – they would have to fix it properly the next day – players on both teams skated by the area, sneaking looks and shaking their heads.

Then I noticed the ref heading for the penalty box, and motioning me to follow. I got two minutes for renovating without a permit or non-unionized carpentry in a union shop or something like that.

A legend was born, or boarded. After the game, Gary took great pains to tell the reporters that "Robinson hits like a pussycat." Laughing, he said: "I don't know why he picks on me like that; I'm a pretty nice guy. Jeez, I wish I weighed about 30 pounds more."

The big boom aside, the series now shifted to Philadelphia and we knew the fans there would get their team back into the Stanley Cup hunt. Even before we left Montreal, reporters were asking Flyers' players and management if the team would bring out its "secret weapon" – Kate Smith singing "God Bless America." Ever since the Flyers had used that song rather than the "Star Spangled Banner," their record in post-season play had been phenomenal. Philadelphia management liked to do it up big when the visitors came to town in the playoffs. There would be lengthy opening ceremonies, designed to soften up the opposition. Then the rink would be darkened and the Flyers would skate out individually under the spotlight as the tension built and the fans went into a frenzy.

And then there would be Kate Smith, either in person or on tape, singing *THE SONG*. Faced with this spectacle, some teams had left their game in the pre-game ceremonies and were easy prey for the aroused Flyers when play eventually did get round to starting. We knew we would be facing all of this and a much more physical Philadelphia team when Game Three started at the Spectrum. Scotty Bowman shifted Pierre Bouchard and Rick Chartraw up front, to give us more muscle. Charty would be replacing Yvon Lambert, who was out with a bad groin. If the Flyers wanted to play it tough, we would gladly oblige them. The players also came up with our own strategy; if the Flyers got involved in a marathon pre-game ceremony, we would ignore it.

We were wound real tight for those two games. The club was staying at the Cherry Hill Inn in Cherry Hill, New Jersey, just across the river from Philadelphia, and most of us couldn't sleep half the time. We spent most of our three days there playing pool to all hours of the day and night, anything to keep our minds off the inactivity.

This was easily the most emotional series I'd ever been involved in up to that point and the adrenalin would start flowing in my hotel room. As Game Three neared, I found that my teammates felt the same way. Normally our dressingroom is a pretty casual place; different guys in various stages of dress or undress, all going through the private little pre-game rituals we have while kibitzing and joking with the others around us.

Not that night. A half hour before the warmups, the whole team was fully dressed in our road reds, impatiently waiting for the buzzer to signal the warmup. We were pacing up and down, champing at the bit, and raring to go. Even after we came back from the warmups, most of the guys had trouble settling down.

True to form, the Flyers darkened the rink lights and individually introduced the players from each team. Now that sounds pretty fair, but what it really meant was that they zipped through our lineup and then we were expected to stand around at our blueline for 20 minutes or so as the Flyers leisurely skated out. One by one. The slow introductions dragged on and on.

I don't know who started it but a couple of our players broke away and started skating. Soon, it was the whole team. We started skating circles in our end. Slowly at first and then building up more and more speed. We were flying.

The TV audience couldn't see anything because the house lights had been dimmed, but we were on all burners and the fans in the Spectrum could see us. Slowly, but surely, they turned from the player intros and started watching us, getting quieter and quieter. By the time Kate Smith had done her thing, the place had lost its wild edge.

On the first shift, Rick Chartraw drove home the point that we were here to play and couldn't be intimidated; he caught Joe Watson in the corner and lowered the boom. Scotty said it best after the game, a 3–2 victory in which Bouchard got the winner: "Here's a guy who hadn't played most of the series and on the first shift of the game, he levels Watson. It was only Joe Watson but it told the Flyers a lot. It told our guys a lot. That's what I'm always asking our guys to do: it's not intimidation. It's simply a way of letting the Flyers know that we're not going to be pushed around."

I beg to differ, Scotty. It was intimidation pure and simple, and it made the Flyers very uncomfortable to be on the receiving end. Charty, considered the team flake by a lot of people, had got his chance and made the most of it. "I was going out there to hit somebody, anybody, on the first shift," he said afterwards. A defenceman, Rick said he liked his right wingers to play tough hitting and back checking.

"I don't want to see my right winger picking up a guy at the red line and then turn around at our blue line and find the other guy going in on a breakaway." With Charty on the right wing, and Bouchard on the left, the Philadelphia defencemen suddenly ran out of room in their own zone. They started dumping the puck out, sometimes without looking, and it was on a play like this that Bouchard and Chartraw teamed up for the winning goal.

It was 3–2 but it could have been 10–2. We knew we were going to win it, and so did all the Flyers with the notable exception of Stephenson who was phenomenal in goal, stopping Murray Wilson, Bob Gainey, and Yvan Cournoyer on breakaways. Midway through the third, with the game still tied, the heavy pressure on the Flyer rearguards paid off. A puck was carelessly cleared to the blue line where Butch Jr. corralled it and whacked it in the general direction of the net. Charty was in the slot, wrestling with Jim Watson. The puck went right through his legs and past a startled Stephenson.

The Cup was one game away. A big game. We were up 3–0 in the series but all three victories had been by a single goal.

Game Four was short on pre-game ceremony but long on Philadelphia heart and the Flyers told us right away that we'd win the Cup kicking and clawing, if we won it at all. Dave Schultz went after Serge Savard right off the opening whistle and both were sent off with double minors. Reg Leach also re-layed the message in his own way when he scored 12 seconds later, blasting one in over Kenny's left shoulder. It was his 19th goal of the playoffs, a record in the pre-Gretzky era. Philly was bumping and grinding and doing what they do best, and the crowd was with them all the way.

The trouble with what Philly usually did best was that it often got away from them. Not happy to enforce and contain, their players would often get to running around, looking for trouble, and the NHL referees were usually happy to oblige. At 3:44, Don Saleski was sent off. At 5:35, Steve Shutt scored and Pierre Bouchard scored his second of the series six minutes later while Bill Barber was serving another penalty.

Tom Bladon tied it late in the period and Moose Dupont gave Philly a 3–2 lead midway through the second, both with Guy Lapointe in the penalty box, but those powerplay goals would be the last of 1975–76 for the Flyers. We broke their backs with a powerplay goal, our third of the game, to tie it with eleven seconds remaining in the second period. And the firm of Mahovlich, Shutt, and Lafleur won it with a pair of goals 58 seconds apart in the third: the Flower at 14:18, Big Peter at 15:16.

Reggie Leach won the Conn Smythe Trophy as best playoff performer for his 19 goals, yet more proof that the reporters upstairs have little idea what happens on the ice. He couldn't have accomplished that feat without the indefatigable Bobby

Clarke setting him up all over the place. And he played for a team that finished the playoffs that spring with a record of 8–8. All the Canadiens did was go 12–1 in the playoffs and the so-called selection committee could find no one from our team? Give me a break. (Well, actually, *Sport Magazine* did. I was selected their playoff MVP and won a four-wheel drive truck.)

Still, we had the one award that myopic writers don't vote for, the Stanley Cup, and we happily guzzled champagne from it in the dressingroom, singing "God Bless America" until we were hoarse.

Two days later, Guy Lapointe blitzed happily into our dressingroom at the Forum, decked out in an orange-and-black Flyers road sweater, chanting "Let's Go Flyers" at the top of his lungs. Bob Gainey, Doug Jarvis, and myself were on our 200th verse of "God Bless America" and Peter Mahovlich's mile-wide grin was punctuated by a cigar the size of my arm.

Montreal's traditional Rite of Spring, the Stanley Cup Parade, was back by popular demand and half a million Montrealers partied with us. We partied extra hard because we all knew something special was just beginning; this team had just started to win Stanley Cups. We fully expected to return the following May, and the one after that. So with Dutchie the cheerleader at the front of the parade, we toasted St. Catherine Street with a couple of cases of 24 and had a great time. A hearse was parked at the corner of St. Catherine and Peel. In its rear window was a pair of Philadelphia sweaters.

How do you recount four straight Cups? Or seasons that ran into each other as we set record after record?

I rifle through the scrapbooks that Jeannette diligently kept year after year, and I'm presented with a variety of images, some surprisingly poignant. The next season started in August for a large group of the new champs. Downtown Montreal had barely been swept clean of the debris left by the Stanley Cup parade it seemed, and we were reporting for the Canada Cup camp at the Forum.

Our photo album for the '76–'77 – the one we finished with

60 wins, 8 losses, and 12 ties – contains two very special pictures. The first is of three generations of Robinsons: me, my Dad, and my late grandfather Henry, then 85, posing proudly in the Canadiens' dressingroom after an easy 9–5 rout of the Maple Leafs. I'd scored twice in the game, my sixth and seventh of the season, and added my 23rd assist of the season.

We three Robinsons are wall-to-wall grins; I can't help but smile every time I see that picture. At the back of the same album is a picture that wipes the smile away, it seems so tragic.

Again, there are three persons standing side-by-side and smiling: Emile (Butch) Bouchard, Pierre's Dad and a former Canadiens' captain; me; and a young hockey star with the Elites du Nord Bantam AA team of Montreal. His name is Normand Leveille and that afternoon, the Truc du Chapeau (Hat Trick) club awarded him with a brand new pair of Super Tacks skates, while Butch Sr. received a painting and I was given a sculpture. Normand made good use of his prize because, five years later, he was Boston's first-round selection, Number 15 overall, in the entry draft after a sparkling career with the Chicoutimi Sagueneens of the Quebec Major Junior Hockey League.

In Normand's rookie season with Boston, a blood vessel burst in his brain and he fell to the ice during a game in Vancouver. He suffered partial paralysis, effectively ending his NHL career. Knowing how his hockey future turned out, the shining optimism on the face of the young boy in the picture tears your heart out.

Looking back on a long career, you rarely see what you think happened because over time memories have become compressed, like various layers of sediment that the archaeologists dig through when they uncover evidence of past civilizations. That big goal in the final against Boston turns out to have been in a semi-final three years later. The big bodycheck on such-and-such a player was in '74, not the '76 final as I might have mistakenly believed for many years. This incident took place *here*, that one *there*. Like a videotape that has been spliced again and again, what once seemed clear becomes an awful jumble of images, memories, and misconceptions.

The headlines from the 1976–77 season tell the story better than I could:

"Habs Play Solitaire as Kings No Match" – a 6–0 domination of Los Angeles in January.

"Shutt, Lafleur play it again" – an 8–1 romp over Cleveland Barons, led by Steve's and Guy's two-goal performances.

"Gambles galore, but Canadiens keep rolling" – a 5–0 suffocation of the Detroit Red Wings.

"Hot reception from a warm Lapointe" – a 6–4 win in which we scored three goals in 2:22 in the third against Philadelphia, stopping their 20-game unbeaten streak and outshooting them 55–27 in the process. Guy Lapointe comes off a groin injury to score two goals and an assist.

"Robinson, Houle pace Habs' romp over Pens" – 9–1 against the Penguins in Pittsburgh, or 19–2 in our past two games. Reggie has two goals and an assist; I have a goal and two assists.

"Pete's cut bleeds Islanders" – Big Peter gets cut with a high stick and we score twice on the ensuing powerplay to beat the Islanders 4–1.

"Stars glimmer but Larry lights way" – I get three assists as we beat the North Stars 5–2 in Minneapolis. The two goals against Ken Dryden equal the number he allowed to the North Stars in four games in the previous season (two shutouts, two one-goal games).

"Canadiens prove they're just too good" – We dismantle the Rangers 8–1 at Madison Square, and I get my revenge on Ken Hodge.

"Grand slam for Canadiens" – We hammer the Blues 8–1 in St. Louis.

After that St. Louis game, Red Fisher of *The Montreal Star* spoke with Mike Shannon, the former third baseman for a couple of St. Louis Cardinals World Series teams. Shannon described the phenomenon of playing for and against a superior team: "I guess you could say I played with a couple of teams which may – may – have been as good as this Canadiens bunch.

"Anyway, we'd go out on the field and we'd know we were

better than the other guys. Worse, they knew we were a lot better. We'd run into teams which didn't want anything more than not to be embarrassed and I guess teams like the Blues and others feel the same way when they play Canadiens.

"That makes things a lot worse. They should go out and play their own game and try to forget how good Canadiens are. That's what I'd try to do; but one thing bothers us. How do you do it?

"What you do is get off the ice as quickly as you can, get out of the arena as quickly as you can . . . and look ahead to the next game."

A phenomenal year, in headlines. Not without its reversals and incidents, either. Like the time in Vancouver – for the Canadiens, it always *seems* that we pick Vancouver as the spot for our tiffs, figuring that geography separates us from reality or something like that. Anyway, on this occasion the team arrived late in the B.C. metropolis, as usual, and the players just grabbed their keys at the front desk and trudged up to their rooms to sleep. Serge and I were roommates and two of the first in their rooms. We had a good night's sleep, went down and had breakfast, and then did a little touring since there was no skate scheduled.

Later that afternoon, we bumped into Doug Risebrough: "Where were ya?" he asked, with his typical brashness.

"Out and about, taking in a little bit of Vancouver. Where were you?" came the innocent reply.

"At practice."

"Uh-oh."

Murphy's Law (Whatever can go wrong, will) has many corollaries. One is: "Just when you think you've gotten away with a minor indiscretion, it will blow up into a major incident." When we joined the rest of our teammates on the bus to the Pacific Coliseum that night, Scotty said nothing about our absence. During his pre-game speech . . . ditto. After all, we were 14 points ahead of our nearest opposition. What could he say? We were about to find out.

Near the end of the first period, Serge and I were on the ice when trouble struck. I had my hands full with Hilliard Graves, a small but pesky winger, when the puck and Ron Sedlbauer popped loose in front of Ken Dryden, all at the same time. Sedlbauer shot, Dryden saved, and then the former scored on the rebound. Worse still, Don Lever scored with two seconds left in the period, a cardinal sin in Scotty's book, and we were behind 2–0, despite outshooting the Canucks 13–6.

Scotty was at his best in the room between periods: "It would seem," he said, chin pointed straight up at the lighting fixture, "that some guys on this team think they're better than the rest. It would seem that these guys got reputations in this league, they're all-stars and they love to read about how good they are in the papers." He was just warming up, his face was pink, going red.

"Obviously guys like this don't have to bless us with their presence at practice like the rest of their teammates because they're too good for us, and the rest of this league.

"Now can somebody tell me, if these guys are so good, such *ALL-STARS*, how come we're losing 2–0 to the Vancouver Canucks? Could it be that the Canucks can't read, that not one guy on their team knows that we have such great stars in our room?

"Graves and Sedlbauer gotta be illiterate. If they knew how great Savard and Robinson are, no way they could have scored a goal like they did."

The psychology behind this kind of attack is interesting. As the recipient, or designated target, you have to sit there and take it; there's nothing you can or will say. You know that somehow you screwed up by not attending practice, even though it might not have been your fault. Your teammates sympathize, but they're not beyond enjoying Scotty's show. When he gets going, it's equal parts humour and inspiration, stuff that will keep the team entertained for weeks. You know that over in the corner, Shutty, the human tape recorder, is quietly snickering and absorbing every word to be used in later monologues: "Savard, what are ya? 38? 39? (Serge is 31.) Yer old enough to be the father of half the guys in the room, fer

Chrissakes, and this is the way ya behave? They're *BABIES*
Serge! Ya gotta be their role model. You keep this up and yer
gonna take 'em all with ya. Look at poor (Bill) Nyrop. He's
lost. He doesn't know where to turn now. Ya gotta be careful,
Serge. Yer formin' young minds."

Serge might bite, throwing in a mock protest: "Hey, watta
about Robinson? I wasn't alone on this!"

And Shutty would be ready: "That's exactly my point,
Serge! Ya perverted a good ol' Eastern Ontario farm boy. Salt
of the earth. If ya can do that to Robinson, what chance do
these kids have?"

The beauty of this situation for the coach is that it affords
him the long-sought opportunity to remind the team that it is
made up of human beings, not demi-gods. At the same time, it
allows him to reaffirm that he's in control by blasting two of the
team's stars. The message is that no one is exempt from the
rules or the coach's wrath if they break those rules. He is yelling at Savard and Robinson, but he's really making a point with
the younger players on the team. We're safe targets; he knows
that Savard and I won't miss another practice in the next ten
years and that we won't pout about this dressing down. He also
knows that when the second period starts, the Vancouver
Canucks will be desperately trying to contain two suddenly
aroused veteran defencemen.

As usual, he's right. We score four in the second, two more
in the third, and beat Vancouver 6–4. Scotty might even have
purposely forgotten to have informed us about the practice,
hoping this opportunity might present itself. Nah, Scotty
couldn't be that devious. . .

It's hard to distinguish one team from another, and even one
series from another, when you play 12 playoff series in four
years, and win 12 of them. I can better remember the events of
the Stanley Cup years 1973 and 1986 because each was pre-
ceded and/or followed by a contrasting bad post-season experience. But 1976 through 1979 tend to run together, the result
of us playing 59 April and May games, winning 49 of them, an
.830 winning percentage. In that run, we beat Detroit, St.
Louis, Philadelphia, Chicago, and the New York Rangers;

Boston three times; and the New York Islanders and the Toronto Maple Leafs twice each.

What really strikes me about the playoff year of 1977 was the St. Louis heat and the tenacity of the Islanders. We beat the Blues four straight to start off our Cup defence. It was quick and surgical, 7–2, 3–0, 5–1, and 4–1; no games close, no threat from the Blues. Everybody sang the praises of our defence, especially the Big Three and this finally got to Serge Savard.

"Robinson, Lapointe, and Savard . . . when is it going to stop?" The rhetorical question hung heavier in the air in the dressingroom than the tropical mist from the showers.

"I'm not upset by this kind of talk because I realize that it's the convenient label journalists pin on teams like ours," Serge went on to explain. "But this team is much more than the Big Three. Bouchard, Nyrop, Chartraw – all three of these guys could play anywhere in this league. The biggest thing that upsets me about this nickname is that the Montreal Canadiens win because we're a team, and by that I mean more than 20 guys. I've played with greater players . . . Beliveau, Henri Richard, Frank Mahovlich, Laperriere, Tardif, and Houle . . . but this *TEAM* is the best." Even then, Serge was sounding like a future general manager.

With all of that talk of the Big Three, we were more like the Big Two-and-a-half in that series. Guy Lapointe was hurt and then Pierre Bouchard went down with a shoulder separation in the first game; so we went with four defencemen most of the time. A rookie named Brian Engblom came up and got into a couple of games for a few shifts, but most of the time it was Robinson, Nyrop, and Savard.

It was so hot it was unbearable and they refused to turn on the air conditioning at the hotel where we were staying. Serge and I took our mattresses and sheets out onto the balcony and slept there. A series to remember. We won it quickly so we could go somewhere more temperate to dry out our equipment.

Up next were the New York Islanders and they promised a replay of the previous year's hard-fought series. We had beat them four straight during the season, outscoring them 16–7, but we were not brimming with overconfidence when the series began. During the regular season, we'd allowed 171 goals to win the Vezina Trophy and the Isles were the only other team in the league with fewer than 200 goals against, ending the season with 193. They'd swept the Black Hawks 2–0 in the best-of-three opening round, then followed that up with a 4–0 whitewash of Buffalo, a team that had given us trouble all season. Last but not least, goalie Billy Smith was riding the crest of a 15-game win streak. That spelled danger if we got too cocky.

They came into Montreal on a high and it was up to us to prick that balloon very quickly, before they could add to their momentum. One thing that picked up our spirits was the return to action of Guy Lapointe and we would need him right away. We won the first game 4–3, outshooting them 38–19. But shots on goal don't tell the tale.

The Islanders led 3–1 in this game, all three goals scored by right winger Billy Harris, and could have gone up 4–1 early in the second period when Jude Drouin deflected a shot wide past the open net. Murray Wilson got us back within one, on a coast-to-coast effort which culminated in him blowing past an Islanders' defender and putting it upstairs on Smith. Guy Lafleur tied it early in the third on a 50-footer and when Jacques Lemaire set up Shutt two minutes later, we had the margin of victory. We had it barely, that is, because Bob Nystrom hit a goalpost late in the game.

What I remember most about those two first series with the Islanders was the work of people like Bob Gainey, Clark Gillies, Bryan Trottier, and Doug Jarvis. And especially Bob Nystrom. There seemed to be an unwritten agreement; whenever we were on the ice, Nystrom and I would belt each other all over the rink. This was Robinson-Dornhoefer all over again, with the main difference being that Nystrom initiated as many hits as I did. With Dornhoefer, I would take the offensive although he certainly never backed down. Bob Nystrom and I must have hit each other nine million times during that series, each one of them a clean shot. It was like hitting a wall; the puck would be going toward him or me and the numbers 19 and

23 would collide: *BOOM*. Over and over again. Clark (Jethro Bodeen) Gillies also chipped in with his formidable size, but Nystrom played it more physical all the time. Clark was still young and fairly new to the league and Charty proved it by blasting him clear over the boards and into the penalty box. A couple of years later, when Jethro stopped growing, there wasn't a player in the league who could do that any more.

Game Two of that series was a similar war and once again, it was one of our classic role players who won it for us. On this night, Ken Dryden and Billy Smith decided They Shall Not Pass and we were locked in a scoreless duel in the third period when Doug Risebrough was sent off with a penalty just after the six-minute mark. Halfway through the penalty, Jimmy Roberts gambled and attacked Jean Potvin at the Islanders blue line as they prepared to mount one more attack against us. The puck hit Jimmy's stick, Potvin's skate, and bounced behind the defenceman. Jimmy sped around him and in alone on Billy Smith, beating him up high to finally give us the lead. I later banked one in off a skate and Peter Mahovlich added a power play goal in the last minute to make it 3–0.

But we knew we had dodged two bullets and, although we were up 2–0 in the series, Billy Smith had been formidable. Now it was back to Long Island. We'd won 17 straight games, going back to March in the regular season, and 11 straight playoff games, stretching back to our last loss to the Islanders in the semi-finals the year before. Yet one loss might bring our house of cards tumbling down.

Denis Potvin delivered that loss, his two goals and assist spearheading a 5–3 New York win that put the wind back in their sails. Two nights later, another all-star defenceman with the number five on his back dramatically sucked the air out of the Islanders. We led 2–0 before the game was three minutes old, and went on to shut down the Islanders 4–0. Guy Lapointe started the ball rolling in the first minute, taking the puck up the ice and, off-balance, sending a one-handed pass across the crease to an unchecked Steve Shutt. At 2:33 of the first, Shutt set up Guy Lafleur.

At the seven-minute mark, Rick Chartraw caught Clark

Gillies with his head down and knocked him clean over the boards and into the penalty box. That shocked the Nassau County Coliseum crowd into near silence. Full silence would come near the end of the period, with a goal by Jimmy Roberts.

There could be no greater graphic example of Jimmy's true grit than the goal he scored with his glove full of blood after his little finger had almost literally exploded. Just before the scoring play, Roberts was banged hard in the corner by Garry Howatt. Jimmy had cut the finger in the previous Thursday's game, had it stitched and, when Howatt hit him, his stick jammed against the boards "and the pressure inside the finger had nowhere to go except through the stitches."

"There was blood, flesh and broken stitches all over the inside of the glove," Jimmy told reporters in what had become his regular post-game press conference since he had scored goals in the last three games. "There was no sense going to the bench as soon as it happened because the play was around their goal and my job is to stay with the play."

His hand hurting like the dickens, he had rounded the Islanders net, taken a pass from Bob Gainey, and put it over Smith's shoulder. He went out and got the finger fixed again, and then contributed hugely to the checking blanket we threw over the Islanders for the rest of the evening. We were one game away from the final.

Of course, nothing is sure against a team like the Islanders and they proved it by beating us 4–3 in overtime, only the second Forum loss in 38 games by the Canadiens, since dropping a decision to Boston the previous October. Steve Shutt had knocked Billy Smith out of the Islanders net in the previous game in Long Island and he'd been replaced by Chico Resch. Resch started the fifth game and played well enough to keep his team in the game as we took leads of 2–1 and 3–2 and never could extend them. That cost us and Denis Potvin sent us all back to New York for Game Six.

I've talked about the quiet men who were our leaders. There were other quiet men, other leaders, on that team, and the single most distinguishing factor that underscored the difference between the Montreal Canadiens and other NHL teams of that era was the fact that we hated to lose. We despised losing and refused to do it.

In Game Six, two other leaders came to the fore. Doug Jarvis and Bob Gainey each may have played his greatest-ever single game in this contest as we edged the Islanders 2–1 to win the series. The Islanders streamed onto the ice to an emotional five-minute standing ovation from a crowd that knew only one word: "Chico, Chico, Chico" they chanted over and over again. Hundreds of times, in fact. We could only stand there quietly waiting for the crowd to quiet so that the national anthems could be sung and the puck dropped.

Once again we stunned the home crowd on Long Island as Doug Jarvis won the opening faceoff cleanly from Bryan Trottier, fed the puck to Guy Lapointe who in turn fed a streaking Gainey. Seven seconds into this game it was 1–0 Montreal. "Chico, Chico, Chico" froze on the lips of the locals as Bo took the Islanders out of the game in the blink of an eye. And nine minutes into the third period, Bo took a feed from Murray Wilson and made it 2–0. The only satisfaction the Islanders had that night was depriving Ken Dryden of a shutout on a Denis Potvin goal with nine seconds left in the contest.

In a game that was 1–0 for 44 minutes, Ken Dryden was a giant, but the real leaders that night were Gainey and Jarvis. Every time there was an important faceoff, there was Doug Jarvis winning it, clearing the puck to a winger or a defence-man, denying the Islanders any chance to get going. Whenever the Islanders pressed in our zone, there was Gainey blasting bodies in the corners or along the side boards, shift after shift, wearing down Billy Harris and other forwards as they desperately tried to tie the game.

We'd beaten the Islanders for the second straight year. We had a great team and yet we knew that if they ever found a scorer, they were going on to greater heights. Later that June, selected Number 15 in the first round, the Islanders had their answer…a forward from the Laval Nationals of the Quebec junior league: Mike Bossy.

We went on to play and beat the Bruins in four straight in a series that turned out to be an anti-climax after the intensity of the New York series. The Bruins had a tenacious team and some quality players like Peter McNab, Brad Park, Wayne Cashman, Terry O'Reilly, and Gerry Cheevers, but we simply outmanned them in every area. Despite the standard Montreal-Boston brawling and an incident where the Bruins accused Guy Lafleur of deliberately shooting the puck at defenceman Mike Milbury causing tough guy John Wensink to threaten the Flower, the series went off without a hitch and we had two Cups in a row.

The 1976–77 season would be a tough act to follow for any team; and yet the 1977–78 edition of the Canadiens might have been the only team able to do so without seeming to skip a beat. How hard an act to follow? Well, that summer, four of us posed with an impressive display of silverware as the NHL handed out its individual awards. Seven trophies were arrayed in front of myself, Bunny Larocque, Ken Dryden, and Guy Lafleur at the Queen Elizabeth Hotel. They were the Prince of Wales, for winning our conference; the Norris Trophy for best defenceman, yours truly; the Vezina, Larocque and Dryden; the Art Ross for leading scorer, Lafleur; the Stanley Cup; the Conn Smythe Trophy for best performer in the playoffs, Lafleur; and the Hart Trophy for the Most Valuable Player in the league, Lafleur.

Winning 60 games would be a daunting challenge but not losing more than eight games would be an even tougher mountain to climb. There were relatively few changes but they did have impact on the club. Jimmy Roberts, now 37, was dealt (again) to St. Louis to make a large contribution as a semi-official player-coach and great influence on a young team. Murray Wilson, injuries seeming to nullify his incredible potential, ended up in Nova Scotia for a spell after scoring only one assist in 12 games. He soon would be on his way to Los Angeles in a "Sam Pollock special" for a Kings' early-round draft choice.

And then came the biggest shock, probably because I was the last to hear of it. Big Peter Mahovlich and Scotty Bowman spent the early part of the new season going at each other with renewed vigour. We had good young players coming up, like young centre Pierre Mondou from Sorel of the Quebec league.

Jacques Lemaire had pretty well taken over from Peter between Shutt and Lafleur, and Mahovlich was not pleased at playing on the second line, and practically not at all on the powerplay, where the serious points were to be had. Some 17 games into the season, he was sent to Pittsburgh in an oddity, a transaction in which all four parties involved had the same first name. Coming to Montreal were Pierre (French for Peter) Larouche and the rights to WHA forward Peter Marsh. Going to the Penguins were Peter M. and Peter Lee, a top-rated centre the Canadiens had drafted from the Ottawa 67s.

Peter and I lived near each other in Kirkland, a West Island suburb, and travelled together all the time, either to the Forum or to the airport. One late November night, he picked me up as usual and we made small talk about the night's game as we headed down the Trans-Canada Highway into town. Peter was in his ninth year with the Canadiens and had been an assistant captain for five.

"You playing tonight?" I asked. This normally wouldn't be a subject of our conversations; Peter would start all games automatically as a star of the team. But this year the feud with Scotty had heated up and Peter had sat out the occasional game.

"Yup. Tonight I'm starting," he answered. "And I don't want you to pound on me too hard."

"Right," I responded, trying to remember accidental collisions with Big Peter that would have prompted such a remark.

"I'm starting for Pittsburgh. I got traded this afternoon." I spent the rest of the ride in silence. I was in a state of shock. When I walked into our room and saw Pierre Larouche suiting up, I knew Big Peter wasn't kidding. A little something in the room died that day.

But even without noted pranksters Roberts and Mahovlich, the team pressed forward. Larouche added another dimension to the team: yet another player who could break open a game offensively at any time. He could take some of the load off

Yvan Cournoyer who was suffering through an injury-filled season. Two years later, Pierre would score 50 goals for us. Young Mondou was also a big help, scoring 19 goals and 30 assists in 71 games and playing good, two-way hockey.

As a result, we finished the season with the second-best total in NHL history, 129 points on 59 wins, 10 losses, and 11 ties. We scored 359 goals, down 28 from the previous year, and allowed 183, 11 more than in '76–77. But we were still miles ahead of the competition, thanks mainly to a record-setting 28-game undefeated run during the season. Yvan Cournoyer was slowing down a little with age and injury; Peter M. and Jimmy Roberts were gone; and the kids like Risebrough, Jarvis, Gainey, Lambert, Lafleur, Shutt, and, yes, Robinson, were just coming into their prime.

The Stanley Cup playoffs that spring were a familiar story. We downed Detroit in five games and swept by the Toronto Maple Leafs in four straight, after they'd caused the surprise of the post-season tournament with a seven-game upset over the Islanders. Once again we were in the final against Boston and this time they took us to six games before we won it on their ice in late May. That made it three and counting, and there was serious talk of taking a run at the five straight of the famed Canadiens' dynasty of the late 1950s. In our last three Cup runs, we'd been 12–1, 12–2, and 12–3. The opposition was creeping up on us, but slowly.

The big news of the coming season would come while the Canadiens were on golf courses all over Canada and the United States. Sam Pollock, the man who put it all together and the best front office man in the sport, was leaving the Canadiens. If ever a dark cloud could hang over a championship team, that was it.

For years, Sam simply had been The Man Upstairs. He took care of business, from A to Z. He took care of the organization and the team and we knew that nobody did it better. That became a comfort to us because it helped us to become the best team on the ice, knowing that the best management team off the ice was fronting for us. Sam's cunning and expertise added to our team mystique; every draft deal he finagled was worth its weight in gold when it came to psyching the opposition. As far as the players were concerned, Sam was there when the chips were down.

In the summer of 1978, Labatt Breweries was putting a lot of pressure on the Bronfman family and their Placement Rondelle company to sell the Canadiens. Labatt was deep in an advertising and sponsorship war with Carling O'Keefe and Molson Breweries and all three were scrambling to acquire hot sports properties so they could shut out the opposition in lucrative sports advertising. The Molson family had owned the Canadiens in the late 1950s and through the 1960s when they sold to Placement Rondelle (a consortium of the Bronfmans, the Bank of Nova Scotia, and John Bassett's Baton Broadcasting of Toronto) and two Molson brands, Export and Canadian, had become synonymous with hockey after years of commercials on Hockey Night in Canada. Over the years, the Bronfman's holding company Edper Investments had taken over Placement Rondelle.

When Labatt made its bid, Molson Breweries heard the alarm bells ringing and feared they might lose their most lucrative sports advertising property. They bid, and they bought, and in August, 1978, the Canadiens changed hands.

During the Bronfman reign (1971–78), Sam Pollock had acquired an impressive equity interest in Edper Investments through stock options and the like, and when the Molson sale went through he was faced with a choice. Divest, and stay with the Canadiens in his current capacity; or remain with Edper. There was no choice, after more than 30 years with the Canadiens he was ready to move on.

Scotty Bowman, seeing his opportunity, made a strong bid for the GM's job but it was awarded to Irving Grundman, a businessman who'd joined the Canadiens in 1971 as part of the Bronfman team. Grundman was not a hockey man, but he had eaten lunch with Pollock almost every working day for seven years and had learned the business inside-out. He was Sam's recommendation for the position and that bothered Bowman a lot.

We could sense it during that season. Scotty was quieter

than he'd ever been before and it seemed to us that he was going through the motions. We kept winning, with a 53–17–11 record for 115 points but this was only good for second place overall. The Islanders finished with 116 points and, if we were to meet in the final, they would have precious home-ice advantage because of that slim single point.

It was a strange year. We kept improving the team make-up even though our points total declined. Three "Baby Bulls" from the WHA's former Birmingham franchise – Rod Langway, Gaston Gingras, and Mark Napier – joined the team, as did another WHA expatriate Cam Connor.

But there was a large hole in the dressingroom as Pierre Bouchard was claimed by Washington in a waiver draft deal that somehow went wrong for Irving Grundman and suddenly there were grumblings that Montreal management was human and could make mistakes.

All that aside, we won the Stanley Cup again, sweeping the Toronto Maple Leafs for the second straight year and then outlasting Boston in a seven-game war that went to overtime in the seventh contest.

After that we faced the fat-cat New York Rangers, surprise winners in six games over the Islanders, and wrapped up the Cup in five.

Four Cups in four years, only one other team had done that in NHL history and they'd won five. We were going to go right after them in 1979–80, the ghosts of the 1955–60 Canadiens. But before we could, the Montreal Canadiens would undergo a summer like no other in recent memory.

ELEVEN

The Flickering Torch

THE CANADIENS' dressingroom at the Forum is equal parts athletes' changing room, museum, and shrine. High on the wall at one end is an excerpt from "In Flanders Fields," the poem writen during the First World War by a Canadian, Colonel John McCrae, who lost his life in the trenches of Belgium.

He tells future generations: "To you from failing arms we throw the torch, be yours to hold it high!" That message has always been taken to heart by the Montreal Canadiens. They've been a hockey dynasty for as long as anyone can remember because they've always made sure the torch was passed like a baton from man to man on a finely tuned 4×100 metre relay team: from Morenz to Joliat to Blake to Lach to Richard to Harvey to Richard to Beliveau to Lafleur and so on. How else do you explain a team that has had only one sub-.500 season since 1950? Where else, in any sport, North American or otherwise, could you find such a tradition of excellence?

On the surface, this rich history and tradition might seem to be the work of nature, a process that almost happens by itself, without much guidance or direction. Nothing could be further from the truth, of course. The Montreal Canadiens have passed the torch so well, and for so long, that some strategy had to be behind it. In this case, the "strategy" essentially was two men, Frank Selke and Sam Pollock.

The torch had a name: work ethic. And the Montreal Cana-

diens practised it upstairs and downstairs long before it became fashionable in the world of sport.

On May 21, 1979, just before 11 P.M., we hoisted Bob
Gainey on our shoulders at centre ice of the Forum. We'd just
been awarded the franchise's 22nd Stanley Cup and announcer
Claude Mouton had come on the public address system to an-
nounce that Bo had been awarded the Conn Smythe Trophy for
top playoff performer.

The torch was burning brightly: we were the proud posses-
sors of our fourth Cup in a row and were the first team since the
Canadiens of 1958–59 in a position to "drive for five." We had
no illusions that it would be easy, with the Islanders climbing
their way to the top of the NHL standings. They'd been upset
by the Leafs in '78 and the Rangers in '79 but their misfortune
couldn't happen three years in a row; they were too good a
team, But so were we; the Canadiens were a quality mix of experience and youth and figured to challenge seriously for Lord
Stanley's hardware come spring, 1980.

And then the flame began to flicker. Just as Sam Pollock's
departure caught us all on the golf course the year before, so
did a string of departures in the summer of '79. The first to
leave the organization was Al MacNeil, the mastermind of our
superb Nova Scotia operation and the man whose job had been
to restock the big club with well-schooled prospects. In eight
years he'd done a stellar job and the wounds of the Henri
Richard incident had healed. The Atlanta Flames came calling
and hired him as their coach before the entry draft.

Barely a week before the draft, a real bombshell: Scotty
Bowman was moving to Buffalo as coach and general-
manager of the Sabres.

While we'd sensed all through the previous season that
Scotty had been deeply upset by the appointment of Irving
Grundman to replace Sam Pollock, on Pollock's recommen-
dation as well, few of the players really believed he'd leave
Montreal. Scotty had been born and raised in working-class
Verdun and was a Montreal boy through-and-through. Al-
though he'd coached in St. Louis, his hockey life was the

Canadiens. But when draft day arrived, there he was, sitting at the table decorated with Buffalo's blue and gold.

Then came the player moves. Jacques Lemaire, 33, and in the kind of shape to enjoy five or more highly productive NHL seasons alongside Guy Lafleur and Steve Shutt, accepted an offer to act as player-coach with the Sierre team in Switzerland. Always a serious student of the game, Coco wanted to start on his post-playing career education in hockey because he fully intended to become a coach or general manager after his playing days were over. Another factor was his increasing shyness in the face of the ever-swelling media coverage and pressure of pro hockey in Montreal.

Thee weeks later it was Ken Dryden, a month short of his 32nd birthday and also with many productive seasons ahead of him, deciding to move on to the "real world." He had a law degree and it was time he got established outside hockey, he decided. I got the feeling that there was no challenge any more for Ken; he'd won six Stanley Cups in eight years, a phenomenal record when you realize that he won his first in 1971 with less than ten games NHL experience, had he'd sat out a season in his celebrated holdout. He'd beat the Soviets in the big series in '72, played for Canada's national team before joining us, and even worked for Ralph Nader. What more could he accomplish?

Last, and definitely not least, the Road Runner did his last "beep, beep" for the Canadiens as a chronic bad back forced our captain, Yvan Cournoyer, to retire. He'd missed much of the previous season with the injury; in fact, Serge Savard had worn the C during the Cup final. Yvan gave it a shot at training camp but the pain told him it was all over.

MacNeil, Bowman, Lemaire, Dryden, and Cournoyer; five certain Hall of Famers left the organization between one season and the next. Name any other team in league history that faced such an exodus between seasons? It was similar to the situation in 1971 when both Jean Beliveau and John Ferguson retired and Al MacNeil moved down to Halifax that summer. The major difference was that there wasn't a Guy Lafleur and

Scotty Bowman waiting in the wings. Montreal's top draft choice in June, 1979, was Gaston Gingras, formerly of the Birmingham Bulls of the WHA, and the new coach hired by general manager Irving Grundman was Bernard "Boom Boom" Geoffrion.

The first, Gingras' draft, was no shocker. Actually, Ron Caron's picks turned up Gingras (27th), Mats Naslund (37th), Guy Carbonneau (44th), and Rick Wamsley (58th), so in the long run, it proved to be a most successful draft.

The shocker was the hiring of the Boomer. Boom Boom had been a coach twice before, with the New York Rangers and with the expansion Atlanta Flames. Both times he'd quit because of the pressures of the job; this time he'd plunged headlong into the most intense pressure-cooker in the sport! To top that off, in Atlanta he'd been handling community public relations for the Flames, keeping Georgians entertained with his half-French Quebec, half-Georgia Peach accent.

The torch might have flickered when Irving Grundman made the announcement, but we knew we still had the tools to take a serious run at the Cup. We were still a force in the league and would continue to be one for many years, staying near the top of the league standings and near the 100-point mark for the next four years.

There were lots of theories as to why Caron and Grundman had hired Boomer. The most popular was the Quebec factor; at the dissolution of the World Hockey Association, four former WHA teams (Quebec Nordiques, Winnipeg Jets, Edmonton Oilers, and Hartford, formerly New England, Whalers) were joining the league for the 1979–80 season. Irving Grundman, it was assumed, wanted to make sure that the Nordiques would not "out-French" the Canadiens and opted for a French presence behind the bench.

The project was doomed to fail from the very start.

Boomer was very much the good liver you see on television in the Miller Lite commercials; a wonderful guy, cheerful, fun-loving. But he was also probably the best example of the saying: "Great players don't necessarily make the best coaches."

In that his long career in commercials has brought him a great deal of notoriety in the communications media, you might find it difficult to believe what I'm going to say next. Boom Boom's greatest difficulty with Montreal, believe it or not, was communicating. He knew what he wanted us to do on the ice but he just couldn't get it across to the players.

When Scotty was coach, our pre-game meetings for an eight o'clock game would start at 6:30 on the dot and run from 20 minutes to a half hour. Everything was broken down: the opponent's offence, defence, specialty teams, goaltending, who's hot, who's not. We skated onto the ice feeling mentally prepared, as well as physically.

As the song goes: "And then came Boom."

Boomer set a record for the shortest pre-game meetings in club history. Most started at 6:30. Most ended by about 6:32. "I don't have to tell you guys what to do; go out there and do your jobs," was his favourite line. His understanding or misunderstanding of his players' commitment to the game hindered him as a coach. As an all-star for many years, Bernie Geoffrion had never needed to be told what to do during a game or to be given as "assignment"" on the ice. He knew the key to success was to go out there and work his butt off, even if he was a natural talent. He assumed that all Montreal Canadiens on the 1979–80 team shared this dedication and professionalism. He was wrong.

I'm not saying that Geoffrion didn't have a clue; he knew his hockey very well. You couldn't play for Toe Blake and not learn your basics. What I am saying is that he didn't have much of a game plan.

Two things conspired to keep us on an even keel. First, we were a team of successful young veterans and many all-stars. Among them Lafleur, Savard, Lapointe, Robinson, Shutt, and Larouche. Second, we had a great crop of young up-and-comers all scratching for more icetime in Mark Napier, Pierre Mondou, Rod Langway, Brian Engblom and Pat Hughes. We still had Bunny Larocque in nets and Ron Caron had gone out and acquired veteran Denis Herron from Pittsburgh to lend him a hand.

We also had Claude Ruel around to teach the kids, run the practices, break down game film, and fill in for Bernie in pre-game meetings after the Boomer had finished his two-minute drill. That was a problem too, because Claude's presence rendered Bernie almost unnecessary. We discovered that we really didn't need that much coaching; but we needed more preparation. We did well, even with Boomer's "non-intervention" style, but we soon discovered that Bernie himself wasn't what we needed either.

On a veteran team that had won four straight Cups, or six in the last ten years, too many players had lived through the "my way or the highway" Bowman regime not to stick their heads above the trench line and cautiously test the battlefield for sniper fire when all was quiet on the western front. It was like a substitute teacher replacing a strict disciplinarian for a day or two; the temptation to fool around was overwhelming.

Also, after years of "I'm boss" and "you play how I tell you to play," Boomer's easier game approach was a problem. What did Boomer in was that too many veterans were questioning some of his moves. Soon "some" became "most" and Bernie was on the way out. Many of our guys spent their entire NHL careers under the iron fist of William Scott Bowman and Bernie's *laissez-faire* coaching style was too much of a temptation to test the boss's authority. When Scotty was coach, the veterans helped him; Bernie had the veterans against him.

Last but not least, Geoffrion had a heart of gold and he treated us like grown-ups. I feel that in order to be a successful coach, you have to be a bit of an SOB and a taskmaster. Always watching. Always letting the players know you are watching. And taking responsibility for all decisions; treating them like kids who need help to cross the street.

Bernie could get mad at us but he couldn't be the SOB who could get the best out of players who didn't want to work for him. When Bernie quit 30 games into the new season, he threw out a few accusations in his meeting with Irving Grundman: Serge Savard was more interested in his horses and business interests than playing hockey; Pierre Larouche was in it only for himself; too many players were coming in at one and two in the morning. He also said that Larry Robinson was the only player he knew would put out 100 per cent every night.

It may have been a flattering comment, but it was hardly true. The team had a work ethic and the boys showed up to play. Another player who put out 100 percent all the time was Bob Gainey but he and Bernie didn't hit it off.

Bo questioned several of the things Bernie was doing or wanted to do and being the leader that he is, often stuck up for players that Bernie was mad at. They had a few loud arguments, certainly not shouting matches, but voices were raised.

One night in Montreal, shortly before he quit, Bernie was really laying into us, telling us what we were doing wrong and other shortcomings. Bo had it: "Hell, we're not getting any direction from behind the bench."

The beginning of the end came during an "unMontreal-like" losing streak that ran from November 25 to December 21. In 12 games, we won only two, losing seven, and tying three for a measly seven points out of a possible 24. Boomer quit December 12, right in the middle of the streak and after a loss to the New York Islanders in Uniondale. That game was the start of a five-game pre-Christmas road trip and when Claude Ruel took over, we promptly went 0-for-North America, losing 5–3 to Edmonton, 6–2 to Winnipeg, 5–3 to St. Louis, and 5–2 to Minnesota.

Maybe the best way to wrap up the shortlived Geoffrion era is to say that the chemistry wasn't there; there was too much of an easygoing atmosphere around the dressingroom and the team and Montreal Canadiens historically have never thrived under such circumstances. We work well under what Ken Dryden used to call "creative tension."

Elsewhere in this book I have written extensively about Piton; how he signed me to my first contract, how invaluable he was as a scout, teacher, assistant GM, go-fer, and go-between. Claude had held many positions with the Canadiens over the years and head coach was one of them. He'd replaced Toe Blake after the 1968 season and won a Stanley Cup the following year.

A year after that, though, the Canadiens finished out of the playoffs with 92 points, tied for fourth place in the East Division with the Rangers. This came about after the Detroit Red Wings basically gave away an afternoon game to New York and Montreal was forced to try to score five goals or more in Chicago against the Black Hawks in the last game of the season. They didn't; in fact, the Hawks scored five goals after the Canadiens pulled their goalie for most of the third period.

A bit of trivia for those who complain about the current playoff system: the first-place St. Louis Blues in the West Division finished with 86 points, well ahead of Pittsburgh, Minnesota, and Oakland, all of which made the playoffs with 64, 60, and 58 points respectively. The NHL has been built on the dumbest playoff eligibility rules anywhere in professional sport, especially since the 1967–68 expansion. It's unfair to blame much of this on Claude Ruel; but that didn't alter the fact that he was the first Canadiens coach to finish out of the playoffs since 1948.

The following year was Boston's, most of it anyway. The Bruins ran away with the East Division and ended the season with a record 121 points, 12 ahead of New York. Montreal finished third with 97, and Chicago, transferred to the West Division in the off-season which saw the arrival in the league of Vancouver and Buffalo, had 107 points. Phil Esposito, Bobby Orr, John Bucyk, and Ken Hodge finished 1-2-3-4 in the league scoring race; Wayne Cashman and John McKenzie were 7–8; and Fred Stanfield was tied with Dave Keon and Jean Beliveau for 10th.

Late in the season, Claude Ruel quit, saying he could no longer motivate the players. He was replaced by Al MacNeil who took the team to the Stanley Cup, despite Henri Richard's unflattering assessment of his coaching ability.

When Claude left, the story was that he'd been too close to the players and couldn't put the distance that a coach needs to function effectively between himself and them. During the interim years with Scotty at the helm, Piton had gotten even closer to the players, especially the kids he worked in practice every day, and many people doubted his ability to change and lead the Canadiens a second time.

A coach of a 38–22–16 team considered a failure? In Montreal, yes. To put everything into context, you have to understand that in the last three decades, and especially the last two, expectations for the Canadiens have been much higher than those for, say, the Leafs. Each team has undergone such crises during that period, but in Toronto they've revolved about a team that's been poorly managed and ineptly coached for a quarter century, and whose results reflect that. In 1962–63, the Maple Leafs finished one point ahead of Chicago in first place in the regular-season standings. In the intervening 25 seasons, the Maple Leafs have never finished above third place in their division. The only other team that achieved a similar level of futility during the same period of time is the Kansas City Scouts-Colorado Rockies-New Jersey Devils and they've been in the league for 12 fewer seasons. And based on last season, they're well on their way to finishing high in the Patrick in the coming years. In those 25 years, for Toronto, Claude Ruel's "low-water mark" of 92 points would represent the second-highest season points total in the club's history (95 points in '50–'51 and 92 points in '77–'78.)

During the same period, Montreal finished first 15 times, and below third only twice. So when I talk about a crisis in Montreal, it usually means the team is not in first place, or just out of it. Montreal fans are famously supportive: they're with you win or tie, but don't tie too often!

In 1979–80, Bernie coached us for the first 30 games, and Claude Ruel came in for the last 50. The "team in crisis" finished the season with 107 points overall. Only Philadelphia with 116 points, and Buffalo with 110, were ahead of us in the overall standings. To top that off, we finished the season with a 22-game unbeaten streak.

But all was not well on the team, win or tie. With Claude at the helm, we found ouselves with a coach who was about halfway between Scotty Bowman and Bernie Geoffrion. He was soft on us, like Bernie had been, especially with the veterans.

And there was also a bit of a language barrier. Claude Ruel was well-liked by his players and we got a kick out of his idiosyncrasies, but he never had the kind of respect, motivated by fear, that Scotty received.

I'll never forget Piton's pre-game ritual. We'd set up pieces of tape on the floor, like the position markers they used to have on TV studio floors. Claude would walk right to the end of the room, turn around and walk back to the exact same spot near the front, night after night. He'd stop dead right on the tape without even noticing it, and we'd all be cracking up. Like Scotty, he'd take us through the opposition strengths and weaknesses and do a good job of preparing us for each opponent.

But Claude had one glaring fault and it cost us dearly. He loved the young kids, the rookies, and second-year men; but he'd never play them. One of the reasons why our late-season streak was so impressive was the fact that he was playing only about 12 guys. Apparently he'd done the same thing as a junior coach, playing his then-star defenceman Jacques Laperriere about 50 minutes a game. Claude had confidence in his veterans and to a certain extent, that's understandable; your veterans will get you there. But over the long haul you've got to use everybody.

When we got to the playoffs, we were exhausted and suffering from a multitude of injuries. We blew away Hartford in three-straight in the opening round, but Pat Boutette kneed Guy Lafleur and put him out of the playoffs. By the time we played Minnesota in the quarter-finals, Lafleur, Pierre Larouche (100 goals between them), Serge Savard, Guy Lapointe, and Doug Risebrough were injured (and Lemaire, Dryden, and Cournoyer were watching on television). That's a huge turnover in twelve months and Minnesota beat us in the seventh game to end our drive for five.

There were few recriminations and no finger-pointing. The series had gone down to the last couple of minutes of the seventh game; we'd played without Lafleur and Larouche throughout, and other players had been injured. It was one of the few occasions when a Montreal loss didn't set off a summer of breast-beating and gnashing of teeth.

It was as if the fans and media got together and said: "We knew you had a lot of injuries and you did your best under the circumstances. But don't let it happen again."

Unfortunately, it did happen again.

Before we got to training camp, there was the matter of the NHL summer meetings and the entry draft and the Canadiens were setting up for the jackpot. Montreal had the first pick in the entire draft and Grundman & Caron Inc. was drooling over a big centre who'd scored 89 goals and added 81 assists with the Regina Pats the season before. Doug Wickenheiser was the darling of the Montreal scouts, the Central Scouting Bureau, and the scouts of the other NHL teams.

There were two other players of "franchise" ability available in the same year; a defenceman with the Portland Winterhawks named David Babych, brother of St. Louis's Wayne; and a tricky play-making centre from Montreal named Denis Savard. Claude Ruel wanted Savard. He'd seen the youngster star for several years with the famous "trois Denis" line – Savard's linemates were also named Denis – and correctly pegged Savard as a future superstar.

What Savard had going against him was size, or lack of it. Montreal was loaded with small, crafty centres – Pierre Larouche, Pierre Mondou, Doug Risebrough, Doug Jarvis – and had two young centres in Nova Scotia – Guy Carbonneau and Dan Daoust – who were looking to move up. What we hadn't had on the club since Big Peter drove me into the Forum for the Pittsburgh-Montreal game was a centre of some size. So the hierarchy went for brawn. To be fair, the Wickenheiser selection was unanimous. Any other GM worth his salt would have picked Wickenheiser first, Babych second, and Savard third that year.

We all know what happened. Wickenheiser wasn't the NHL player a lot of people thought he'd be; Babych has since been traded from Winnipeg to Hartford; and Savard has close to 1,000 points in eight NHL seasons.

The '80–'81 season began the same way the '79–'80 season had ended: with half the club in the infirmary. When we went into a slump in late November and early December, losing four home games, the fans were asking the age-old quetion: "What's wrong with the Canadiens?"

In a word: injuries.

I remember once hearing a hockey "analyst" blurting out "real good teams overcome injuries and should never use injuies as an excuse for poor performance." What crap.

When the 1980–81 Canadiens played without goalies Richard Sevigny and Bunny Larocque, as well as Guy Lafleur, Pierre Larouche, Pierre Mondou, Yvon Lambert, Doug Risebrough, Guy Lapointe, Serge Savard, and myself for long periods of time, chances were the team performance levels would drop. It would fall off for two reasons – first, the replacements would never be as good as the regulars; second, the extra responsibility taken on and ice time logged by the remaining regulars would eventually result in diminished performance throughout the whole team.

It was one of those years for me. I missed 11 games between November 16 and December 10 with a separated shoulder and both Savard and Lapointe were out for parts of that period. I returned for a game in Pittsburgh against the Penguins and the "Larry Robinson Pittsburgh Penguins disease" surfaced again. (I wrote earlier that Penguins' centre Syl Apps Jr. once broke my nose, and then a former Penguin and then-teammate Denis Herron broke it a second time the same year.)

I was hardly back from the shoulder injury when defenceman Dave Burrows got his stick up, breaking my nose on a cross-check. Hello Pittsburgh, the team I could never smell coming!

The Flower was having the same type of year. He almost killed himself rehabilitating his injured knee in the off-season, re-injured it at training camp, and when he finally did return, was sidelined a couple of games with an eye injury after being clipped by Charlie Simmer's stick.

That injury out of the way, he pulled his groin, missed two

more games, and then went on to catch a puck under the left eye
. . . in practice.

Larouche, like Lafleur, had suffered injuries too but was
healthy again. Except he wasn't playing. During a January
road trip out west that saw us get hammered 9–1 in Edmonton,
tie Calgary 4–4, lose to Los Angeles 4–1, and beat Colorado
5–2, Pierre was dressed in only the Rockies game, and
benched in the third period to boot.

He was not happy, and when Pierre Larouche was not happy, it tended to spread to Guy Lafleur. And when Guy Lafleur
was not happy, headline writers were busy. The team became
embroiled in a feud that involved the coach and several
veterans and it all came to a head when Guy's frustration over
his injuries boiled over.

Guy went public with his frustrations, most spurred by a
seemingly endless string of injuries. (He was knocked out of
action eight times that season.) Guy told a radio announcer he
was upset because there were "too many extra guys on the
team, too many bodies." He didn't have much of an argument
there, though. The injuies we'd suffered up to that point in the
season made our dressingroom look like the set of M*A*S*H.
We were carrying all sorts of bodies – rookie defenceman
Gaston Gingras and, for a while, Bill Baker, the U.S.
Olympian. But it was young defencemen like these and Brian
Engblom and Rod Langway who were taking care of business
for us through injuries to Lapointe, Savard, and myself.

"It's been like this for the last season and a half and it makes
it had for Claude to coach properly," said Guy.

Rookies like Chris Nilan were up with the team and goalie
Rick Wamsley was called up a couple of times to sub for either
Bunny Larocque, Denis Herron, or Richard Sevigny when
they were hurt.

What had steamed Guy was that when the injury situation
seemed to clear up, some prominent veterans were benched by
Ruel. Both Guy Lapointe and Serge Savard were either benched during games or left out of the lineup and that upset many of
their teammates. Serge seemed to be the fans' whipping boy,

too, and the Forum faithful really came down hard on him on several occasions.

Another criticism at the time, and this appeared in the press, was that Ruel was relying too much on Bob Gainey for advice on how to run the team. This seemed silly to the extreme but it was the kind of thing that bothered the Flower.

It all came back to Larouche, Lafleur's regular centre now that Lemaire was in Switzerland.

"We are becoming much too defensive," Lafleur said on radio after Ruel sat out Larouche in a game. Larouche and Lafleur had been the club's only two 50-goal scorers the previous season. The Flower said slashing Montreal's offensive potential to produce a possibly marginal defensive improvement was stupid hockey. This sort of lent credence to the Gainey advice rumours, in that Gainey was a defensive player.

The word was that Pierre Larouche wasn't playing because his defensive game left a lot to be desired. On this point, I heartily endorsed the Flower's view that this reasoning was incredibly stupid. Defensive players were a dime-a-dozen. But players with Larouche's great moves and soft hands were rarer than diamonds.

If we wanted to win anything, snipers like Steve Shutt, Mark Napier, Lafleur, and Larouche would have to be firing from everywhere. We had enough Langways, Robinsons, Engbloms, Savards, and Lapointes to take care of business in our own end.

Montreal management never went out of its way to convert a defensive player into an offensive threat. Defensive players automatically had a role on our team; the unfortunate thing is that this didn't seem to be the case for offensive talents. Suffice to say, Lafleur was not alone in his comments about Larouche sitting out. For years, Larouche has carried that rap around the NHL with him: good score, no check. It began in Pittsburgh, followed him to Montreal and later Hartford and the Rangers. You'd think they'd learn to appeciate a guy with almost 400 NHL goals.

Purely offensive talent is hard to find; only seven or eight guys out of 400 or so are capable of scoring 50 goals or more a season, for more than one season. Larouche got a bad rap because he was a player who'd made it to the NHL on his offensive style, and who was then forced to change it when he got there. Wayne Gretzky and Mario Lemieux are certainly not the strongest backcheckers in hockey, but you don't hear them getting criticized for it.

With Peter Mahovlich, Yvan Cournoyer, and Jacques Lemaire gone, we certainly could use Pierre's scoring touch and Guy was right to make the point.

Another sore point with the team as the season wore on was Bunny Larocque. Ruel had lost confidence in him, dressing Denis Herron and Richard Sevigny as 1–2 and even bringing up rookie Rick Wamsley when injuries felled either, or both of that pair.

When Ken Dryden had retired after the 1978–79 season, Bunny quite rightly figured he'd be our number one goalie, after five years apprenticeship as number two. He was wrong. Just before the 1979–80 season opened, the club acquired Denis Herron from Pittsburgh for Pat Hughes, and Herron quickly became our team starter. When Peter Lee of Pittsburgh skated over Bunny's hand in December, the injury forced him out of action for six weeks and allowed Sevigny to establish himself. When he returned, Bunny was somewhere between number two and number three on our goaltending depth chart and chafing at the bit.

His first game back was against Chicago on January 21 and he was pulled after giving up three first-period goals. Ten days later, he lost 4–1 in Los Angeles and didn't play for another three weeks. When he tied the Blues 2–2 in St. Louis, that was the last straw.

"Get me out of here," he told Ron Caron and Irving Grundman.

"You don't want me, the coach doesn't trust me, and a change of scenery would be the best for everybody."

Just before the trading deadline in March, Bunny was sent to Toronto for Robert Picard, the former Montreal junior and number one draft pick by the Washington Capitals. Bunny ad-

mitted to us that the seemingly endless string of injuries had
finally got to him.

"I couldn't stand it any more," he said. "It seemed that every
time things would be going good, there'd be another damned
injury or something like that. After a while you start wondering if it all isn't inside your head. You need a change."

He got it. From the penthouse to the outhouse and with the
Leafs he could no longer complain about lack of action.

It was the other half of the trade we couldn't figure. Even
Claude Ruel seemed taken aback by the news that Picard was
coming to Montreal. At the time, we were essentially going
with four defencemen: myself, Serge, Rod Langway, and
Brian Engblom, and Guy Lapointe was working himself back
into shape after a long injury layoff. Bill Baker had been up and
down from Nova Scotia a couple of times and had acquitted
himself well; we didn't need another defenceman.

But the club fooled us again by sending Baker to Colorado
for a draft choice. That made room for Picard, sort of.

"I have my four top defencemen and Guy Lapointe is almost
back to 100 percent," said Ruel the diplomat. What he was really thinking was: "What do I need this guy for? He didn't do
anything in Washington and Toronto; the word is that he's a
prima donna and he led the Leafs with the worst plus-minus at
minus-25."

What Claude said was: "I want to see Picard on the ice with
the team before deciding where I'll work him in."

Ruel loved reclamation projects though, and you could see
the wheels turning when he added: "He's a good young prospect and a strong man. Don't forget, Serge Savard is 35 years
old and can't play forever." Whether he knew it or not, Picard
was coming to Claude Ruel University, all classes held after
practice – "We specialize in turning so-so talent into bona fine
NHL players."

As for Lapointe, he'd missed almost 11 weeks of the season
with a severe charley horse and subsequent muscle spasms
before he returned to action late in the season, so Picard got
into the lineup earlier than expected.

If our General Hospital soap opera wasn't humming along
beautifully by then, both Guys would liven up the plot in

March, just as the season was winding down and we were preparing for the Stanley Cup playoffs.

Injuries had weighed heavily on both players and for the first time in seven seasons, the Flower would fail to score 50 goals. The media openly speculated about his "rocky marriage" and there were items about Lafleur and Larouche doing the town's hot spots until all hours. In late March, Lafleur and his new teammate, Picard, had a late supper together and then retired to Thursday's, a popular club, for a nightcap. Driving home later that night on Highway 20, heading for the western suburbs, Guy apparently fell asleep at the wheel. His Cadillac careened off the highway and into a large Frost retaining wall. One of the fence posts came through the windshield like a javelin and just nicked Guy's ear. He was otherwise uninjured.

Quebec hero or not, quite a few of his teammates were surprised by the general tone of the reaction to the accident. We were upset when the media reported that there was supposedly a second person (a woman) in the car when it wasn't true. But we were more upset to hear all of this talk about Guy's loss to the Canadiens as a player took precedence over relief that Guy the human being had survived. It shows just how much some people overwhelm reality with fantasy. Guy the hockey player was fantasy; Guy the human being was reality.

Never mind whether he was lost or not to the Canadiens and what this would mean to our playoff chances; we were just glad he was alive and not seriously hurt.

Then it was Guy Lapointe's turn to add to the soap opera. A year before, Guy and Ruel had words after he was benched during a Rangers game. Two days later, he missed a pre-game skate and was left out of the lineup the same night, and then missed a trip to St. Louis and Winnipeg. He sat on the bench in our final game against Minnesota in the playoffs and told the media he wanted out of Montreal. But he and Claude had apparently patched up their differences in the off-season and lived through an uneasy truce, part of that the result of Lapointe's injuries.

Late in the season, Pointu returned to the team. Just after his return, he met with Ruel and the coach told him he wasn't happy with his play and would suggest that the team not protect

Lapointe in the NHL waiver draft the next fall. "Hell of a way to build your confidence, eh?" Lapointe commented. "Especially after I was out for 11 weeks and 40 games."

In a Saturday night game in late March, he was on the ice for five goals in a 6–2 Forum loss to the Rangers and found himself in the press box for our game the next night against the Nordiques, in Quebec City. Then Mario Tremblay came down with a knee injury and Lapointe was called down from the press box and told to dress. He didn't play a shift in our 4–0 loss and was raging after the game.

"I can't afford to miss ice time at this stage of the season when we're getting ready for the playoffs," he said. He went on to say he didn't expect to play in our next game against the Islanders because "they're a second-place club and I wasn't good enough to play against a tenth place club (Quebec) tonight." He was right.

In my mind, our management was panicking. For the second time in his career as head coach of the Canadiens, Claude Ruel was showing that he couldn't take the heat. Here was a five-time all-star and a valuable man on our defence and they weren't letting him play. Worse still, I felt this sense of panic in regular season would be multiplied in the playoffs when the real pressure was on.

The tone of the media commentary, fed by management, was that some of the Canadiens had become fat cats, playing as if their jobs were guaranteed. That kind of attack is hard to defend against because nobody consciously goes through the motions; his teammates won't let him. What had happened was that our team game was falling apart and everybody was trying to do everybody else's job to make up for it. In hockey, you're only as good as the guy next to you. As defencemen, we were only as good as the guys in front of us.

When we won the four straight Cups, we were led by superstars like Lafleur and Dryden but we never relied on them to carry the team. We won because we worked together and everybody contributed. The fat-cat accusation or intimation was a red herring; you couldn't accuse Lapointe of that because he'd missed half a season. And if other players were behaving that way, it was wrong to use Pointu as a message board. He was right to be angry and you could see that management was trying to set him up when Irving Grundman over-reacted.

"I consider Lapointe's remarks last night an insult to the coach and the hockey team," he said after the Quebec game. "I talked with Claude today and I'm going to meet with him again tomorrow and then we'll decide what to do with Guy Lapointe."

Our next game was against the Islanders and we won it 3–1 before a full house at the Forum. Gaston Gingras, who'd been out since late February with a rib injury, was pressed into action and so was the Flower who'd received the medical OK a couple of hours before game time. Lapointe sat on the bench and I played most of the game on right wing, taking Mario Tremblay's place. We wrapped up the season in Boston with a 4–2 win and sat back to wait for our playoff opposition. We were third overall and that meant we'd play the 14th-place team, or the third-last qualifier.

That turned out to be the Edmonton Oilers.

During the season, they'd whacked us good, 9–1 in Edmonton, but we'd been without many regulars that night. We knew we had to get to them early. They were a good young team, prone to making lots of mistakes in their own zone, but with Wayne Gretzky, Mark Messier, Jari Kurri, Paul Coffey, and Glenn Anderson, they could fill the net at the other end. Their goaltending was a question mark and we felt we could exploit that weakness.

Edmonton was a 14th-place team, but they'd finished only four points out of tenth and had lost only three of their last 26 games of the season. They were a 14th-place team in the first half of the season, not in the playoffs. They were young, they were hungry, and they were superbly coached.

And, thanks to Richard Sevigny, they were motivated. Sevigny, The Great Communicator, gleefully told reporters before the series opened that "Guy Lafleur would put Wayne Gretzky in his back pocket." He was wrong.

Guy disappeared in this series under a checking blanket named Dave Hunter. Everywhere Guy went, Hunter went.

Every time Guy turned around, Hunter was in his face. Meanwhile, Gretzky was tying us in knots at the other end of the rink, tying an NHL playoff assists record with five as the Oilers banged us 6–3 in the opener. I had a miserable night – I was on for five goals against – and I had a lot of company. Serge Savard was on for three goals against and every time he touched the puck, the Forum fans booed.

Behind the bench, Claude Ruel was having his lunch eaten by Glen Sather. He responded to Sather's checking blanket on Lafleur by going to three lines and leaving our top checking centre, Doug Jarvis, on the bench for the last two periods. We were the home team and had the line-change advantage but still Ruel couldn't find a way to get Lafleur free of Hunter.

In the second game, we did a better job on Gretzky, holding him to two assists, but this time we were stopped at the other end. Andy Moog, a rookie, stoned us in a 3–1 loss, allowing only a Gaston Gingras goal early in the second period. They scored two long ones on Sevigny and even though we had 41 shots on net, we were heading for Edmonton down 2–0 in a best-of-five series and praying for a miracle.

We lost 6–2. Our four-man defence of Savard, Robinson, Engblom, and Langway was worn out by now. Sevigny was again beaten early on some long shots (we found out after the game he'd broken a toe in the pre-game warmup) and we were headed for the golf course in early April for the first time in memory. The Big Three was going to be broken up, and other regulars from the late '70s were going to move as well. Last but not least, Claude Ruel wouldn't be back as coach.

Meanwhile, as unused as we were to finishing our hockey season this early, Guy Lafleur and I decided to join the Canadian team at the world hockey championships in Sweden. If we ever needed any indication that 1980–81 was the Year of the Snake Bite, we got it on Guy's first shift.

Alan Eagleson and other Team Canada officials had gone to the International Ice Hockey Federation directorate on the same Saturday night we were eliminated and asked that Team Canada be granted a 12-hour extension to the deadline for filing its final roster. They got permission to add three players – two skaters and a goaltender – and when the

Canadiens and Chicago were knocked out, the Flower, myself, and Tony Esposito were on our way to Stockholm. Team Canada wanted us to play against the Soviets in three days' time and we spent almost two sleepless nights flying from Edmonton to Stockholm, arriving four hours before a game against the Netherlands, a team primarily composed of Canadian expatriates who'd played junior.

Canadian coach Don Cherry greeted us at the rink and told us to turn around and go to our hotels to sleep.

"Rest up for the Soviets, get used to the change in time zones; we can take care of these guys with what we got."

"No way," we argued. "We came to play and the sooner we get on the ice, the better."

On Guy's first shift, he picked up a pass in the neutral zone and turned to move up ice. At that very moment, Don Cherry's version has it, a "no-talent goon" named Rick Van Gogh, a guy who'd played Junior B in Ontario, hit the Flower with a vicious elbow right in the face. Guy went down like he'd been pole-axed, a three-stitch cut in his nose. My version has it that it was a good check and Van Gogh got the Flower with his shoulder.

If that wasn't enough, a childish prank played by yours truly almost turned very ugly. Don Cherry described the scene in his bestseller *Grapes*:

Despite the adversity, I was proud of our guys, especially Lafleur. He was giving it his best shot and so was Larry Robinson, except that Larry fell victim to one of his own little pranks and we were all the worse for it. In a giddy moment after practice, he decided to play Martian. He gathered a bunch of extra-long Q-Tips and inserted them in his ears and ran around shouting, "Look, I'm a Martian!" It got a few good laughs until he tried to remove the Q-Tips from his ears. Apparently, Robinson forgot they were extra-long and when he reached for one of them, he accidently drove the thing into his ear, right into the ear drum. Blood spurted out of his ear and the doctor had to be called.

Robinson was given pain-killers and sent back to his hotel room to recuperate. Unfortunately, he couldn't recuperate fast enough for us. He missed three games but worse than that, the

poor guy was suffering excruciating pain. (He told me that during the first night he had never been in such agony in his life.)
"If I had a gun," he told me, "I would have shot myself."

Don got all the facts right, except the part about shooting myself over the pain. It was more like doing it for the stupidity of sticking Q-Tips in my ears. Anyway, when I got back to the team dressingroom a few days later, they were all lined up on both sides of the room, standing at attention . . . with Q-Tips in their ears. None of the extra-long variety, though.

We lost to the Soviets 8–2 the first time we played them, but then came back to tie them 4–4 in the medal round game, and considered the tournament to be a modest success. It was more of a success for Guy and myself; we were two weeks removed from the Canadiens' post-mortems in a city of "Quincys." It seemed that everybody wanted to play coroner and examine the cadaver.

While we were in Europe, Claude Ruel resigned and I greeted the news with relief. On the one hand, we'd probably have Claude back in his best function, intermediary, the guy who worked between the head coach and the players. Claude could get back close to the players, something that he couldn't do as head coach, and he could work hard with the kids. On the other hand, we could go out and hire a coach with more talent behind the bench, a better game strategist.

During that summer, the boos still ringing in his ears, Serge Savard retired. Serge is fond of saying that I took his retirement worse than he did, and he's partially right. I know that I was even more upset about the boos that showered down on him in the Edmonton series than anything else visited on us that year. I adored the man; I'd played with him for seven years and felt he'd made me into the hockey player that I'd become. As a young defenceman at first, and later as a veteran defenceman who liked the offensive gambol (and gamble), I made so many mistakes and he was old Steady Eddie, right there to cover up at all times. I was the one who took off and got all the goals and praise . . . and he got little credit for making it all possible. I still can't believe that Serge Savard never won the

Norris as the league's best defenceman at least once; but at least he got the Masterton and Conn Smythe, two trophies earned under pressure.

It was getting near the end of the line for Guy Lapointe too. His two-year-old feud and injuries were working against him and Irving Grundman gave all indications that he'd entertain serious offers for Pointu. The Big Three had become the Big One-and-a-half, and counting.

That bothered me a lot, as well, because it appeared that the Canadiens' management was doing its best to belittle Lapointe. In his heyday, Guy was a great defenceman and not too far behind Bobby Orr. He rushed, he played the body, he blocked shots (and had two eye injuries to show for it); he was there in the heavy traffic and he had one of the best point shots in the game. Guy Lapointe simply did everything, and the people who compared him to Park and Orr did him a disservice; he was better than Park because he could do more.

I look at a teammate of the 1980s, one they say will win a Norris Trophy one of these years – Chris Chelios. If Chris can refine his game on all levels, become a headier hockey player who picks his spots on offence and defence, he'll be another Guy Lapointe. And that's the supreme compliment I can pay him.

The summer of '81 would be a difficult one. The year before, we'd been done in by injuries against Minnesota but everyone seemed to understand. Guy Lafleur and Pierre Larouche had 50-goal seasons and gave every indication that they would repeat the following season. We went out and drafted the number one junior in the world, supposedly, and he'd give us size and offenseive punch up front. Young talented centres like Keith Acton and Pierre Mondou were coming along while defencemen like Engblom and Langway rose to the fore.

Then along came 1980–81 and a lot of the promise went unfulfilled. Pierre Larouche, playing spottily in 61 games, scored 25 goals and 28 assists, far short of his 50–41 – 91 of the previous year. And injured some eight times. The Flower scored only 27 goals and 43 assists in 51 games.

In the playoffs, Guy had one assist in the three games against the Oilers, Larouche two passes in the first two games before he was benched in the final. Neither could look ahead to 1981–82 with the same kind of optimism of the year before. For the first time in both of their careers, there would be doubts. Yvon Lambert, steady as a rock on the left wing for years, was benched for poor play in the playoffs, and Steve Shutt had seen his production fall off too.

Last but not least, Doug Wickenheiser had played only 39 games, scoring seven goals and adding eight assists. Claude Ruel didn't like him, didn't think he was a quality NHL player, or a decent number one draft pick. Whether or not that was Claude's way of protesting the club's refusal to draft his choice, Denis Savard, no one knows. What we do know was that the young man who came to camp with such promise in September, 1980, returned home to Saskatchewan quite disillusioned the following April.

Meanwhile, down in Uniondale, the Islanders were finally fulfilling the promise of the late '70s and began putting together a dynasty of their own. They finally found their sniper, a "can't check his suitcase" Quebec league star named Mike Bossy. He put the Islanders over the hump by giving them the great natural scorer they'd always needed. There were others like Morrow, Gillies, Persson, Nystrom, Bourne, and Goring to back up Trottier, Potvin, and Smith, but Bossy was the one who made the difference. I think they came the closest to resembling the Canadiens team that won four straight; speed, defence, work ethic, and scoring ability – both teams were about even right across the board.

We played each other tough and clean through the late '70s and into the early '80s. We held the upper hand in our Cup years, they in theirs. We were similar in many respects and that mainly had to do with the fact that Al Arbour was coaching on one side and Scotty Bowman on the other, and both had been together for so long in St. Louis. Both stressed tough hockey but tough hockey isn't dirty hockey. It's going into the corners and coming out with the puck. It's catching a guy with his head down and nailing him. It's taking your shots and coming back later with your own.

The difference, in most part, was Bossy. The Natural. The guy they said couldn't check his shadow. All he could do was score 50 goals a year, every year. Who gives a darn if he never checked in his life? He was very underrated as a junior; Laval Nationals had nobody and Mike and goalie Bob Sauve took them to the league final.

I got to know him a lot better during the 1984 Canada Cup because I roomed with him the whole series. Just fooling around with the goaltenders in practice, Bossy would take his shots and they'd complain that their hands hurt when they caught the puck. He was one of the hardest and most accurate shooters I've ever seen.

The intimidating thing was that he could put a good move on you, so you were in a quandary. You knew that he could really fire the puck like some of the league's best shots, but less mobile skaters. And he had the speed that could beat you, especially because he had a great pair of hands and could get inside you. So what do you do? It wasn't a pleasant thing for an NHL defenceman to contemplate.

In my years in the NHL, I saw only one player with faster hands than Bossy and that was Steve Shutt. He had the quickest hands I've ever seen; he always seemed to be able to get his stick on the puck, no matter where it was.

So it was now the Age of the Islanders. The Canadiens Era had ended and we would start to rebuild. We were still highly competitive; arguably one of the top three teams in the league. But we were a different team. Pollock had left in 978; Bowman, MacNeil, Lemaire, Dryden, and Cournoyer had followed a year later. In 1981, Serge Savard joined the exodus and Pierre Larouche, Yvon Lambert, and Guy Lapointe were eyeing the Exit/Sortie sign over our dressingroom door with some anxiety.

Whatever happened in the coming months, the team that would call the Forum home that fall would be vastly different from the one that had proudly carried the Stanley Cup in May, 1979, just a short 24 months before.

TWELVE

The Darkness

THERE's a word in French that describes the next few seasons – 1981 through 1984 – for the Montreal Canadiens.

Noirceur.

Some of its meanings include blackness, darkness, gloom, and despondency. In our case it was "all of the above" – The Great Darkness – as we entered into the period of my career with the club where the fortunes of the Montreal Canadiens were at their lowest ebb.

I'll always remember the three seasons ('81–'82, '82–'83, and '83–'84) as those that went against the grain, mine and the team's. It was a time where long-time friends and teammates left the Canadiens and new players replaced them. It was a time of negativity.

Having read this much, I'm sure that you have realized that I am proud of being known as Mr. Positive. I have always taken a great deal of pride in everything I do and I work hard to maintain my own performance and standards. The same thing had always been true for the Montreal Canadiens. Under Frank Selke and Sam Pollock, a dynasty had been built before I was born and maintained throughout my lifetime; one which always demanded that each succeeding generation of players reach down and give more of themselves than even they thought they had to give.

Looking back now on 1981–82, I can see that we began

to go into decline as a leading force in the NHL. At least
that is the impression I still have five or six years after the
fact. I admit the mind can play tricks. A look at the record
book shows that the Montreal Canadiens finished the ensuing season, 1981–82, with 46 wins, 17 losses, and 17 ties
for 109 points, good for third overall in the league
(Islanders 118 and Oilers 111) and 1st in the Adams Division, 13 better than second-place Boston.

But I can't look back on that era in terms of success. Perhaps
the best way to describe it is having to go through some very
unpleasant years. I have been playing this game for the number
of years I have because it was fun for me. But I can't look back
on those days as being fun. It's nice to get away from the rink
once in a while.

For 80 regular-season games, we were still a team to be
contended with and we all thought the team was a valid contender for the Stanley Cup. There was, and could be, no
thought of decline.

However, the darkness would descend in the playoffs. The
main reason for the negativity in the Montreal point of view, of
course, stems from the fact that the regular calendar is seen as a
six-month-long preparation or exhibition season for the real
thing, the playoffs. No matter how well you do from October
to the end of March, you'd better still be playing and playing well in late May. The fans feel that way and so do management and the players. The banners that hang high at the
Forum are for Stanley Cup victories only; no division or
conference pennant will wave in the Forum rafters like they
might in other arenas.

So, despite the fact that only six other teams in NHL history
have ever had at least one season where they accumulated 109
points or better, as we did in 1981–82 (Boston, Rangers, Buffalo, Philadelphia, Islanders, Edmonton), when we lost to
Quebec that April, the season was filed under "Disasters,
Montreal Canadiens (1981–82)." In keeping with those sentiments, I also look back to that period with a sense of frustration
and lack of accomplishment.

The 1981–82 season began for us in late spring, with the

appointment of Bob Berry as head coach of the team on June 3. A hometown boy, hometown being the Town of Mount Royal, an exclusive suburb just off the northwestern slope of the large hill that dominates the Montreal skyline, Berry was returning to the Canadiens' organization as something the club had not had since Scotty Bowman had shuffled off to Buffalo. A disciplinarian.

"Discipline was one of my top priorities in hiring a coach," said Irving Grundman at the press conference. We all knew he was feeling the heat of the Edmonton sweep.

"It is something our club has benefited from in the past and something we have to get back to. He's lived through some old times and some new times . . . he's about the right age (37) . . . I know this man does a lot of preparation and is a student of the game."

I would certainly beg to differ with that assessment, but more on that later. The press conference was very upbeat in mood and had to be; the town and the hockey media were in surly moods. You could almost sense a desperation in Irving Grundman, a man who knew that upper managment at Molson was not happy with the latest turn of events.

Bob Berry had started in the talent-rich Montreal organization after an all-star career in Canadian university hockey with Montreal's Sir George Williams University. He wore number 23 for the Canadiens for two games in the 1968–69 season and, a year later, was moved to Los Angeles. He was more of a presence with the Kings, playing 539 games for them over eight seasons; scoring 159 goals, 191 assists in regular season and two goals, six assists in 26 playoff games. He was known as an honest, working left winger, the kind of a guy whose presence on a second or third line would strengthen most clubs.

When his playing days ended he moved on to coaching with a stint in the American Hockey League and was named head coach of the L.A. Kings at the beginning of the 1978–79 season. When he resigned in late May, 1981, to accept the Montreal offer, his record with the Kings was 107–94–39 for a winning percentage of .527, best-ever by a Los Angeles coach in the franchise's history. Berry was true to his word, his discipline-above-all style turned the Southern California Beach and Marina Club into a serious hockey contender for a couple of seasons. In 1980–81, the Kings finished with 43 wins and 13 ties for 99 points, only four points behind us in the Norris Division, and tied for fourth overall.

How tough a disciplinarian was he?

"In Los Angeles, I instituted a $500 fine for any King who showed up at the rink with a suntan," he said. That got a laugh at the press conference.

"Guess I won't need that here. I am going to have some rules, like curfews and I'm not going to change my coaching philosophy to suit any individual. We'll make sure everybody is on time for everything; that's not too much to ask from a professional athlete."

He was a hundred percent right, of course. Bernie Geoffrion trusted players to behave like adults and professionals and some took advantage of him. Claude Ruel tried to stay too close to some players and was burned for his efforts.

When I heard Berry's words, I could only nod and say "Amen." This sounds like a guy who knows what he's doing. Bob Gainey and myself had talked about this on many occasions and both had agreed that the club could use a stern hand on the reins.

But then Bob Berry blew it in the next breath . . . "I don't think it will be any more difficult coaching here than in Los Angeles. As a coach, you adjust your philosophy to your present situation but not to the point that you make basic changes in the way you do things."

Coaching in the NHL in Los Angeles and Montreal is, and isn't the same. It should be, in that both coaches are dealing with hockey players with much the same background, playing the same sport. It's difficult in Los Angeles because you don't get a lot of practice time and there's a different attitude toward the game. Also, the travelling schedule of the Kings means that constructive time which could be spent in practice is spent at an altitude of 35,000 feet, criss-crossing the continent. And travelling is hard on you, so you have to handle things differently on the West Coast.

Montreal doesn't have those problems, being located right in the middle of the East Coast travel network where most cities are an hour's flight away. But in Montreal, everyone expects a lot more of you as coach or player. Here hockey is a tradition. You have to look at it that way and it's mentally harder on a player.

I've mentioned this elsewhere in the book but it bears repeating. During the 1976 Canada Cup, mostly centred in Montreal, Denis Potvin found himself playing for the "home team" for a month and it wore him out. A little exasperated, he asked me how I could survive here for so long because there is no escape. "You can't to anywhere or do anything without someone knowing who you are and acknowledging you. It's relentless. You can't leave the game at the rink."

Say hello to the Montreal media. Anyone who equates NHL coaching in Los Angeles and one newspaper article a week – if the Kings were lucky enough to get that "splash" in a market that included the Rams, Dodgers, Angels, and Lakers – to the media fishbowl in Montreal and the reams of daily "copy" in the print and electronic media, had problems plugging into basic reality.

Hockey is very much a mental game in Montreal; we all need extra time to get away from the rink and the extra attention or we won't last the season. Bob Berry would find out the hard way.

The man in the lightweight summer suit who stood tanned ($500 fine?) and self-assured on the podium that day, and later posed confidently with Irving Grundman for the photographers, would soon be brought to heel by the realities of Montreal hockey, a world totally beyond the control of a simple head coach.

(Like they say in TV: Fade to black. Advance to an image of the same coach three years later, in a post-game interview. His head is down, his shoulders hunched, and he puffs nervously on cigarette after cigarette. He is the model of self-doubt and lack of confidence.)

The scene is one I can't forget: Bob Berry, chain-smoking between periods, looking like he'd been gutshot if we lost a game. It got so bad that he couldn't hide the negative effects and that got to some of the players.

Bob's problems stemmed from two basic facts. No matter what he felt about coaching in Montreal, he was intimidated by the fish bowl. Secondly, and worse for him because this led to problems with the team's performance, he was trying to coach a style of hockey that was outdated.

Bob Berry wanted us to play man-on-man, and the most charitable thing I can say is that it doesn't work in today's hockey. Teams that play man-on-man just don't go anywhere because there's just too much movement in the game. The "new" hockey, North American version, had been pioneered by Bobby Hull and an army of Swedes and other Scandinavians with Winnipeg of the World Hockey Association, and had been brought into the NHL along with the Jets and two other teams, Quebec and Edmonton, in the WHA-NHL expansion of 1979.

The game changed substantially, especially with young sensations like Wayne Gretzky and Marc Messier (and later the Stastnys) leading the way.

As a defenceman, I had less to complain about in that I could play my basic game without too much modification. But a lot of forwards were misdirected, trying to adapt to Berry's game. They pretty well tried to follow the man-on-man situations, even though it led to frustration and, eventually, poor results.

Our forwards would end up chasing the other guys all over the rink. Edmonton and Quebec would pull a lot of old basketball plays on us like pics and moving pics with a great deal of success. (This is where an attacking player without the puck or ball stops to one side of a defender, allowing the ball or puck carrier to cut around him to the outside while simultaneously shielding the defender from moving out against the attacker. Also known as a moving screen.)

The result for us would be trouble and panic. We still were winning a lot of games on talent; but more often than not when we came up against teams with a flow offence like Edmonton, we'd be standing around a lot while they crisscrossed or checked off on us. As a result, Edmonton ate our lunch. During the Berry era it was all we could do to stay close to the Oilers, let alone beat them. His system just doesn't work in this day and age and he proved it once again in Pittsburgh after he left the Canadiens.

That's why when Jacques Lemaire finally replaced Berry as head coach in February, 1984, he was so successful, so quickly. He got rid of the man-to-man and we did what everybody else did, zone defence.

Another major reason why Berry's system couldn't work had to do with our team make-up. We no longer had the blinding speed we had been noted for in the mid-70s. To play man-on-man you have to have a quick team; usually in basketball, the man-on-man teams have quick guards pressing up front and big guys back deep. We had the big defencemen, but as time went on we didn't have the quick forwards who could stick their faces in front of rushing defencemen and then get back in time to defend. People like Lafleur, Larouche, Napier, and Acton went elsewhere, to be replaced by the Walters, Smiths, and Wickenheisers.

Another sore point, and perhaps even the thing that bothered me the most about the years I played for Bob Berry was that practices never changed from the day he started to the day he left. We had the same practices, day-in, day-out. After the five-minute warm-up, we'd skate in one direction. Then we'd skate the other way. That would inevitably be followed by two-on-ones, one-on-ones, two-on-twos, and three-on-twos. It was always the same.

It got to the point where I just disliked going to the rink because it was so damn boring. About the only relief from the monotony came when Berry would break down the power play, getting us to work on specific elements of it. Strangely enough, we'd never do that for any other aspect of our game, individual, or team.

When did it all start to break down for him? It's hard to say. In practice and in the room, Bob yelled and screamed a lot but never really got his message across. His problem was that he'd get mad at somebody and go over to talk to him, but he could never look that person straight in the eye. He always looked down at the ice or away when he was talking to you. It gave the guys a sense of insecurity. His.

Nobody worked harder at being our coach. Bob looked at films for hours. He pored over scouting reports. He analysed. He did everything he could. Unfortunately, he was also experiencing marital problems at the time and that made things worse. He had nowhere to go to leave the game behind for a couple of hours, no place to get away from it all and it showed. Some mornings he'd come in looking like he'd just been dragged through a wringer-washer backwards. You could leave the building very late one night, and come in early with the birds in the morning; Bob Berry would be there when you left and when you returned. As time went by, he became more and more nervous and insecure and it reflected on the team.

In the end, that's basically how it was. All the players were wondering how long it could go on. Truth to be told, it seemed that Berry instinctively got off on the wrong foot with his very first act of authority, appointing Bob Gainey captain of the team after Serge Savard formally announced his retirement in August, 1981.

We ourselves couldn't have picked a better man to replace Serge as captain than Bob Gainey but we never were given the chance. The various possible candidates for the job would have included the Flower, Guy Lapointe, and myself but none of us was the type of leader who would wear the C with the distinction of Savard, Yvan Cournoyer, Henri Richard, and Jean Beliveau. All of these men has been elected by their peers, as Bob Gainey surely would have been. But that was taken away from us and there was resentment in the room. When the press conference was called to make the announcement, Bo wore a three-piece suit. The rest of his teammates wore jeans and polo shirts in a subtle protest.

The captain of the Montreal Canadiens always has been a

player's player. While he may be used for two-way message traffic between players and management, he was always seen as a player first, a management-messenger second. In 1980–81, the management-to-players part of the pipeline had sprung a major leak as Serge Savard stood up to Claude Ruel to defend teammates on more than one occasion. I've always wondered if Irving Grundman passed on this information to Berry with the strong suggestion (read order) that he appoint Gainey; just in case the players fooled everyone and elected someone like Guy Lafleur as captain. A free-wheeling and shoot-from-the-hip (or lip) veteran like the Flower could have done a lot of damage to a rookie coach's authority, especially if his comments had the C stamped all over them.

Two years earlier, when Serge Savard had been sidelined with a broken bone in his foot, Gainey wore the C with distinction for a large part of the regular season and into the playoffs. However, when he replaced Savard for three games during the 1980–81 season and tried to rally the troops, he ran into some flak. Several veterans resented his attempts of taking or imposing control. Whether or not Bob Berry knew about these things is a question I've always had.

Bo acknowledged the disagreement at the press conference:

"I did have a problem last year . . . things that I was trying to control weren't under my control. I think a lot of those problems have been alleviated. I think there are a lot more players with a common attitude this year. On a club like ours, you have a lot of different players with different interests. I think we have to be careful that we don't force a player into a mold that isn't him."

I can't say often enough that Bob Gainey turned out to be a magnificent leader and captain, a leader on the ice and off. But the players had the impression that someone in management just didn't trust us to have the good sense to elect him ourselves. Going into the 1981–82 season, there were a few noses out of joint.

My season, and those of Guy Lafleur and a couple of other Canadiens got off on the wrong foot with a loss to the Russians in the second Canada Cup. But we quickly rebounded and buoyed by Bob Berry's "hands on" direction, the Canadiens got off to a great start in regular season play. We were red hot.

After nine games, we had six wins and three ties. You might wonder why I'd pick the ninth game and not the tenth or fifteenth. Because in the ninth game we annihilated the Philadelphia Flyers 11–2, taking a 6–0 first-period lead and running away. Other scores in the first half of the season included 10–4 (Vancouver), 9–0 (Colorado), 7–0 (Boston), and 9–0 (Buffalo). Does that sound like a team in decline?

In the midst of the team's overall good fortune came some moe good news. Winnipeg GM John Ferguson, an old friend, had lured Serge Savard out of retirement and the Senator would join the Jets. Fergie had originally selected Serge in the October 5 waiver draft, gambling $2,500 that Serge might be talked into playing but nobody thought anything would come of it.

First and foremost, Serge was convinced he had taken the right decision to quit the game after 14 seasons with Montreal. Second, Savard had signed an agreement with Irving Grundman that said Serge would not play or work for any other NHL team during the 1982 season. In return, Serge would receive the full salary he would have been paid had he played the option year of this contract.

The Winnipeg GM started working on his old friend and fellow horse lover, stepping up the pressure when he received some bad news in his camp. Team captain and veteran defenceman Barry Long discovered a circulation problem in his hand during the pre-season and the word from the doctors came back quickly: Long would need delicate surgery and was gone for the entire campaign. Ferguson was stuck with a very green defensive corps and desperately needed a veteran who could do two things; 1) still contribute as a player, and 2) help settle down the Jets blueline Kiddie Korps – David Babych, Tim Watters, Moe Mantha, Don Spring, and friends. I was extremely happy for Serge.

Another old friend was not so fortunate. The Black Cloud which had followed Guy Lafleur refused to dissipate as his wretched luck continued. This time he suffered an eye injury in a rare loss, 4–2 to the Kings in Los Angeles, and that would keep him out of the lineup for a while. That injury helped contribute to a lousy atmosphere on what was a winning team.

There are some similarities with that period and the season just concluded, but one shining major difference. At this writing, I have just returned from a ten-day holiday in Jamaica; one which began a few days after our abrupt, and much deserved, elimination from the 1988 Stanley Cup chase by the Boston Bruins. The 1988 season, which was a good one and I'll write about it later, ended negatively for us in the playoffs. What should have been something positive, recovering from my leg injury, playing well, winning the division, and finishing second overall in the league, all went down the drain with a bad playoff experience.

The 1981–82 Canadiens had their share of bad experiences in the two previous playoffs, losing to Minnesota and Edmonton back-to-back. But we still were a successful and consistent team when you took in the whole picture, even though we were probably heading, unknowingly, for a decline at the end.

There was one essential difference between the two seasons.

What I can't shake is the overall unpleasant feeling, or bad attitude that reigned in the dressingroom at the time. This year, even though it ended negatively and we had occasions where players had their disagreements with the coach, we had fun when we were winning because we had a pretty good group of guys and we enjoyed being together.

Back then, however, even when we were winning, there was a lot of bitterness.

Guy Lafleur was frustrated over his seemingly endless string of injuries. Pierre Larouche was in and out of the lineup as Bob Berry tried to transform us into a more defensive-oriented team and to gain full control as a disciplinarian. Guy Lapointe, a solid contributor with the Canadiens throughout his career, had had a running feud with Claude Ruel the previous two years and that had spilled over into his relationship with upper management. He felt that no matter how he played – good, bad, or indifferent – they were looking to ship him out. And happy-go-lucky Steve Shutt, one of the guys in charge of lighting up the dressingroom, was having meetings with everybody – the coach, the general manager, his agent – because all of a sudden he was spending some game time in the press box.

While playing well as a group, we were a team heading for trouble. Just before Christmas, we pulled what we called the "New England quickie" – games on successive nights in Boston and Hartford with a 90-mile bus ride in between. Pierre was not used in the first game – his fifth straight in the press box – and let his feelings be known on the bus to Boston. It was loud and beery and would be all over the papers in Montreal the next day.

Larouche had scored 9 goals and added 12 assists in the 22 games of our first 33 that he had played. He could still be a solid contributor but Montreal had caught the dreaded "defence before anything" disease and a terrific natural scoring talent was suddenly being described as a "liability."

The "system" didn't suit Guy Lafleur, although he became a more complete hockey player because of it, and it certainly didn't suit Larouche. What management seemed to have forgotten was that both of these guys had scored 50 goals during the 1979–80 season, and we needed that offence. Several seasons later, Larouche would have some great seasons with the Rangers because they knew better than to put limitations on him.

Larouche was popular with his teammates and the fans, but when management puts its mind to it, it can change such perceptions. The result was a frustrated hockey player who carried those frustrations over into his game and made the situation even worse. They call that self-fulfilling prophecy – say if often enough and it will come to pass.

The bus rolled into Boston and our regular hotel, the Sheraton, and the bus ride tirade continued. In fact, Irving Grundman later said he had not heard the comments on the bus and that Larouche got into trouble for what was to happen at the hotel. Most professional sports teams have a hard and fast rule. Players cannot drink in the team's hotel bar; it's reserved for coaches and management. The reasoning is very simple: to avoid run-ins that may be sparked by higher spirits, no pun intended.

That night, Pierre not only went right to the hotel bar, he did everything but pee in all four corners to stake out his territory. When management discovered him and asked him to leave, Pierre loudly and defiantly refused. The GM and coach could pretend they "hadn't heard" his bus outburst. But this incident was in public and they couldn't ignore it; a week later Larouche was wearing the green and white of the Whalers. They didn't force a defensive game on him in Hartford and he scored 25 goals and 25 assists in the remaining 45 games of the season.

Irving Grundman was a little desperate to get rid of Larouche and this was known around the league so he got few takers when he made his first round of phone calls. Right up to the end, it was thought that Powerful Pierre would end up in the blue-and-white of the dreaded Nordiques. In the end, Grundman engineered the Whalers swap and got fair value – Hartford's first pick in the 1984 entry draft. The Canadiens already had their eyes on this tall beanpole named Mario Lemieux who would be eligible that draft year and just might develop into something. If only the Whalers could stay at the bottom of the overall standings until then.

Unfortunately, Hartford was four spots too good overall, and Lemieux (Pittsburgh), Kirk Muller (New Jersey), Ed Olczyk (Chicago), and Al Iafrate (Toronto) were gone before the Larouche trade was finalized in the person of Petr Svoboda. The same draft also turned up Shayne Corson, Stephane Richer, Patrick Roy, and Graeme Bonar but, by then, Irving Grundman was long gone.

A couple of months later, it was Pointu's turn. Like the "other Guy," Lapointe had suffered a series of injuries, of varying severity during the past three campaigns. Like the Flower, he had engaged in a running feud with Claude Ruel and had upset management. And like Bob Berry, he had gone through a long and emotional divorce. All of this grief showed in Guy's game sometimes; he was forcing and seemed determined to do it all so management would change its opinion of him. Like me, he was bothered greatly by the departure of Serge Savard and the treatment accorded him by the fans in the Edmonton series.

Through injury and benching, Guy missed ten games in the first half of the schedule. Midway through the season, we went into Uniondale for a game against the defending (two-time) Stanley Cup champion Islanders and Pointu had an unbelievable game as we beat them 5–4. During one penalty-killing shift in the third period when we were hanging on to a 5–3 lead, he stayed on the full two minutes, blocking shots by Denis Potvin and Mike Bossy – another way of taking his life in his hands – flattening Bossy with a check, and keeping the slot in front of Richard Sevigny clear of New York forwards. At the end of the period, with their goalie pulled for a sixth attacker, it was Lapointe who cleared the puck out of danger and down the ice to preserve the win.

There was no doubt in my mind that Guy Lapointe was still a major part of our defence. Then, in late February he suffered a separated shoulder in a game against the Rangers. Rod Langway was also out at the time with a knee injury and that enabled Berry to give lots of ice time to young guys like Gaston Gingras and Gilbert Delorme.

I have nothing against either player, both Gingras and Delorme contributed when they were with us; in fact, Gingras became a rarity, a player traded away from, and back to, the Canadiens. But neither of these players was half a Guy Lapointe. Gas had a tendency of trying to beat one guy too many on a break; losing the puck, and getting caught far up ice. And Delorme would skate miles to hit somebody and take himself out of the play, over and over and over again.

More important to the team, Pointu was a leader and was needed in the room, especially by players like Gingras and Delorme. He was going on 34 and still had a lot of hockey left in him but the decision seemed to have already been made. He wouldn't be returning to the lineup, even if his shoulder got better, so he began meeting with Grundman, urging a trade before the March 15 deadline.

If Canadiens management didn't recognize Lapointe's worth, other hockey executives did and interest was expressed by several teams, including the Philadelphia Flyers. As it turned out, he was traded to St. Louis and the room never seemed emptier.

Guy was the last "true hometown boy" left on the team. He was raised in Montreal's fabled East End and came from a long line of firemen and policemen; when his "off-ice" buddies congregated at the Forum, they always seemed to be in uniform. Guy came up through the Immaculee-Conception sports organization headquartered in Parc Lafontaine, where Maurice Richard played as an amateur, and only learned to speak English when he spent a year in Houston.

His bilingualism proved to be painful for another Canadiens draft pick, a guy named Brian Lavender who got his kicks from making fun of Guy's accent and struggle with a new language.

"One day in practice, I caught him with his head down and hit him a beauty," Guy laughed. "I knocked him clear over the boards. It was amazing how much my English improved with that one play . . . nobody made fun of it after that."

A wonderful friend was gone and, in the space of nine months, the Big Three had become the Big One. That is not to say the Canadiens' defence would fall apart; we still had Rod Langway and Brian Engblom, two potential all-stars, as well as the good young kids and we were solid up front. But now the guys who had arrived after our last Stanley Cup win were starting to outnumber those who wore championship rings.

What made it easier for the fans and media to accept all of this turmoil was the fact that we were still winning. But you got the impression that they were paying close attention and were looking for an excuse, any excuse, to let us know. Late in the season we played a Forum contest with the Vancouver Canucks and (King) Richard Brodeur stoned us, 4–2. (One of these two teams would go all the way to the Stanley Cup final that spring; it wasn't us.) We were all over the Canucks but Brodeur stopped almost everything and the crowd was on us something fierce. I got my share, even though I scored one of our goals, and the players were pretty upset after the game. It was only our second loss in 28 games. As Rodney Dangerfield would say: "Boy, what a tough crowd!"

There were other reasons for the loss; we played the game without Guy Lafleur (foot) and Doug Risebrough (knee), and Pierre Mondou and Rod Langway had just returned from their own knee problems and were not at a hundred per cent. A couple of days later, I came down with a groin injury and we headed into the playoffs with a lot of question marks. More importantly, it would be our first playoff against the Quebec Nordiques, the team that had become our archrivals in three short seasons.

Ever since the Nordiques had entered the league in the "WHA draft" of 1979, we had lived an uneasy existence.

In Quebec's first season, we were the defending Stanley Cup champions and the Nordiques were a WHA team trying to become an NHL team. We finished the season at the top of the Norris Division with 107 points; they at the bottom of the Adams Division (Buffalo, Boston, Minnesota, Toronto) with 61 points and out of the playoffs. Different divisions, few games between the two teams, a very new team versus an established one – all of these factors meant that there was little to no animosity between the two teams. Games between the two teams were almost festive affairs, especially for the crowds.

All of that changed in 1981–82. First, league realignment meant that Montreal and Quebec were now in the Adams Division, along with Boston, Buffalo, and Hartford.

Second, we had slid from our position as defending Stanley Cup champion and Quebec had risen from the lowest depths of the NHL to become a middling good team. The club had leapt forward with the acquisitions of Pete and Anton Stastny, two Czechosolovakian defectors, and Michel Goulet – a former teammate of Rod Langway, Gaston Gingras, Mark Napier, and Rick Vaive with the Birmingham "Baby Bulls" of the WHA – was coming into his own. As well, a rookie from the Sudbury Wolves of the OHA, Dale Hunter, had scored 19 goals and 44 assists in his first season with Quebec in 1980–81 – and added 226 penalty minutes – so the club was very respectable up front.

Third, the Nordiques had appointed Michel Bergeron as head coach at the start of the 1980–81 season. A former midget coach in the Montreal area, he had guided the Trois-Rivieres Draveurs of the Quebec Major Junior League to Memorial Cup finals in 1978 and 1979. A players' coach and one of the best men I've ever seen behind the bench during a game, Bergeron alone was worth a couple of players to his team.

Fourth, we now were going to play eight regular season games against Quebec and if that couldn't build up any animosity, nothing could.

By playoff time, the Battle of Quebec was in high gear. And although a lot of it could be attributed to the happenings on the ice, it seemed much of it happened off the ice, in the newspapers and on radio and television. The media jumped on everything, sometimes subtly and sometimes not. Much was made of the rising young "francophone" superstars in Quebec, especially Bergeron, General Manager Maurice Filion, and President Marcel Aubut.

And look who was running the Montreal Canadiens, the so-called Flying Frenchmen. Bob Berry and Irving Grundman. Couldn't hockey's most storied team anywhere find a francophone capable of coaching, or managing, or running the whole operation? That ethnic theme hung over the Quebec-Montreal games and was played up in the media.

We were the established team, the one with the history of accomplishments that could fill several volumes. Yet it seemed that we were always on the defensive when we played the Nordiques. I remember reading several years later that Marcel Aubut admitted to his team that he adopted the French-English strategy and felt bad about it. But he added, his club had to do something, or anything, to gain recognition and a following in a province that had been exclusive Montreal territory.

I never got caught up in the French-English thing, I never have. But I could see Mario Tremblay and guys like that who had grown up in French areas really getting upset over that kind of stuff. I grew up in a French-English area outside Ottawa and was comfortable with the two languages: I never thought of people as language first, person second.

The real detriment to the whole situation was the media circus that grew up around it. That's what the Battle of Quebec really came down to. It wasn't our team against their team; it was our media against their media. Their media would try to dig up as much dirt against us as they could to get things going, and vice versa. After that, the coaches would get going at each other, especially the Tiger. But that was just Bergeron trying to get our team to lose its concentration, and it worked in a lot of cases.

In today's language, Michel "Le Tigre" Bergeron was a shit disturber. And I say that with full respect.

To me, you can practise all you want and play all you want. Most coaches are able to properly prepare you before the game. But the ones who can win and lose games for you are those who are true generals behind the bench, who are able to "see" the game and make adjustments on the fly. Michel Bergeron is in this category; he was a tremendous bench man and you could see it when you played against him.

I wrote earlier in this chapter that Bob Berry's man-on-man system was a problem against "flow" teams like the Oilers and the Nordiques, but so was our overemphasis on defensive play. That continues to upset me to this day because we sacrifice offence for defence.

Ever since the Jarvis and Gainey "superchecker" days, followed up with the additions of Guy Carbonneau, Chris Nilan, Brian Skrudland, and Mike McPhee, no longer did the Montreal Canadiens go in and establish a game. In no game that we played, home and away, did we go out and say: "Okay, we're going to establish our game plan and let them check us." Instead, at all of our meetings, whatever we did was built around who Jarvis and Gainey, or Carbo and Gainey, were going to cover.

Building a team game plan from the goal on out can be effective if you're a new young team, if you don't have a lot of scorers, and if you're trying to build a system and gain respectability. For us though, it meant stifling some natural goal-scoring talents (Larouche and Lafleur among many) and forcing "natural" hockey players to adapt to a "safety first" style.

It didn't work badly against the Nordiques because Carbo was always playing against the Stastny line, and after the Stastny line, there wasn't much. Our other lines were pretty well balanced and we had the advantage. However, if the Stastny line was being played a lot, say 30 or more minutes a game, that meant that our checking line was on for the same time, and our scorers had sharply reduced ice time. The same thing happened in 1987–88: Jean Perron always wanted Claude Lemieux on Michel Goulet. The problem is that you can't have a game plan when that happens. You end up with one of your players following the changes at their bench and jumping over the boards each time he sees "his number" come up. If he's a right winger, it can screw up the assignments of all the other right wingers.

Some other forwards get so little ice time that they hardly break a sweat. As a result, the team can't establish momentum.

Going into that first best-of-five series against the Nordiques, the media had a field day in black and white because the contrasts were everywhere: Red vs Blue, French vs English, Grundman vs Aubut, Berry vs Bergeron, the Nordiques' "European" or "modern" style versus Montreal's "old-fashioned" Katie Bar the Door defence, and number one (Montreal 109 pts) vs number four (Quebec 82 pts). The latter was the least significant; the only real difference between Quebec and ourselves was that we had played very well in our own division, which was becoming known as the "Black and Blue Division", and their flow game had served them better against the rest of the league.

During the season, we played almost to a stalemate; they usually handled us with ease in Quebec, we repaid the compliment at the Forum.

Six years have passed but some of the images of that series are still sharp. One is me trying to get some sleep at our "northern hideaway" in the Laurentians where the team was closeted away from all outside distractions. The beds were too short, and I had to push a chair up against the foot of the bed for extra leg room.

Another is me relentlessly playing a video game into the wee, wee hours of the morning after Game Five and Dale Hunter's overtime goal at 22 seconds of the fourth period that sent us packing. The video game was a car crash spectacular, and every time one of the little cars was totalled, I was hoping I was in it.

In between those two pictures were five games of a schizophrenic hockey series that we should have won, but didn't. And nothing hurts more than knowing you have lost to an inferior team because it means you didn't do all you could do. When I say schizophrenic, I use up my entire dictionary of psychological terms and schizophrenic is exactly what this series turned out to be. Up and down, in and out, with no sense to it.

We breezed through the first game in Montreal, 5–1, their lone goal coming midway through the third when we were coasting 5–0. Carbo and Gainey handled the Stastnys, Mario Tremblay and Mark Napier got a pair of goals each, and it appeared the series would be a 3–0 blowout. What iced the game for us was the two we scored shorthanded while Pierre Mondou was serving a penalty. Mario set the tone with his first goal just 56 seconds into the game, and they couldn't even get a shot on our net until the ten minute mark. By then we had established our game and they couldn't do a thing about it.

It looked bad for the Nordiques. What could they possibly do in the face of such opposition, a strong defensive team that had shut them down and controlled the game at will? They couldn't win the series without a win in Montreal and it didn't seem that they could get that close. On top of that, Peter Stastny would miss the second game because of a bruised kidney suffered in the first game. It looked like a Montreal sweep.

So naturally we went out and lost 3–2 in a game where their goalie Dan Bouchard stoned us, and we stoned ourselves with our overconfidence. Experience should have taught us that Michel Bergeron was a genius at motivating his players. Deep down, we probably knew it. Still, we came up flat and headed to the Colisee now needing to win a game in their rink.

Game Three was a preview of the series finale and confirmation of the value of Dale Hunter. If we had any doubts about his ability and leadership before, we had none after the 2–1 loss at the Colisee. (It's amazing how quickly his own team could forget; after they traded Dale to Washington at the 1987 June Draft, they finished out of the Adams Division playoffs for the first time since 1981. It was no coincidence.)

Simply put, Dale Hunter is an asshole on skates. And I mean this with full respect.

Peter Stastny is definitely the Nordiques team leader and has been since he and brother Anton arrived in North America; I'll have more to say about him later. But he had sat out the second game of the series and was not in top condition for the third. The Nordiques turned to Hunter and he didn't disappoint them.

Dale Hunter is a guy that you love to hate. But you'd love to have him on your team because he is a real team player and willing to do it all to win game in, game out. He'll get you a clutch goal, he always wins a big faceoff, he kills penalties, plays on the powerplay. He is just an SOB, that's all. If he gets hurt in a game, you really don't care – and that is perhaps the best testimony of how good he is at getting under your skin, disrupting your game.

He would get under my skin on occasion and once got me so mad I was ready to go over the penalty box partition at the Forum to get at him. During a skirmish, one of those things with six or seven bodies all coming together at once, Hunter and I got to shoving and pushing and tugging and he got his stick up under my nose: "I'm gonna take your damned eye out!" he snarled.

I went nuts. Nobody had ever proposed surgery to me in such a way before. I swear if I would have gotten to him, I'd have killed him. When I got back to the bench, some of the guys were laughing. "Your face was redder than the goal light."

Beyond that incident, Hunter and I regarded each other with

a wary eye and a lot of respect. I can't exctly say he mellowed but when his brother Mark joined us it seemed that his game changed a tiny bit. Having Mark with the Canadiens was a big plus for us. Guy Lapointe, who now was a Quebec coach, told me that Dale really didn't like playing against Mark. He wasn't the same, and was a much better player against other teams because Mark wasn't there. The three Hunters were very, very close, but Dave was in the Smythe Division with the Oilers and almost out of sight, out of mind. With exhibition, regular season, and playoffs, Dale and Mark could play each other 15 times a year. That was a strain on Dale, the middle brother, more than kid brother Mark. It really got bad when Dale and Mark came together in a scramble for the puck and Big Brother put Little Brother out for the year with a serious knee injury. And we would later trade away Mark Hunter to St. Louis for a chance at drafting Jose Charbonneau ahead of the Nordiques. That is probably Serge Savard's worst deal since he became GM.

To get back on track, Dale Hunter stepped into the rather large hole left by a sub-par Peter Stastny and was the single-most important contributor for the Nordiques in their series win. He scored both Quebec goals in Game Three, a 2–1 win that had our backs pinned firmly to the wall. More importantly, he did all of the other things he excels at to keep us off our game. With veteran defencemen like Dale Hoganson, Pierre Aubry, and Mario Marois playing like they were possessed, and Bouchard stopping nearly everything we had, Quebec was one game away from putting us out of the playoffs.

That one game wasn't Game Four though. We silenced the Nordiques half of the Colisee with a 6–2 victory that resembled the cakewalk of Game One. We were all over the ice, stifling their game and taking a comfortable lead. They couldn't handle us and when the teams returned to Montreal for Game Five, the players on both sides knew that everything favoured us. So what were we doing tied with Quebec 2–2 as the siren went to end regulation time?

In the room before the overtime, we agreed that we couldn't play too defensively or conservatively because the game had come down to the first break wins. Home ice went out the window. There were no more psyche jobs; just two tired and emotionally drained teams going down to the wire knowing that only one of them could win.

So, of course, in the best Montreal tradition, we started our defensive specialists: Gainey, Jarvis, and Hunter up front; Langway and Engblom on defence. This was the first time as a Montreal Canadien defenceman that I hadn't started an overtime period in the playoffs. As it turned out, I never got on the ice.

Instead of laying back and waiting for them to come to us, we pushed into their zone right away. One of their defencemen took the puck from behind the net and threw it up the boards where Brian Engblom pinched in to keep the puck in the zone. Both Brian and Doug Jarvis were kicking the puck along the boards when Michel Goulet got his skate on it and it jumped out to Dale Hunter. He and Real Cloutier took off on a 2-on-1 against Rod Langway. Rod played it perfectly, and when Hunter tried to pass it across to Cloutier at the last second, Langway deflected it away.

But two bad things happened. Langway and Cloutier took themselves out of the play, and the puck bounced right back to Hunter. His momentum had carried him too deep to do anything with the puck so he circled behind the net and tried to stuff it in the short side as Rick Wamsley came across. Rick was there on time to freeze the puck and I thought "no sweat" as I got up to jump over the boards for the inevitable line change.

I couldn't believe my eyes when the red light came on. And then the referee was pointing into the net and The Longest Summer had begun. And so had the downward slide, because the Blue had defeated the Red and that was the worst thing that could happen to the Canadiens now that the Nordiques were in the NHL.

They went on to beat the Bruins in the division final before losing to the Islanders but Dale Hunter's dribbler had forged a subtle change. They now were seen as the team with the future in Quebec; we were the team on the down slope. And nothing could panic our head office more than that kind of belief. They proved it by going off and having the worst draft year in a decade for the Canadiens.

Were the Canadiens and the Forum seen as too English? Let's draft some Quebec juniors to show we're plugged into the province. Picking 19th and 31st overall, Irving Grundman and Ron Caron selected Alain Heroux of Chicoutimi and Jocelyn Gauvreau of Granby as their first two picks. Neither ever played a game for the parent club. Later in that draft came a number of U.S. collegians who would play some with us, but spent most of their early careers stocking Sherbrooke in the American Hockey League: Kent Carlson, Dave Maley, Scott Sandelin, Scott Harlow, Ernie Vargas, and Michael Dark. (As this is being written, Caron has reunited Carlson, Harlow, Vargas, and Dark in the St. Louis organization.)

While it wouldn't be fair to categorize that draft as a total disaster for Montreal alone, the 1982 crop was probably the worst in the decade, the Canadiens still could have done a better job. Between Heroux (19) and Gauvreau (31) were Pat Flatley (21), Yves Courteau (23), Gary Leeman (24), and Peter Ihnacak (25). After Maley (33) came Paul Gillis (34), Tomas Sandstrom (35), and Richard Kromm (37).

The supreme irony, of course, was that the "French" Nordiques went to the Ontario Hockey League for their first two selections, defenceman David Shaw of the Kitchener Rangers and centre Paul Gillis of Niagara Falls, and both made it to the big team, although Shaw since has been traded.

The point is simple: in a straight role revreasal, the Nordiques now were acting, and the Canadiens, reacting. Not a position of strength. Although the players certainly felt we were the much better team on the ice, and most hockey observers outside the province would agree, Canadiens management had developed a nervous tic and always seemed to be looking over its shoulder. With reason; hardly a day went by that summer without speculation in the media about a new management team – one story had Scotty Bowman returning as GM, another had the club reaching into the collegiate ranks for a new coach.

The players did not escape lightly either. Everywhere we

went we heard two things – "who's getting traded?" and "how on earth could you lose to the Nordiques?"

Eventually, even the Longest Summer drew to a close and training camp beckoned. As I prepared to return to the Forum, I instinctively knew that it would be a deadly serious affair. All of us would be glad to return and be given a chance to make up for the loss to Quebec. But there were lots and lots of question marks. Doug Wickenheiser had never really worked out, no thanks to management and the coaching staff. Would he finally be traded? We had also lost our offensive spark. The Flower had just come off two consecutive 27-goal seasons, after six straight 50-plus years. Steve Shutt was in the 30s now, not in the high 40s or 50s, and although Mark Napier had scored 40 in 1981–82, he was very publicly unhappy with his contract. We needed to beef up our front line, especially to play in the black-and-blue Adams Division. But where would we find muscle, talented muscle?

Both Napier and Rod Langway were unhappy with the Canadian dollar and Quebec taxes, the highest anywhere in North America at the time. They were making noises about playing in the United States where the dollar was worth 100 cents and the taxman had the good sense not to kill their golden goose. It was pretty much a foregone conclusion that Rod was going to force Grundman and Caron into a trade; but what kind of trade?

Even after a summer of speculation, I was stunned at the magnitude of the transaction that Irving Grundman announced September 10, 1982. Gone to the Washington Capitals were Doug Jarvis, Craig Laughlin, Rod Langway, and Brian Engblom. We were getting Ryan Walter and Rick Green. Also gone was Doug Risebrough, to Calgary for an exchange of second-rounds picks in 1983 and the Flames' third-round choice in 1984. Irving explained to the press that Langway was going to go under any circumstances, which led them to believe that it was Langway for Green straight up. If that was the case, then we gave Washington three players, and a second team all-star in Brian Engblom, for Ryan Walter. And that was too much.

Brian and Rod had been a pair the year before and probably the most effective defence duo in the league. Doug Jarvis was still the best defensive centre in the league, and one of the best faceoff men anywhere, while Laughlin was a no-nonsense winger who could check and score the odd goal. Also gone was Risebrough, an inspirational third and fourth-line centre and a veteran who could help.

What struck a nerve was the fact that it seemed to me they had totally overrated three players, all defencemen: Gaston Gingras, Gilbert Delorme, and Robert Picard. Gingras was the best offensive player of the trio but prone to spectacular lapses in judgment. And I've already discussed Picard's and Delorme's penchant for taking themselves out of the play to deliver thumping bodychecks. None of the three was as good as Langway or Engblom. I had played with Ryan Walter and Rick Green at the world championships in Sweden the year before and knew they were quality players. But I knew the team had been weakened, and not strengthened, especially in the short term.

At the time, it was a lousy deal. It made us a lot worse before we got better; especially after it was announced a week later that Denis Herron was off to Pittsburgh for his second stint with the Penguins. Six players were gone in the space of a week, eight in a year if you include Larouche and Lapointe. The signs weren't good.

Somebody at Molson Breweries was paying attention. Barely a month into the season, Ronald Corey was appointed President of the Montreal Canadiens. It was the beginning of the end of the Irving Grundman era at the Forum. And it was the beginning of almost two years of frustration for yours truly.

The most obvious result of the trade was behind the blue line and it showed in the year-end statistics for the 1982–83 season. We went from 109 points, third overall and first in the Adams to 98 points, fifth overall and second in our own division. In 1981–82 we had allowed 223 goals against, winning the Jennings Trophy – which had just replaced the Vezina as the team goaltending award – by a comfortable margin of 27 goals over the runner-up Islanders.

In 1982–83, with Langway, Engblom, Jarvis, and Herron all playing in the Patrick Division, we allowed 286 goals against, a whopping increase of 63 goals or almost one a game.

We were seventh in goals allowed and Irving Grundman and Ron Caron were still trying to say the trade had short-term advantages. Had we been able to trade one of either Picard, Gingras, or Delorme instead of Engblom – the latter two because I don't think Washington wanted Picard back – it would have made more sense for us.

Grundman knew that trade had to come-up roses for Montreal before the year was out once Corey was appointed. It didn't. As I mentioned earlier, we finished second in the Adams and met Buffalo in the first round of the playoffs. They waxed us three straight, including back-to-back shutouts by Bob Sauve at the Forum

The seeds of our discontent had been sown during the regular season. All of a sudden, we were "leaderless." That accusation came up from an unlikely source, Bob Berry, after a particularly disappointing loss to the Nordiques in Quebec. After the Nordiques scored a pair of third-period goals to win 3–1, he told the press: "I was disappointed in Guy Lafleur, but he wasn't the only one. Larry Robinson is another. We have 20 leaders in the room and none on the ice."

Good old Bob. I doubt he could even look the media guys in the eye when he made that statement. I was steamed, especially since our lack of success was a team effort and it started behind the bench.

Berry had gone on to tell the reporters: "We had 19 giveaways in the first period alone. How are you supposed to win games playing that way? . . . I'll tell you what we have: we've got lots of questions. Every system we use, we've got questions – but nobody gives me any answers." The next day was punctuated by a tough 90-minute workout (when the coach runs out of imagination, make the players sweat) and a meeting between Berry and Grundman. News Flash, stop the presses: Grundman endorses coach!

His comments were just what I needed. A year before, with Serge Savard gone and other veterans not contributing like they had during our four-straight Cup run, I began to hear my first boos at the Forum. After Berry's remarks, I heard some more. Six years and more booing after the fact, I can say I took it in stride and that it didn't really bother me. And I can sell you some land in Florida real cheap if you believe that whopper.

After one incident, a Forum game with the Maple Leafs that we tied 4–4, I was asked by a reporter if it was getting to me.

"I can't say I don't hear the fans," I told him. "I'd be deaf if I didn't hear them. But I try not to let it bother me, because I was here when they were doing the same thing to Serge Savard. If they can do it to Serge . . . as great a player as Serge was . . . I consider it an honour. If that's what it is, then great! They can boo me all they want."

In other words, it hurt like hell.

A couple of weeks later, we played the Rangers at the Forum and we fell behind 2–1 in the second period, mainly because Glen Hanlon was stoning us. About seven minutes into the third, Reijo Ruotsalainen came down my side into our zone and I lined him up on the boards. The Finn is quick and I didn't get all of him as he threw out a pass that Vaclav Nedomansky tipped into the net. 3–1.

With about five minutes remaining in the game, we were on the powerplay when the Rangers tried to clear the puck out of the zone. I stepped in front of the clearing shot, stopped it, and drilled one right through Hanlon's legs. The fans cheered wildly and my frustration boiled over. It wasn't quite as blatant as the "Eagle's one-finger salute" but I gave the Forum the stick and chugged to the bench where I sat down and refused to talk with the world. When the game's three stars were announced, I was number three. And I was in the dressingroom, refusing to come out for the customary acknowledgment. Who needed it?

I showered and dressed in a blur and gritting my teeth, steamed out of the dressingroom, telling the media that I'd talk the next day, and went home. I didn't trust myself to speak that night because Canadiens fans and management weren't going to like what I had to say. It was one of my smarter moves in a long career.

It isn't easy to feel unloved and unappreciated after years at the top. And it's the hardest lesson to learn when it has been all yours almost for the asking. Guy Lafleur, Serge Savard, Guy Lapointe and many others learned that lesson in Montreal before me. Others would follow me.

Strangely enough, from that point on, things quieted down for me and the Forum crowd and I enjoyed a solid second half of the season. That self-satisfaction came crashing to earth in early April when Buffalo blew us out.

Within days of the playoff disaster, Irving Grundman, Ron Caron, and Bob Berry were gone.

It was time to rebuild, said Ronald Corey. And who better to do the job than some Montreal veterans?

THIRTEEN

On The Way Back

I F RONALD Corey had learned anything in the business world before joining us, it was that an organization like the Montreal Canadiens must always be true to its history and its origins.

One of his first actions as President of the club, even before dealing directly with the current team and its management, was to bring back the team's history – in the flesh. He had a special room built for retired players and their families and welcomed them back to the site of many of their, and Montreal's, former glories. It was a very smart and popular move; a gathering of Dollard St. Laurent, Doug Harvey, Jean-Guy Talbot, and the Richards at the Forum on game night brought history back to life and added to the Montreal mystique, for the fans and the players. I always wondered why such clever hockey men as Frank Selke and Sam Pollock had never thought of it.

Corey's move was brilliant in its timeliness. The Nordiques may have defeated us a year before and may have rocked the Canadiens organization at the management level. But our bedrock was their glaring weakness: we had a history and they didn't. We could use that history against them.

Many factors, some hockey-related, others not, were at play that spring as Corey set about rebuilding the team's front office. First and foremost, it was fairly obvious that Molson Breweries was calling the shots. Beer wars had finally caught up with hockey and Molson was very determined not to lose any Quebec market share to Carling O'Keefe because of the improved image of the Nordiques. Marcel Aubut's strategy of making the Nordiques Quebec's French team had worked to some extent; it was now obvious that the Montreal Canadiens were going to have to respond to his challenge because a lot of Quebecois had bought his bill of goods.

There was no shortage of talent out there if the Canadiens' president chose that route – French-Canadian players had played prominent roles in the NHL from its earliest days and beyond. But, truth be told, they had for the most part been shut out of the league's front offices by an Old Boys Network that was mostly English-Canadian and centred in Ontario.

Two names that always came to mind when I speculated on former teammates who had the right stuff to move on into coaching or managing were those of Serge Savard and Jacques Lemaire. Both had played the game with distinction and were Hall of Fame bound. And both had impressed me with their grasp of the science and art of hockey during the many years we shared together.

That previous spring, Jacques Lemaire had coached the Longueuil Chevaliers, a brand new franchise, to the Quebec Major Junior League final against Pat Lafontaine and the Verdun Junior Canadiens. With Berry out, a strong lobby had arisen to get Coco appointed coach of the Canadiens. Since he had retired as a player, he had coached two years in France, served as an assistant coach at Plattsburgh State University in New York, and coached in Quebec junior.

There was quite a lot of speculation about the top job, as well, but few people thought of Serge Savard at first. After all, he was still under contract as a player to the Winnipeg Jets. Imagine my surprise then, when my former roommate was appointed Managing Director of the Montreal Canadiens.

Serge was coming to Montreal and it was a good thing for several reasons. First, he knew what it had been like for other generations of players, joining the club as he did in the late 1960s and then leaving under the circumstances he did.

Serge had matured in much the same way I had, watching the Canadiens' lifestyle change. I remember his comments on the subject: "When I was growing up, playing for the Canadiens was everything. When I started in the system, nothing else mattered. Maurice Richard, Henri Richard, Emile Bouchard, Jean Beliveau, and Toe Blake, that was what it was all about. I started at the same time as Carol Vadnais and after we'd both been here for a year, Sam Pollock decided that one of us would go and that ended up being Carol. He played great for Oakland, and later the Rangers and Bruins, but I always remembered him saying he'd walk all the way to Montreal from Oakland just to play for the Canadiens again.

"Back then it was a great thing. But then it began to change.

"In my last few seasons at Montreal, there were problems at all levels. In Sam Pollock's day, those problems had a way of being quickly handled before they got bigger. No more. Coaches were coming and going. Players were talking and complaining to the press. The situation seemed to be getting worse every season as my career wound down.

"The draft and a bigger league were partly to blame. When I started, a rookie played hard and kept his mouth shut, otherwise he'd find himself in Houston or some other farm team. The money got big after you were established. Now with the 21 teams and big signing bonuses, it was hard to keep the same values. If a kid wasn't working out and you told him so, the next day you'd read in the newspaper that his agent wanted him traded somewhere where his talent would be appreciated.

"And in a way, the kids were right. Playing in Winnipeg showed me that there is life after the Montreal Canadiens. It's still the NHL. You still play the game, you still get paid. There might not be quite the same prestige of wearing the red, white, and blue, but that was a minor consideration for many young players."

So Serge was coming in with his eyes open. And for the first time in two or three years the players seemed happy with a management decision. There was no second-guessing in the media.

His first task was to appoint a coach and he had conversations with his former teammate Lemaire. "I don't feel ready to be head coach right now," Coco told him. "I'd be happy to serve my time as an assistant." What a lot of people didn't know was that Lemaire had been offered the Hartford Whalers job late in the previous season but he had turned that down too.

When all was said and done, Bob Berry returned as head coach with Jacques Laperriere and Jacques Lemaire as his assistants. The mood was upbeat, the Canadiens were on a roll. Canada's most popular NHL team (according to a poll the previous winter) was back on the rails.

Go figure.

The result of all that new positive feeling at the Forum turned out to be Montreal's worst regular season in 40 years; a Murphy's Law of seasons; whatever could go wrong, did. And often.

It began with the NHL entry draft. Selecting 17th in the first round, the Canadiens chose Alfie Turcotte, a solid little centre built like Marcel Dionne and a former teammate of first overall pick Pat Lafontaine with the CompuWare midgets of Detroit. Lafontaine had gone to the Quebec junior league while Alfie went west to Portland. They both met in the Memorial Cup tournament that spring and Alfie showed a lot of promise in leading the Winterhawks to the championship. The Central Scouting Bureau had rated him 11th and the Canadiens' scouts 9th. Why was he still around when Montreal picked?

We found that out when rookie camp opened ten days before the regular training camp. Alfie was as wide as he was tall after a summer of pizza and milkshakes. He would never really make it with the Canadiens, even though he showed flashes of talent.

When Serge became Managing Director, he had received the good wishes of many of his new colleagues. But that was about all they would give him. He was on the phones right away trying to swing some trades before the draft, hoping to improve his position. But it was in vain. Nobody was interested in waking up the Canadiens. After years, decades, at the top, the Forum was beginning to learn how the other half lived. Serge would finally make his big trade in late October.

Turcotte was just one disappointment heading into Savard's first season as head hockey man in Montreal. Many more were coming.

Another reversal that was hard to swallow was a wrist injury suffered by Rick Green. It shelved him for 73 games of the regular season and we missed him a lot. I have already expressed my feelings on the Big Trade from the point of view of the players we gave up, and the Professional Hockey Writers Association expressed theirs after the 1982–83 season, awarding Rod Langway the Norris Trophy as the league's top defenceman. I felt then as I do now, we gave up too much.

However, with regard to the players we received, both Ryan Walter and Rick Green quickly became major contributors to our team. Green especially was solid as a defensive defenceman and a major reason why we would win the Stanley Cup two years down the road. At the beginning, however, we wondered if he ever would play for us. Greenie was out of our line-up for nearly the entire 83–84 season; when we skated out for games, journeymen like Jean Hamel and Bill Root took a regular turn at the blue line every night.

We were halfway though our exhibition season when the other shoe dropped. Ric Nattress, a second-year defenceman who had contributed in the previous season, was suspended 40 games by league president John Ziegler as the result of a conviction for smoking marijuana as a junior in Brantford. That was later commuted to 30 games but the damage was done to us, and especially to Nattress's confidence. He never seemed the same when he finally returned.

If that didn't shake up Serge, then came news that Chris Chelios, a valued defensive prospect who currently was playing with the U.S. Olympic team, had been charged with purse snatching while playing at a tournament in Anchorage, Alaska of all places. Chelios was scheduled to join us after the February Olympic Games in Sarajevo, Yugoslavia.

Those charges were almost immediately dropped but the incident contributed to an unsettled feeling that seemed to spread right throughout the lineup. You had the impression that Serge Savard was waking up every morning, turning to his wife and saying: "All right, give me today's bad news."

During one intra-squad game, there were brawls all over the ice. Doug Wickenheiser vs John Newberry in a battle of centres; defenceman Bill Kitchen vs centre John Lavers; Chris Nilan and Jeff Brubaker, in three separate scraps; and Robert Picard vs a rookie named Blair Barnes. Bob Berry had been watching the session from the stands but it got so bad he had to come out onto the ice to put an end to it.

We weren't three games into the season when veterans like Wickenheiser, Napier, and Picard found themselves on the bench. Barely two weeks later, Serge swung his first big trade; Napier was gone to Minnesota along with Keith Acton for Bobby Smith. Two of the three players involved, Smith and Napier, were happy with the trade. The third, Woody Acton, wasn't.

A scooter and a disturber in the mould of Ken Linseman, Acton was a solid team man and popular with his teammates. He had been unfairly fingered by a disgruntled Guy Lafleur a year earlier as one of the reasons why the Flower's production had fallen off. All I can say was that Woody gave a hundred per cent every time we played and you can't ask for more. It took Woody a long time to get over the shock and disappointment and I'm glad he finally was traded to Edmonton where there's a competitve atmosphere much like ours.

In Smith, we were finally getting the big centre we had wanted since the Wickenheiser draft four years before. At 6'4" and 210 pounds, Bobby was expected to improve our offence and especially our powerplay which had been sputtering for a season or so. He helped right away with 15 goals and 7 assists in his first 20 games.

But if Serge Savard and Bob Berry were looking for a quick fix, they wouldn't get it.

Smith did contribute, as did a splendid sophomore Mats Naslund, and some rookies were showing their stuff, among them Craig Ludwig on defence and John Chabot and Greg

Paslawski up front. But injuries to players like Steve Shutt, Mark Hunter, Tremblay, and Mondou kept our offence off-balance all season, especially since Naslund, Mondou, and Tremblay had played so well together.

Outmanned on defence, and with Lafleur and Shutt way down in production and often outmanned up front, we struggled. Bob Berry tried to cure the disease by yelling and screaming and that didn't work. By now the team had tuned him out. His anxiety was starting to show.

"Never in my seven years of coaching have I seen a team as tough to movtivate," he complained to the media, something he had rarely done in previous seasons.

"I can't understand how we can play so lousy. I don't know why I have to beg some of those blankety-blanks to play when they're making that kind of salary."

In early December we had won only two of nine games and even the team president was being hounded in the newspapers. That's how the Montreal media work – controlled hysteria. We knew we were playing poorly; yet we all seemed to be working as hard on the ice as we had before. But the results weren't there. Then four days before Christmas came Serge's second big trade as GM of the Canadiens: Doug Wickenheiser, Gilbert Delorme and Greg Paslawski to St. Louis for Perry Turnbull, a bruising forward who would give us even more weight up front. It was, as one Montreal columnist wrote, the end of the Wickenheiser Era.

Unfortunately for Doug, as nice a guy as you'll find anywhere, his name came to symbolize a four-year period of frustration for Montreal. It was unfair for all of our ills to be dumped on him and I was glad he'd finally go somewhere where they wouldn't dump on him all the time because the club drafted him and not Denis Savard. His failure to become the dominating big centre that Montreal needed led to dismissal of Grundman and Caron, the Turcotte draft and, later, to the Smith trade. But blaming all of this on one player would be stupid.

Doug Wickenheiser was all of 22 when his purgatory on ice in Montreal came to an end.

The acquisition of Turnbull was what has since become
known as an Adams Division trade. He was the type of player
who should do well in the small rinks in Buffalo and Boston.
He was tough, a decent skater and had a good shot; all of which
explained three straight 30-plus goal seasons with the Blues.
When the trade was made, he had scored 14 goals for St. Louis
and only Bobby Smith, with 19, had scored more for our team.
Wickenheiser, who had scored 25 goals the season before, had
5 goals and 5 assists.

But Murphy's Law was still at work.

When Turnbull joined the team, it was soon obvious that he
wouldn't fit in to our style of play. From that point on in the season, Wickenheiser outscored Turnbull (7–21) 28 to (6–7) 13.
Even Greg Paslawski (8–6 – 14) outpointed Turnbull the rest
of the way. The Blues would go on to eliminate the Red Wings
in the first round of the playoffs and take Minnesota to overtime in Game Seven of the Norris Division final, a modest
success for a team that hadn't even attended the NHL entry
draft the year before. By playoff time, Turnbull was sitting out
as many games as he was playing.

For us, it was just a matter of time before the inevitable
happened.

In late February, we were still lurching along on a one-win,
one-loss rhythm when Serge Savard called the media together
on a Friday night conference call. "I have released Bob Berry
as coach of the Canadiens. Jacques Lemaire is the new head
coach. Any questions?"

We were 28–30–5 after 63 games. The last time the
Canadiens had suffered 30 losses was 1950–51 when the club
finished third behind Detroit and Toronto with a 25–30–15 record in a 70-game season. (That club went on to the Stanley
Cup final nevertheless.) In 75 years of NHL play, the club had
suffered through exactly two 30-loss seasons, the other being
1939–40's dismal 10–33–5 showing.

Enter Jacques Lemaire. Although we would end the year
with a 35–40–5 record, the sub-.500 team that arrived in post-
season would little resemble that which had lurched along in

semi-futility during the year. The names were the same; only the players had changed.

First, our five-man defensive rotation would immediately improve 40 per cent with the additions of Rick Green, finally back from injury, and Chris Chelios, joining us after the Olympic Games. Over the year, newcomers like Mike McPhee and John Chabot had proven their worth while the players acquired in trades, notably Bobby Smith and Ryan Walter, were fitting into the system. And young veterans like Mats Naslund, Mario Tremblay, and Pierre Mondou were doing a great job filling in for Steve Shutt and Guy Lafleur who both were struggling.

Late in the year, we called up Quebec City native Steve Penney after Rick Wamsley was hurt and Richard Sevigny struggled. Penney lost the four games he played and had an average of 4.75 per game. But he played well, making a lot of big stops. However, nobody in their right mind could predict that he would have a 2.20 average with three shutouts in 15 playoff games.

We still felt better than in previous seasons. Jacques Lemaire was head coach and we felt we had joined the modern age in hockey It might even be possible to reverse the trend of previous years: great season, abysmal playoff.

There were 17 games remaining in the season when Lemaire took over as head coach. He went to work right away in changing our system. We didn't have any scoring punch, we knew that, and the only way we were going to beat clubs was to play his 1-2-2 system. Instead of a futile man-to-man chase all over the ice, his first innovation had us playing zone defence all over the ice, like a basketball press. The trick was to block off the middle and clog the lanes, forcing everything out to the perimeter. Teams like Edmonton and Quebec would discover that we could play with them now. We forced the other teams to the outside and made the ice smaller. What we lost in speed, we made up in size and weight.

Jacques was an excellent psychologist when he started. He got input from the players, asking them for their ideas and communicating more openly than any of his three predecessors. I still say he was able to communicate more easily with us and get his message across because he had been a player.

It was like night and day in the room and at practice. Suddenly we were working on a variety of game elements. Jacques had learned his job well in the four years he'd been away and proved to be a fine teacher. He was the best coach I'd had since Scotty Bowman and might even have eclipsed Scotty had he stayed longer than he did. I even kidded him by saying he was an awful lot like Scotty, even in his mannerisms. He handled the team behind the bench in much the same way as Scotty. He was a very, very smart hockey man.

His arrival meant a major change for the remaining veterans of the Stanley Cup era in that this would be the first time a former teammate had coached us.

I was interviewed shortly after the coaching change. I was asked: "Is it very difficult for a veteran player who played with someone for so many years to find himself being coached by him?"

"Yes. I find it hard; mainly because Jacques and I practically lived together for four or five years. We had cottages up on the lake (Lac Labelle) and hung around together. Even today, his wife Michelle and Jeannette get along very, very well together."

What's the hardest thing about the transition from fellow teammate to coach? Just like in the working world, a co-worker is promoted and suddenly must deal with you from a position of authority. It's a big change in your normal relationship. All of a sudden, the new boss, your close friend, is giving orders and expecting them to be carried out. And hoping that you'll co-operate and help him out while all of you get used to the change.

In hockey, the former-player-become-new-coach suddenly has to be a bit of a prick. Like putting on curfews and that kind of stuff to assert his authority. Overall, I think Jacques handled it well. While he was open to suggestions from us, he took control of the team; Coco wanted to be and was the boss. What he said was Gospel. It was difficult for me because we had been close and his new duties meant he had to establish some distance between us. We couldn't be that close anymore. I probably found it much harder than he did because I like to joke around a lot with Jacques, that's the way we had been as players, and he had to keep a separation. He knew only too well that Claude Ruel had floundered not once, but twice, because he wanted to stay closer to the players and his friends than a coach should.

It proved that Jacques Lemaire had learned his trade well in his four previous coaching jobs. It also didn't take long for him to establish the player-coach separation between the two of us.

Our first real difference of opinion, and an incident that really had me steaming occurred on a trip into Toronto. We got in the night before and during our check-in at the hotel I asked around: "Is there a meeting or anything on tomorrow morning?"

"Nothing."

I was rooming with Ryan Walter, a notorious good guy. Ryan is a born-again Christian and one of the most sincere people you ever might want to meet. Strictly a by-the-book man, in all senses of the phrase.

He and I got up the next morning, took our time showering and were in the coffee shop having a leisurely breakfast when Jacques Laperriere stopped by: "Hey you guys, you're late for the meeting."

"What meeting?"

"We've got coffee and doughnuts and video all set up in a room." When we got there, Lemaire fined us for missing the meeting. The club took the money off my paycheque and I was just livid. I steamed about that for two weeks because he tried to say it was our mistake and even Lappy admitted it wasn't our fault. I can kid about it now but I was furious at the time.

I was so mad that I didn't trust myself to talk to Jacques about it. Even today, I wonder if it was just his way of getting to the younger players; target Robinson and Walter because Larry and Ryan won't defy you – you can trust them to let it blow over in the long run – and show the kids that if they screw up, it won't go easy on them. There were other veterans and former teammates on the team like Mario Tremblay, Bob Gainey, Guy Lafleur, and Steve Shutt and I guess Jacques figured implicating them wouldn't have the same impact. In the Flower's case, it might have started a war. (That would come anyway.)

In that way, Lemaire was a lot like Scotty Bowman. Single out one or two wrongdoers and punish then publicly for something trivial, something that could be forgiven but something that would still get the message across. And when the players did something silly or semi-defiant, punish them privately and quietly, without making a big fuss.

That happened a year later in Vancouver. We had lost against the Canucks and had a three-day layoff before our next game against L.A. so Jacques put a curfew on after the game. Everybody was cursing him; Mario and I pointedly stayed over at The Keg across the street from the Westin Bayshore until about two or three in the morning and got joyfully hammered. The next day, Jacques quietly suggested that we do an extra 30 laps during practice. When we left the hotel for a post-game sandwich, he had probably guessed our intentions and confirmed his suspicions with a late-night call to our rooms.

But that is a situation all coaches face; it wasn't particularly unpleasant or unusual. His actions proved that by then, he had established himself as a coach, and was no longer just a former teammate. We all recognized that and respected him for it.

The real source of my personal frustration was a standard hockey complaint – Lemaire played me less than Berry or Ruel. He wanted more icetime for his young guys so I had less. Chelios had just arrived and Craig Ludwig had shown he deserved to play too. I was mad about it because I wanted to play more – which is normal. I would have a similar run-in three years later with a coach I respected a whole lot less; but that's a different story.

In April, 1984, with Jacques Lemaire in charge, the Canadiens were ready to go places.

The 1984–85 season proved to be the season where the Battle of Quebec hit its peak, or scraped the bottom of the barrel, depending on your point of view. During the season, you couldn't pick up a Montreal newspaper, English or French, where the comparisons weren't being made between the surging Nordiques and their "brilliant" team of marketers led by president Marcel Aubut, and the "struggling, once-proud" Canadiens, "desperately seeking to counter the Quebec success."

It seemed that everywhere you turned, the media were reporting the results of yet another opinion poll on the subject. O'Keefe beer sales were on the rise, Molson was dropping. The Nordiques were gaining new fans. The Canadiens were stagnating. Still, we were at least twice as popular as Quebec, so the real uphill climb was theirs, not ours.

We wound down the season much like we started it, win one, lose one, but there was a huge difference in attitude. Our last game was at the Boston Garden on a Saturday afternoon. The Bruins were still mathematically in the fight for the first place although it appeared that the Sabres had it locked up. All indications pointed to Buffalo-Montreal and Boston-Quebec matchups. Buffalo had handled us easily during the season while we had played .500 against the Bruins.

When we went into the Gardens, we were out to prove ourselves and were not in the mood for any Boston guff. That point was made abundantly clear when Ryan Walter got involved in three fights, two of them with Terry O'Reilly. We lost it 2–1 but it wasn't a game between a first or second and a fourth place team. The teams were equals on that afternoon. That Boston win, and another on Sunday night combined with a Sabres loss, propelled the Bruins into first place.

That was great news for us. We felt we could beat the Bruins.

Boston had blown its wad in a late-season push for a first place. After playing 35 and 40 minutes a game for a month, guys like Barry Pederson, Rick Middleton, and Ray Bourque were exhausted and Terry O'Reilly, the club's captain and inspiration, was hurting from a chronic bad shoulder injury that he had aggravated during one of his scraps with Ryan Walter on Saturday.

Jacques Lemaire's game plan was simplicity itself: "Get in front of Ray Bourque wherever he is on the rink. Make him skate around you or through you but make him skate. And every chance you get, dump the puck in on his side in their zone and get all over him."

It worked like a charm. With Steve Penney making the saves he had to in our end, and players like Mike McPhee, Mario Tremblay, Bob Gainey, and Chris Nilan all over Bourque in his own zone, we swept the Bruins 2–1 and 3–1 in Boston, and then 5–0 back at the Forum. Meanwhile Quebec was doing the same thing to the Sabres, a three-game white-wash, and we were finally going to get our chance to avenge the 1981–82 playoff loss to the Nordiques.

In the last chapter, I spoke about the value of a Dale Hunter to a team like the Nordiques, especially when a Peter Stastny was injured or playing sub-par. My point was that Hunter never got the credit he should for being the heart of his team.

If Dale was the heart, then Peter Stastny was the team's soul. He rarely had a sub-par game for them and in my mind is prob-ably the best overall player to come out of Europe in the 1980s. And that includes great talents like Jari Kurri, Mats Naslund, Kent Nilsson, and a host of others.

Quebec's number 26 is simply a great hockey player. He's tough, he takes and gives out the hits. He's a good faceoff man and he never throws the puck away; he controls it. And he's a leader. I remember in the 1984 Canada Cup, he gave a speech in the dressingroom before we were to play the Russians. All I can say is that if we had played the game right after that speech, we would have had guys going through the walls to beat Team Soviet. Peter came across as a real leader.

It is one thing to have a lot of respect for a player, because you will respect individual players for various reasons. In Peter's case, that respect meant we had to gear everything we did as a team to a defensive plan built around him and Michel Goulet.

Goulet needs a great centre playing with him, perhaps even a bit more than a Mike Bossy needs a Bryan Trottier. During his career in Quebec he's been called a floater, lackadaisical, or unmotivated because he has the Frank Mahovlich style of playing the game without a fuss and then, bang, popping in two or three just when you thought you had him under control. He can skate and has a terrific shot, but he does come across as a bit of a moody player. Come to think of it, most goal scorers are moody players. Look at Stephane Richer, Pierre Larouche, Guy Lafleur; are you going to tell me these guys aren't moody?

Attitude is all-important in hockey, as it is in most sports. You have to want to play and have fun playing every night if you're going to perform. And that gets to be difficult for a goal scorer, because he's expected to pop in a couple on almost every other shift. That's a tremendous amount of pressure for a Richer in Montreal and for a Goulet playing in Quebec City.

Our strategy usually was to try and add to that pressure by staying right on him. We had our problems with this because he hung back a lot, coming in as a trailer behind Peter and Anton Stastny. With his burst of speed and shot, the smallest opening led to a goal.

Another contributor for the Nordiques was Peter's younger brother Anton, a solid winger. The major difference between the brothers is that you could hit Peter all night long and never disturb him; he has the physical and mental toughness to take a pounding. But Anton could be disturbed by the heavy traffic and easily distracted. I don't think he has the same strong character Peter has, but he certainly has the moves.

I distracted him a lot in the first period of Game Three. He came toward our blue line on the left wing and was half-turned to take a pass a little behind him when I came across laterally to check him. I had my ass up high and both feet planted and he turned around just in time to catch the full force of the hit. He went down like a ton of bricks and stayed on the ice for five minutes. I got him with everything, my hips, back, elbows. It was one of those checks that is so technically perfect that when you hit the guy, you don't feel a thing.

Full credit to Anton; he was back for the second period.

With Bergeron behind the bench and the Stastnys, Goulet, and Hunter up front, the Nordiques were definitely on the rise and a formidable opponent. But we knew we could beat them because their defence wasn't strong. And this time the pressure was on them; they were the favourites and that can make a huge difference.

That didn't mean they couldn't or wouldn't get up for us.

One player who always played his best against us was Pat Price. He was one of Bergeron's favourites and thrived in Quebec for several seasons. He would never try to do too much and was very effective inside their zone. Another defenceman who was solid was a rookie, Randy Moller, a member of the World Champion Canadian junior team in 1982. In spite of his youth, he was very steady, never forcing too much, and very strong in front of their net. And Dan Bouchard was his usual hot-cold self.

The pre-series hype was spectacular and despite his best intentions, and his shyness with the press, Jacques Lemaire was sucked into the Michel Bergeron Media Circus. Jacques had never talked to the media when he played, and probably hated talking to them even more when he coached but he had no choice now. Michel got his goat with his usual fiery statements and Jacques ended up in a headline war. As the series advanced, the press and coaches fought harder than the players but that couldn't last. We were the pawns and our turn would come.

Game Six of the series was scheduled for Friday, April 20. It was Good Friday, probably the holiest day on the Roman Catholic calendar and Quebec province still had a lot of practising Catholics. What happened at the Forum that night was far removed from the peace and brotherhood that religious holiday stood for.

We went into the game leading an up-and-down series 3–2. Quebec had won the first game, and then we had won the next two and held a 2–0 lead in Game Four at home before Quebec roared back and won in overtime. They returned to the Colisee full of renewed hope and we shut them out 4–0. It was now our series to win.

So, of course, we played like we didn't want to win it. Peter Stastny's first-period goal had given them a 1–0 lead and Bouchard had turned back 18 shots when all hell broke loose late in the second period. The instigator was Louis Sleigher, a journeyman who would develop a fatal habit of arousing the Canadiens at the wrong time in important playoff games.

A scrum developed behind our net after the puck had been frozen; with players like Sleigher, Mario Tremblay, and Jean Hamel jostling each other after the whistle. Dale Hunter lay on top of Guy Carbonneau for a few extra seconds and that got it going. Fights are rare in 1–0 playoff games for a simple reason; coaches spend their entire time behind the bench and between periods reminding players that a stupid penalty can kill you. But Hunter is Hunter and Sleigher, apparently, had never gotten the message either.

In the ensuing bench-clearing brawl, Chris Nilan hammered Randy Moller, cutting him badly; Mario Tremblay broke Peter Stastny's nose with a series of rights, and even spare goalies Richard Sevigny and Clint Malarchuck threw punches.

Just when it appeared that tempers had cooled and the teams would return to their rooms, Sleigher sucker-punched Jean Hamel, breaking his nose. Hamel went crashing to the ice, injuring his shoulder, and was out for the playoffs. That lit the fuse, and gloves, sticks, and fists went flying in all directions. Mark Hunter, Tremblay, Nilan, and a host of others tore after Sleigher and a second round of fights broke out all over the ice. Referee Bruce Hood could do nothing more than take notes.

The next problem developed from poor communication between the referee and the minor officials charged with tabulating the penalties.

Even though the intermission was extra long, the teams were not advised that Nilan, Tremblay, Sleigher, and Peter Stastny had been assessed game misconducts. All four returned to the ice as the third period was about to resume. The minor officials who knew about the penalties didn't know that those four had not been told.

Sleigher was a red flag to us and Mark Hunter immediately went after him. Mark was sidetracked and ended up in the same pile-up as his brother Dale, but Mike McPhee caught up with Sleigher and started roughing him up while Richard

(The Terrible) Sevigny charged Dale Hunter and Brawl II was under way.

When the smoke had finally cleared, Mark Hunter and Sevigny joined Nilan and Tremblay on the sidelines while Peter Stastny, Dale Hunter, Moller, and Sleigher were among the Quebec missing.

That changed the game around totally and even though Michel Goulet scored his first goal of our series three minutes into the final period to give them a 2–0 lead, we blew five straight by Bouchard in ten minutes and won 5–3. Life was worth living again and the worst season in recent memory was already fading in the public consciousness.

We went on to lose to the Islanders, and they to the Oilers, but that was probably the best summer since our Stanley Cup victory in 1979. We ended the playoffs on an upbeat and with Serge Savard and Jacques Lemaire at the helm, things were looking up for 1985–86.

The new season was a good one, we finished atop the Adams Division standing ahead of Quebec, but what stands out several years later is something that took place late in the second month: Guy Lafleur's last hockey game as a Montreal Canadien.

We started the season off with confidence, determined never to repeat the debacle of the previous year. Lemaire was in full control and the benefits were there for all to see.

Jacques Lemaire's game preparation is meticulous. He studies video or game film as well or better than anybody, maybe even better than Scotty. He can break down what a team does; and then devise a way to counter it using our resources; such as the 1-2-2 zone that served us so well during the previous playoffs. Jacques sees a lot more than the rest of us when he watches a hockey game. (I got first-hand evidence of that during the 1987–88 season when I had the opportunity, through injury, to sit in the stands with him during games in Detroit and Vancouver.)

If any negativity lingered from the previous year it centred on the Flower. As the playoffs went on and Lafleur's performance dwindled, he was played less and less by Lemaire. Both talked and agreed that Guy's icetime would increase with the quality of his performance and that's how the new season began.

Although both had played on the same line for three straight Cups, they were never close. They never really hung around much together away from the rink. Jacques was a friendly man but pretty much a loner. I also think that being from the Old School, he didn't approve of some of Lafleur's behaviour during the glory years when he played and he certainly didn't like that act later as a coach.

At the time, Lafleur was the biggest thing in sports in Quebec, a place where they adore their sports heroes. When you're famous, everybody comes around. Guy got caught up in the fast lane and that didn't help. But nobody ever really said anything to him either.

By the time Lemaire became coach, the Flower had struggled for several seasons. The last half-season he played was painful. With every game he played without scoring, it got worse for him, the team, fans, management. Everybody wanted to see him do well, to score.

It was like a cancer; and it wasn't because he wasn't trying. He was playing hard, skating hard. That last year he played he was skating better than the previous year. I think the real problem was that Guy got to the point where he was trying to think out what had previously come naturally.

Steve Shutt said the same thing last year. He and the Flower went back together on a touring Purolator NHL oldtimers team, travelling all over the place and Shutty said Guy was firing the puck like he always did. The first three times they got together, Guy was like he was when he quit; trying to squeeze the sap out of his stick. Once he stopped thinking about the game and the pressure he became the same old Flower we all had known, just flying all over the ice, and scoring goals off the crossbar, the posts. Steve thought Lafleur could still be playing in the NHL he was so far ahead of the other oldtimers.

What I wouldn't give to see him back in uniform, even at 37, and as this edition goes to press Guy is training for a comeback with the Rangers. I think he'll make it.

Jacques and Guy were on a collision course that fall. In October, Steve Shutt was traded to the team of his choice, the Los Angeles Kings and it was a sad group of old friends who gathered at the Mise au Jeu to say good-bye. But we were happy for Shutty because he had chosen the Kings and Serge went out of his way to accommodate him. The parting a month later with Lafleur was less friendly.

I don't think we'll ever know exactly how or why Guy quit and exactly what was said. I'd love to know the true story. Everybody has their own opinion and maybe only four people know what it was really all about. What it came down to was that Guy said he could no longer play with the diminished ice time he was getting from Lemaire and that he was getting out of hockey. He would retire to a front office job.

The two of us had been drafted on the same day and it was the end of an era that touched me personally when Guy announced he was quitting. We had been involved through thick and thin for many years, including during our celebrated contract dispute. To this day, it's a big mystery to me why he never stuck around. I would have liked for us to have the same length career. There is absolutely no doubt in my mind that he could still contribute as a player; it was just a question of getting his confidence back.

I never really got a chance to talk to him about it. When he retired it was like a big wall went up between us. I got the impression that he no longer wanted to be closely associated with the players. The following summer when he had his blow-up and said he didn't want to hang around the club like a celebrated clerk for $75,000 a year, he made a clean break. That statement will hang over his head for a long time.

Several other changes took place just prior to or during the 1984–85 season. First, the Perry Turnbull experiment was called off and he was sent to Winnipeg for veteran winger Lucien DeBlois. Second, we drafted our first Czech, an 18-year-old beanpole named Petr Svoboda who would spend most of the next season playing alongside yours truly, sort of like a second son. Third, Jean Perron, a former university coach and assistant to Dave King with the Canadian Olympic Team joined us as an assistant to Jacques Lemaire.

And fourth, I became a living legend. (Easy for you to say, Robinson . . .) The year 1985 was doubly important in the history of the Canadiens as the team's 75th and the Forum's 60th anniversary. The club decided to run a contest with several newspapers and radio stations so fans could vote on the all-time Canadiens team. Named to the team after all the votes were tabulated were Jacques Plant in goal, Jean Beliveau at centre, Dickie Moore at left wing, Maurice Richard at right wing, and on defence the immortal Doug Harvey and the very mortal yours truly! Larry Robinson, living legend. I had a hard time believing it − all of the other players selected came from the glory years of the 1950s, which is what you'd expect from such a competition.

On January 13, 1985, at a special banquet at the Queen Elizabeth Hotel, I was presented with a special oil painting of myself and I told the 1,800 hockey fans, who included Mayor Jean Drapeau and Prime Minister Brian Mulroney: "This is a great honour for me. I've been involved in a lot of Stanley Cups and I've been nervous before a lot of games. But my knees are shaking right now. (I wasn't kidding. Talking to a hockey banquet in Eastern Ontario is not quite the same thing as addressing the Mayor, the Prime Minister and 75 years worth of Montreal Canadiens.)

"I'm a little farmboy, or a big farmboy depending on who you're talking to, so I'm not really accustomed to making very long speeches.

"I'd like to thank everybody very much. And I'd like to make a special tribute to the one person who has meant a lot to me and that's my wife Jeannette." (At that point, the memory of the pork chop dinners at the Vaillants' in Kitchener was very clear to me. And there wasn't a dry eye in the house. I had 'em where I wanted 'em.)

"And now to get serious. (The place cracked up.)

"I'd like to thank all of the players that I've played with over the years. This is a team sport and indeed without all the great players I've played with and alongside, I wouldn't be here today.

"I would like to especially thank Guy Lafleur and Serge Savard who have meant a lot to me over my career." (And no, I was not bucking for a raise, honest.)

My knees still shaking, I sat down. The look I got from Jeannette was priceless.

As I mentioned before, we finished first in our division and took out the Bruins in five games in the playoffs. The Nordiques also advanced and we met again in the playoffs.

This time it went to seven games and overtime at the Forum. Steve Penney was not the same goalie he had been a year earlier, although he did turn in some good performances for us in post-season. This time it was Quebec's turn; Peter Stastny scoring at 2:22 of overtime to eliminate us.

But this time it was different. It seemed that both clubs and the media had learned their lesson after the Good Friday Horror Show the year before. While the Quebec-Montreal rivalry was still there, we both appeared to respect the other a lot more and the media stayed on a more even keel. Quebec won it, but fans on both sides seemed to accept the fact that a victory in OT in Game Seven was the closest of margins, and that the rivalry would get healthier as time went on. We still had our fights and took the extra shots, but that was because this was the Adams Division, not just the Battle of Quebec.

Ever since then our rivalry has been on more of an even keel.

It wasn't easy taking to the golf course after losing to the Nordiques, but it also wasn't anything as traumatic as the Summer of '82. Maybe we were all growing up. "We'll get 'em next year," we said to ourselves as we stowed away our gear for the summer, the eternal cry of the playoff loser. And we meant it.

Little did we know that a big change would take place during the off-season. To the surprise of all, Jacques Lemaire decided in July that he could no longer function as head coach of the Canadiens. His intense shyness and aversion to the media made him very uncomfortable. He never liked dealing with them; even when he was playing.

"Serge, I'm sorry but I just can't get used to that part of this job," he told Savard.

"I would like to stay involved with the hockey side, but get somebody else to lead the hockey team."

Serge reluctantly agreed, and Jean Perron became our fifth coach in the six years since the departure of Scotty Bowman.

Life is never dull at Atwater and St. Catherine.

FOURTEEN

Stanley Revisited

JULY 27, 1985 was a gorgeous Montreal summer day; the kind where one might find me on a golf course, in a pool, or on a horse, chasing after a hard ball with a polo mallet in my hand.

On this day, however, you would have found me in Serge Savard's office at the Forum. Earlier that morning, the phone had rung: "Larry, it's Serge. Can you come down and see me? Something's up."

"Sure, I'll be in as soon as I can get there."

"As soon" meant about 90 minutes. When I got to Serge's office, Bob Gainey was already there.

Serge began talking. He was as serious as I've ever seen him and that's saying a lot. Although he enjoyed a good laugh as well as the next guy, Serge always had a more mature aspect about him. They didn't call him the Senator for nothing.

"We wanted you to be the first to know that Jacques will be no longer with us.

"He feels he has done all he can do and would rather move behind the scenes. I know this is sudden and a surprise because he never indicated this to anyone before, but I'd like you two veterans to help out during the transition."

As Serge spoke, I wondered what he meant. What transition? Jacques Laperriere was a heck of a guy and good with the defencemen; well liked and popular. But now that he had decided to move on to something else, there didn't need to be any major change. After all Coco was still in charge . . .

"In his place we're announcing that Jean Perron will be appointed. He'll be the Canadiens next head coach."

You could have knocked me down with a feather. It was Jacques Lemaire who was quitting. Jacques Laperriere was staying.

"Are you serious?" I said, unable to really believe that our best coach since Scotty Bowman was leaving the club after not much more than a season. Jacques Lemaire had quickly proven himself and had the respect of all the players. The man coming in to replace him couldn't make the same claim.

One of the themes of this book is the coach-player relationship and how I lived it. The most salient fact is that it is almost impossible to put your finger on the precise reasons why some coaches win over their players and others don't. The chemistry of such a relationship is hard to figure; you can't melt down the components and then recombine them into the perfect coach. It defies description. How do you explain such varied people as Ted Sator, Jacques Demers, Michel Bergeron, Jacques Lemaire, and Glen Sather: all different styles, all winners?

All have had the players on their side. Call it respect, trust, loyalty, common commitment, fear . . . whatever they used, it worked.

Perhaps the best way to describe the Jean Perron era with Montreal Canadiens is to say that he was a coach that I never really could get a handle on. It was probably less his fault and more mine, but here was a man who was my coach for three years and I never felt I knew him. It was not for lack of communication, we spoke on several occasions, most of them friendly; but something just didn't click.

The best thing is to start at the beginning – Jean Perron's appointment. While I heard every word that Serge Savard was saying to us that morning, I truthfully could not understand the appointment of Perron. In my mind, he didn't have the credentials, even though I've argued this point with several people. Here was a man who had basically come out of nowhere, having coached a university team.

Jean had joined us the year before as an assistant, after wrapping up a term as assistant to Dave King on the Canadian

Olympic team and after taking the Moncton Blue Eagles to the Canadian university championship final three times. If you sat and recited those facts to me in the Canadiens dressingroom, it would prove that you knew more about Jean Perron than I did.

The significance of coaching in the Canadian university ranks escaped me. Very few hockey players ever came out of Canadian university hockey and into the NHL. On the other hand, several NHL coaches had been in the CIAU as it's called, among them Tom Watt and Mike Keenan.

If you get the impression that I'm biased, that's fine. I feel I can explain my point very clearly. Although I might acknowledge that men like Dave Chambers (who coached the Canadian junior team to the 1987–88 world championship) and Dave King (the perennial Olympic team coach) have made their livings as coaches, and rightfully so, I still will point out the huge gap between coaching in amateur and professional.

I happen to believe that there is a world of difference between amateur and pro, and there is also a wariness on both sides, a mistrust. Pros look down on amateurs, even though some are paid big salaries. The amateurs like to think that the pros have corrupted the game because their only consideration is money.

To my way of thinking, the difference between coaching in the amateur ranks or professionally is this: It's never easy to coach but it's a lot easier going to the rink knowing that there's just a championship at hand, so to speak. When you're a professional coach, the pressure to win is such that your livelihood almost can be on the line with each passing game.

The CIAU or NCAA pressure-cooker is a tiny teapot compared with the stress of 80 to 100 games a year in the big leagues. While you might argue that Dave King or Jean Perron have faced pressure to perform in international or school hockey, and have been professional coaches since they graduated from university, there wasn't such a premium paid for winning, if you know what I mean. They were paid as teachers, not as much for delivering victories.

The argument comes back that a university coach who can't win will eventually be fired, just like the pro coach. I guess that's true, but all you have to be is competitive. Be in the running. If you win, naturally it's better. That's the difference between amateurs and pros. And that's why if you come in with four or five Stanley Cups as a coach, I think that is a hell of a lot more significant. And you have to be a lot more than just competitive in the pros unless you work for Harold Ballard.

But it is nothing like the NHL. We have 21 teams and 10 of them let their coaches go sometime during or immediately after the 1987–88 season. They were: Mike Murphy, Los Angeles; Doug Carpenter, New Jersey; Jack Evans, Hartford; Andre Savard, Quebec; Bob Murdoch, Chicago; Mike Keenan, Philadelphia; Pierre Creamer, Pittsburgh; Jean Perron, Montreal; Jacques Martin, St. Louis; and Herb Brooks, Minnesota. That is a turnover rate of almost 50 percent. Did ten hockey coaches in all of the CIAU lose their jobs last year?

That's what I mean about pressure.

Perhaps the most underrated coach in the NHL is the best, Glen Sather. All he has done has won the Stanley Cup four of the last five years. He doesn't have a college background; instead he was a journeyman NHLer. But all the best "scientific" coaches on both sides of the Atlantic have tried to beat him without success.

Is there a lack of respect by professionals like myself for non-professionals? I think there is to some degree and I'll admit the obvious: everybody was a non-professional at one time. I think hockey coaching has to be learned or experienced in stages, just like playing. There's a difference between a midget and a junior, and a junior and a semi-pro, and a semi-pro and a pro. As a player who progressed through all of these stages, I saw others reach their top level and drop off. The same happened with coaches, too.

At each level, the skills improve a little bit. The speed of the game, however, increases a lot. And that's the same speed a coach has to coach at. The opposing argument is that coaches only have to be mentally quicker and it's easier for them to adjust than for players.

I'm not sure that's true.

I am willing to admit that college-trained coaches may have the advantage today. The game is a lot different now. It's more like basketball and now it involves a lot of play-calling, diagramming, reading, and studying. These are areas where college coaches traditionally have been strong.

And Jean Perron was strong in this part of the game. He was always studying the opposition, trying to figure out what they were going to do in certain circumstances. The fact that he had been a great student of the game is what got him to the NHL. But that is only one aspect of coaching. Many other coaches have been good technicians and unable to keep their jobs for any period of time. Knowledge of the game and its various components is not enough.

I want to move slowly and carefully here because this is being written after Jean Perron has left the Canadiens. In three years as head coach, all Jean did was win the Stanley Cup once, guide us to first place in our division and second overall in the league, and keep us competitive. On paper, he was very successful. At least that's what the writers would have you believe.

In the aftermath of his departure from the Canadiens, much has been said by the media about players "running the team" and how it is practically impossible for a coach to exercise any authority anymore. My name was prominent in many of these new reports because of two incidents – one in 1986 and another in 1988 – where I disagreed publicly with his coaching method or style. The conclusion by some or many was that I was trying to run the team. Nothing could be further from the truth.

I have been a team player ever since I started this game and I have never put myself above or beyond the team for selfish interests. If I spoke out against Jean Perron, or against the direction in which the team was going, it was because I was deeply concerned about the team's welfare, not mine.

I spoke out when I did because I felt the club needed it at the time. I was speaking out as much for and to the club as I was for Larry Robinson. And right now I hope that I'll be able to explain what I mean clearly so that the reader will understand exactly what went on at the time.

I would also like to think that this is an analysis of the last three years rather than a criticism of it or one man.

First, I had to try to reach my real feelings about Jean Perron's arrival as head coach of the Canadiens. A friend and I were discussing it and he finally phrased the question in a way that I could see how I really felt.

"Are you more upset with Jean Perron becoming head coach, because you honestly feel he doesn't have the background; or with Jacques Lemaire quitting the team?"

After thinking about it for a few minutes, I had to admit I was more upset with Coco's resignation. And I wasn't alone. Jacques had been with us a little more than a year and the players trusted him. We were going places and trusted him to help lead us there. With Jacques, there was no second-guessing.

Whatever I felt about Jean Perron's credentials, he was part of the new wave of college-trained coaches coming into the NHL as the old guard like Don Cherry, Scotty Bowman, and Harry Sinden were on their way out. The game had started to change and guys like Tom Watt, Jean Perron, and Mike Keenan were quickest to pick up on the changes.

Earlier I wrote that I instinctively trusted professional coaches more because they had usually come up through the ranks like I had. But I have worked with some very intelligent hockey men who were college-trained coaches. A case in point was Tom Watt, a good coach who got a bum rap. He never had great teams to work with and deserves a shot at a good team. I worked with him in the 1984 Canada Cup and I was quite impressed.

Tom Watt did a superb job of going over all the teams and breaking down their games on video. Both Jacques Lemaire and Jean Perron were superb in this area too. I still can't figure why Watt isn't a head coach in the NHL today.

Perhaps the best way to make sense of all of this for the reader is to establish the three basic points that affected me, the team, and Jean Perron as head coach.

Point One: like many veterans, I had a hard time getting used to college-style coaches.

Point Two: I did not dislike Jean Perron. In fact, I found him to be a very nice, if shy, man. He was fair and aboveboard with me in all of our dealings.

Point Three: Jean Perron came into his job with a strike against him. As an assistant, he had not gained the respect of some veterans on the team. After three years, that attitude had spread throughout the room. That's what hurt him the most in the long run.

Jean knew it would not be an easy thing to win the confidence of some of the veterans. When he was an assistant to Jacques Lemaire, he had run-ins with some players, especially when he was left to run practices. Nobody took him seriously, but that happens sometimes with assistants. It's like having a substitute teacher at school – party time! Jacques Laperriere, the other assistant, didn't help much in this area. He was too nice; he never got involved with authority and didn't want to ruffle any feathers. So during Perron's practices, guy weren't listening, they were fooling around, and occasionally they would yell back at him if he tried to maintain order.

Under normal circumstances, this would be devastating to a new head coach. But training camp 1985 could hardly be called normal circumstances. The Montreal Canadiens were about to undergo a major youth movement.

While we were losing to the Nordiques in seventh-game overtime in the Adams Division final in 1985, a lot of future Canadiens were still playing hockey. In the American League, the Sherbrooke Canadiens had made the playoffs with a late-season charge. They were led by three free agents, centres Randy Bucyk and Brian Skrudland and defenceman Mike Lalor. After their Quebec Junior teams were eliminated from the playoffs, Stephane Richer and Patrick Roy joined Sherbrooke and the team went on to win the Calder Cup. All five would be given a serious look at our next training camp.

They were not alone. The Memorial Cup playdowns were held in Quebec that year and three of the four teams involved were led by Montreal draftees. Claude Lemieux of the Verdun Junior Canadiens, Sergio Momesso of the Shawinigan Cataractes, and Graeme Bonar of the Sault Ste. Marie Greyhounds were labelled "can't miss" by the scouts. Add to that group a

very talented Brantford forward named Shayne Corson and a
Swedish forward named Kjell Dahlin and there were at least
ten blue chip rookies coming to camp. There also would be a
tough kid named John Kordic from the Portland Winter Hawks
whom few people knew anything about.

And greeting them was a rookie coach.

Jean knew it would be a hard row to hoe and called his veterans together right away. He said he wanted the contribution
of the veterans such as Bo, myself, Ryan Walter, Bobby
Smith, Mats Naslund – basically the guys who've been
around for six or seven years. He said he was a rookie coach
and he was going to make some mistakes.

I got the impression that his desire to open this channel of
communication was honest. Some guys thought it was an act,
that this was a little speech to make it look good when he really
didn't intend to ask for our input. But he proved himself over
the years, especially in that first season. He would listen to
what we had to say.

Camp was interesting, to say the least, and when the season
opener rolled around on October 10, a lot of the new kids were
staying – Skrudland, Lalor, Richer, Momesso, Dahlin, Roy,
and Bucyk. They had played hard and earned a shot; but they
also had been blessed with blind rookie luck, a rash of injuries
to veterans. As the season got going, Lucien Deblois, Mario
Tremblay, Steve Penney, and Ryan Walter were out with injuries and the kids got a lot of icetime.

We started with a couple of wins and travelled to Boston on
the first Sunday night of the new season. It was still a close
game when Chris Nilan butt-ended Rick Middleton in the
mouth, breaking his bridge. When Knuckles' ten-minute
attempt-to-injure penalty was over, the game was out of reach.
He subsequently was assessed a ten-game suspension and that
was the beginning of the end for him in Montreal. Chris was
one of the players who had tormented Jean Perron the year
before and their relationship went downhill from then on.

After that loss, and missing yet another veteran, we headed
straight for the Adams Division basement. Perhaps the lowest
point of that stretch was a Saturday night game in Hartford

where the Whalers had us down 7–2 after the first period. We eventually lost 11–7 and some of the younger players showed their stuff – Momesso, Dahlin, and Richer – but, as the score indicates, things were not going well.

Strangely enough, though, the bad times led to good times. All of those injuries to veterans proved to be a good thing in the long run because the club was forced to play the rookies a lot and they gained experience and confidence with each game. Momesso and Dahlin were especially effective up front and Kjell looked like a "Kjoe-in" for the rookie-of-the-year award with his great offensive play.

But the rookies wouldn't escape the injury bug, either. First to get hurt was Stephane Richer, out with an ankle injury in early November. Until that point, Steph had been one of our top scorers and playmakers and appeared well on his way to a 30-goal season. He sat out for several weeks and his enforced absence seemed to work at his confidence; he figured he had lost his spot in the line-up. When he returned, he played badly. It was hard to figure.

The next rookie to get hurt was Sergio, the big friendly Italian kid from west-end N.D.G., who suffered a knee injury that doctors feared would end his career. He was one of the few rookies who got along with both his fellow rookies and the veterans and his loss was important.

Jean Perron was head coach of what was, in effect, two teams. One team comprised the veterans who had been there for several years before. The other was the large rookie contingent. Normally veterans easily overwhelm rookies because they outnumber them by a large ratio. Not so with us in 1985–86. We had seven new guys as well as young guys like Petr Svoboda, Chris Chelios, Tom Kurvers, and Steve Rooney who had been around for only a year or so. The team was divided almost right down the middle by age and experience.

One of the points of contention was starting goaltending. Steve Penney had a terrible start and it almost was a blessing when he suffered a groin injury that disabled him. That left veteran Doug Soetaert and Patrick Roy in the nets and Patrick was getting the lion's share of the action. Patrick would play great, especially in close where he was like a big cat pouncing on every puck. But in a lot of games, he would give up a spectacularly bad goal on a long shot, the kind of goal that sucks the air out of a team.

Several veterans were upset, especially since Doug Soetaert was the best of the three goalies and the most consistent, and was getting little icetime. When Doug started playing more, we started winning more. We played well between December and mid-February but you could hardly call us consistent. We could go into Philadelphia or Long Island and whip the Flyers and the Islanders, and then turn around and lose home games to Minnesota, New Jersey, and Los Angeles.

Nobody knew which Montreal Canadiens team would show up on any given night.

Jean was in a tough position. He was new to the team as head coach and, like the rookies, had to feel his way around. Had he been able to play it tough with everyone, at all times, I'm convinced he would still be the coach going into the 1988–89 season. What hurt Jean then, and later, was his inability to instill discipline: he didn't have an iron fist. He couldn't come out and say: "All right you guys, I'm the frigging boss here and if you don't frigging like it, there's the door."

Back then, it was easy for him to handle the rookies because they were new, too, and didn't really know their way around. When the team screwed up, the guy at fault was most likely to be a rookie. Brian Skrudland or Shayne Corson would get a minor penalty and another one for yapping at the referee, and miss the rest of the game while they "thought about discipline," as Perron said. But Chris Nilan would do the same thing and wouldn't miss a shift because the coach was afraid of him. Jean didn't treat everybody equally and, at first, a small group of players almost openly defied him. As time went on, this group would get bigger.

Our rookie-veterans split came to a head during a late-February road trip. We had played a terrible Forum game against Hartford and had flown out west the same Saturday night to prepare for a Monday night game against the Oilers. We lost 3–2 in a game where both teams slept on the ice for long periods. We then flew to Vancouver for a Wednesday night contest against the Canucks. During Tuesday's practice, Chris Nilan and Stephane Richer bumped and then squared off as Nilan hammered the rookie with several shots before we could get them separated.

The media were on us like vultures and the standard "it was only the heat of the moment, everybody's friends now" line as we came out of the dressingroom was sounding a bit forced, to say the least.

To his credit, Perron let the team sort it out. Several conversations were held between rookies and veterans and one fact was crystal clear to all of us. If we didn't get our act together, and soon, we'd lose it.

We were in a struggle for third and fourth place with Buffalo and Hartford and we could end up last and out of the playoffs. We went on to win the next two games in Vancouver and Los Angeles and we flew east in a better frame of mind. We were promptly bashed by the Islanders at Uniondale and then by the Blues at home and the pressure was back on.

Rick Green and Chris Chelios had been out for a long time and that was starting to show at the blueline. Also, Mats Naslund and Kjell Dahlin both went into a slump at the same time and we had to look to other players to pick up the slack. Worse still, Doug Soetaert was injured, Steve Penney was barely recovered from an injury, and Patrick Roy was Patrick Roy, a rookie who could stun both the opposition and his teammates on any given night.

We picked up Gaston Gingras from Toronto and after playing in Sherbrooke for a spell, he reported to Montreal and played better than he had his first time here.

Late in the season, we were back on a downslide when we headed off for our last major road trip of the season. Actually it was like two separate road trips: a first leg to Winnipeg and St. Louis, then into New England for back-to-back Whalers and Bruins.

We have always played well in Winnipeg and one reason is the fact that the fans cheering for the Canadiens usually outnumber those cheering on the hometown Jets by as much as three-to-one or four-to-one. Although he still had a gimpy knee, Doug Soetaert wanted to play against the team that had traded him so he started for us. We played well at the beginning, taking a 3–1 lead after one and leading 3–2 going into the third period.

When a team's snakebit, you have to wait for the venom to work its way right out of its system. Trying to rush the situation only makes it worse, as we discovered that night. We weren't more than 20 seconds into the final period when one of their players skated behind our net, flipped the puck out in front and it went in off Gaston Gingras' skate. About a minute later, Craig Ludwig deflected one in past Soetaert and Doug kept checking his shirt to see which team he was playing for. The final was Winnipeg 6 Montreal 4.

We flew to St. Louis that Wednesday night and would play the Blues on Saturday. St. Louis became boot camp. Jean Perron delivered a lecture about pride and effort and then put us through two 90-minute workouts that had guys gasping on the ice.

I blew my stack. This was Bob Berry all over again with punishment practices and no rhyme or reason. Red Fisher of *The Gazette* was in the right place at the right time (or wrong time, depending on your point of view), when my frustrations came pouring out.

"If he skated the hell out of us because he was unhappy with our performance against Winnipeg, why didn't he start to do it after St. Louis beat us in Montreal? Or after Hartford beat us in Montreal? Or a month and a half ago? Is he telling us we're out of condition after the 73rd game of the season?

"Losing games is always a problem. We've got lots of problems. And the only way of solving problems is to get some discipline on thie ice. Discipline is not to give up three-on-twos or two-on-ones to the other team – and making the most of ours. I don't know how many of them we've had in the last few games, and each time the pucks seem to be going into our net. On the other hand, I don't know how many times we had them on the other teams with nothing happening."

Guy Carbonneau was also upset and made a few comments

in the French press and, suddenly, the rumours started flying thick and fast about a possible coach change. I wasn't looking for one and neither was Guy; we just wanted the team to get its head on straight.

Whatever the case, Serge Savard convened a special veterans meeting at our hotel in St. Louis. Nilan, Gainey, Smith, Naslund, Walter, Deblois, and myself attended. The only guy who really spoke up was Lucien Deblois.

"I don't think Jean is doing a very good job and I know for a fact he's not getting the respect in the room," he said. We may have agreed with him, but nobody else really said anything.

Lucien was in and out of the line-up and a lot of what he was saying could be construed as personal frustration.

Serge was pretty succinct.

"It's time you guys shut up and started playing hockey. I'm not going to change the coach so don't even think about that. I chose this coach and I'm going to stay with him. It is up to you guys to get this team going again."

One point I feel I should make is, no matter what we felt about the coach then or now, or what he felt about us as individuals or a group, Jean Perron had class. He never singled out a player for any reason; he never spoke against any of us. He was very good that way. That is why to this day I regret saying those things in public; I meant them and they had to be said somehow, but I should probably have gone to Jean instead of talking to the media. The fact is, when I spoke, I never thought it would be treated like it was.

We played much better the following night but still lost, this time 3–2 to the Blues as Rick Wamsley just stoned us. (Doug Wickenheiser got the winner for them so there was a bleu-blanc-rouge ribbon wrapped around that one.) An encouraging sign was that Steve Penney had played well for us. However, that would be his last game of the season as he aggravated a groin injury that would sideline him for the rest of the year.

Up next was the New England tour. And more bad news.

We lost the first game in Hartford 3–0. The game was scoreless for the longest time before the Whalers scored late in the second period. Our shots hit goalposts, legs, sticks, bums, you name it, and Hartford was able to put the game away with two goals in the first minute of the third period.

It was a very demoralized team on the bus to Boston that night.

Everyone was on edge. Serge Savard and Jacques Lemaire arrived at the Sheraton and the talk again was about a coaching change, even though the veterans knew that Serge was committed to backing Jean Perron all the way. There was something going on, though, because Serge, Jacques, and Jean got together for a long session that night in the Managing Director's room.

Their solution was apparent the next morning when Claude Lemieux showed up in the lobby. His exile to Sherbrooke, the product of a terrible training camp the previous September, was over. He played that night, and played well in a 3–3 tie that broke our losing streak.

During that game, Mats Naslund and Keith Crowder went crashing into the boards near the end of the glass and both emerged unhurt. Not so starting referee Dave Newell. He was caught between Mats and the glass and damaged some ribs and his back, forcing him out of the game. He was replaced by a former Nordique and a current AHL referee named Paul Stewart.

In the second period, Stewart called back a Boston goal scored against Patrick, claiming it had been knocked into the net with a high stick. The replays showed it hadn't, but we were only too glad to take the point. The losing streak was over.

Two weeks later, we gathered at "Alcatraz," the Sheraton Hotel on Ile Charron, an island in the middle of the St. Lawrence River midway between Montreal and south shore Boucherville. It was playoff time and we were getting ready to play the Bruins.

Nobody knew what to expect; we had eight rookies playing regularly in the line-up and a large contingent of veterans who weren't. We also had Chris Chelios and Rick Green, both returned from injuries and that had to cheer up everybody.

One thing was certain. For this playoff year, Alcatraz was the ideal way to bring everybody together.

A lot of players hate the whole idea of forced togetherness that some teams institute during the playoffs. I was pretty much used to it, remembering playoff headquarters in Ste. Agathe during the Stanley Cup years of the 1970s. It is good to get together during this time because it helps focus the players. It also gets us away from the house and all the telephone calls from friends and acquaintances looking for tickets and other things.

The negative side is that young and healthy married couples are separated and a lot of psychologists will tell you that is not good for a relationship. A lot of the telephone calls turn into an exchange of frustrations on both sides and put some people in pretty bad moods.

But considering our rookie-veteran split, and the various incidents that had taken place during the year, it was better for the team to take a chance on some marital discomfort and bring the players together as a group. The reader must realize that we are members of two families during the hockey season. Quite often, we're with the guys on the team more than we're at home. You'll have squabbles with your kids and squabbles with your wife, whatever, and you might not be with them as much as you are with the other players.

So ask yourself: Isn't it normal that you'll have disagreements on a team like ours?

As the playoffs got under way, everything was planned so that the veterans would take the rookies in hand. Bob Gainey and myself were the leaders of the Big Brother movement because Jean Perron had asked us to pitch in. Also contributing were Bobby Smith, Mats Naslund, Ryan Walter, Mario Tremblay, and Lucien Deblois.

The drill was fairly consistent. We would have all our meals together, bus into town for practice and to take care of some business, and then get together in the evenings at the hotel for team meetings, to go over video, or have a few drinks and watch games in other series.

On our first night there, Perron got us all together in a meeting room and had some of the veterans explain their Stanley Cup experiences to the younger players. Bob Gainey was team captain and he went first and talked about what it meant to be a Stanley Cup winner; the feelings you had riding in a Stanley Cup parade. He talked about his experiences and the work it had taken to be a champion and how it was worth it for all of the individuals involved.

My message was a little more immediate: "This is a once-in-a-lifetime shot for a lot of NHL players. A lot of guys play all their lives and never get a clear shot at winning the Stanley Cup. Some of us won't be together again and you never really know what next year will bring. You have to take your best shot while you're here; I think we have a really good hockey team and we can go all the way."

After I spoke, Bobby Smith got up. "When I was with Minnesota, we beat the Montreal Canadiens and we went quite far in the playoffs. We were real happy because we felt that we had the team of the 1980s and we'd be right back the next year and the year after that. We ended up almost missing the playoffs the next year and were never again the strong team we had been in 1980. There is no such thing as we'll get 'em next year. Do it now, if you can."

Whatever we said, it seemed to work and the team came together as a unit as the playoffs moved along.

The rest is all colour images running into each other. Taking out the Bruins in four straight with John Kordic handling Jay Miller several times and Claude Lemieux scoring big goals.

Going down to the wire with Hartford, the upstarts who had surprised the Nordiques. Great series on both sides of the ice; Guy Carbonneau, Kevin Dineen, Ulf Samuelsson, Patrick Roy, Mike Liut and Steve Weeks, Mike McPhee and Rick Green . . . and finally, seventh game overtime at the Forum and a backhand by Claude Lemieux high over Mike Liut's left shoulder to send us on our way.

After beating Hartford, we knew we could go all the way; we had the talent and the confidence to beat anybody and everybody.

Up next were the Rangers, a team we hardly knew, and the images I most clearly retain are a combination of Mike McPhee and Bob Gainey shutting down Pierre Larouche while Patrick Roy "Roo-Ah! Roo-Ah! Roo-Ah!" goaled the game of his life at Madison Square in the third game.

And finally as they say, the final. Another big red machine with the C on their chests. Familiar faces; Lanny McDonald, John Tonelli, and Dougie Risebrough, busting their behinds to push the Calgary Flames ahead of us, and Brian Skrudland's back-breaking, record-setting overtime goal in Game Two, while many in the Saddledome crowd were still at the concession stands. Nine seconds! The guys on the bench hadn't even had time to sit down.

Thinking back, we must have been quite a shock to the Flames. All year long, all everyone could talk about in the league was how big the Flames were, how they would wear down other teams with size and relentless grinding. And then we skated out onto the ice and pound for pound, we were bigger. And faster.

That memory must have lingered two years later, as Cliff Fletcher traded for even more size in 1988, fully expecting to meet us in the finals once again. What is that they say about the plans of mice and men?

Last but not least, there are the memories of two months in Alcatraz, and special shirts given to the team by Sheraton management. They were publicly introduced on our four-hour flights to Calgary and back. They went really well with Blues Brothers shades and a rose behind the ear. Right Serge Boisvert?

As I said, it all blurs.

What comes through clearly, though, are the many occasions when we could have lost it because we were still a team overladen with rookies on the ice and behind the bench. We were a very talented team, and still are, but we came close to losing it that year.

Forgotten in the celebrations and the Stanley Cup parade was the fact that there still were too many incidents of panic on the bench in the middle of close games. We may have beat

Calgary 4–1 to win the final, but late in the third period of the fifth game in Calgary, when they scored two goals in the last two minutes to get within one at 4–3, there was a lot of screaming on the bench and behind it.

You wouldn't believe the fear on the bench after they scored their first, and then their second goal. I got up and started walking up and down the bench, screaming "Relax, relax." Talk about mixed messages. Patrick Roy saved our bacon with a save off Jamie Macoun with less than 15 seconds left in the game.

Those moments of indecision would come up again, in other seasons, and would prove costly.

We outlasted the Flames, but it was a lot closer than anyone would want to admit, even though the series only went to five games. I was certainly glad it ended when it did. By the time it was over, I had had more than 100 cc's of blood and fluid taken out of my elbow. I had an inflammation of the bursal sac and everytime I banged the elbow, it would swell up like an eggplant. The first time they drained it, they took out three needles full of fluid; after that it would flare up every time I hit it.

Still, we won it, my sixth Stanley Cup, and easily the most gratifying.

When the final siren had gone, I was out on the ice in a sea of red shirts and there was Bo handing me the Cup. I was so emotional I just broke down. I couldn't think of anything for a while.

Forget the money, the travel, the media, and the time away from your family. When, finally, the other 20 teams have been defeated and you're skating out there with the silverware, you know what the hard work was all about.

As corny as it might sound to some people, that's what makes the game worth playing. Anybody who says they're playing for the money is just kidding himself. Money's nice, but it sure isn't everything. Then again, I've tried going to the grocery story with my Stanley Cups but they don't want to give me anything.

A short time later, I was sitting in that dressingroom in Calgary, watching a bunch of young hockey players in various stages of undress spraying each other with champagne and beer. With the weird strobe effect you get from television lights and all those cameras, it was almost like being in a time warp. The last time had been seven years and three days before, May 21, 1979, to be exact.

In a bit of a daydream, I could see the Ghosts of other teams; the guys hollering and whooping and hosing each other down with suds: Shutty, Sharty, Ken, the Flower, Big Pete, the Dougies, Yvan, Pointu, Yvon, and Powerful Pierre. Serge Savard.

The Senator was there in Calgary but this time he was wearing a three-piece suit.

It was a room full of new Canadiens, kids most of them, just like the young group that had partied so hard in the Spectrum in 1976, singing "God Bless America" until our voices were just a croak. Kids who would, like we had, probably go on to other Cups, other championships, with or without me.

Brian Skrudland, an emotional kid, a young leader and a worker. A guy who never stops, a guy who reminds everybody of a blond Doug Risebrough and in Montreal, that's a compliment.

Claude Lemieux, a pressure player who scored ten goals in the playoffs, including big overtime goals against Hartford and the Rangers. Tough, feisty, and with the kind of mouth like a Ken Linseman that can drive you to distraction.

Stephane Richer, a super sensitive kid with all the tools to become another Guy Lafleur if he ever matures enough to handle it.

Mike Lalor, a good, basic defenceman. A six-footer who plays even bigger because he is deceptively strong.

John Kordic, one of the toughest guys in the league but very bright and quiet. Respected by the opposition because he doesn't take cheap shots.

Sergio Momesso, before he was injured and they put several pounds of Gor-Tex in his knee, a very hard worker with good offensive skills.

Patrick Roy, very good instincts, incredibly quick, but still a goalie in search of a style. If he ever shows consistency, he will be up there with Fuhr and Hextall every year.

David Maley and **Steve Rooney**, typical big American college-trained wingers.

Kjell Dahlin, a Swede with the softest hands I've seen in a long time and great offensive instincts.

Shayne Corson, a junior who didn't play in the Cup playoffs that year but a real good one who would make a major league contribution for the longest time.

Everywhere you looked there were kids. Naked to the waist, or still fully dressed in the fabled red visitors' sweater because they were too excited to even get undressed. The immediate future of the Montreal Candiens strutted around the dressingroom.

There were also a lot of transition era Canadiens, guys who had been with us for a long time, or who had come over from other teams, after our last Cup win in 1979: Ryan Walter, Bobby Smith, Rick Green, Mats Naslund, Chris Nilan, Guy Carbonneau, Mike McPhee, and Craig Ludwig. It was their first Stanley Cup and you never forget your first, especially if you had waited such a long time for it.

But there were still some 1970s Canadiens in the room that Saturday night. After seven years of frustration, of having learned what it was like to live on the other side of the tracks, Bob Gainey, Mario Tremblay, and I could look at each other and know what each other was thinking, without having to say a word.

They talk a lot about passing the torch in Montreal.

We were back.

FIFTEEN

A Hard Act To Follow

T HE CHARTER flight back home from Calgary in the early morning hours of Sunday, May 25, 1986, was a 2,500-mile long party.

Young guys like John Kordic, Serge Boisvert, and Gaston Gingras paraded around in their Alcatraz cut-away shirts and shades, knocking back beers and mellowing out in the best California tradition. There were a lot of wives and team management types on the flight so the festivities never really got out of hand, even when Doug Soetaert gave the sleeping Naslunds, Mr. and Mrs., an unscheduled sudsy wake-up call somewhere over northern Ontario. A good time was had by all at 33,000 feet.

I partied with the guys but I also spent some quiet moments by myself in my seat, sipping quietly on a beer and enjoying the vibes. I was also thinking: "Would this be the time to go? Nothing could be better than leaving a winner." Larry Clark Robinson would celebrate his 35th birthday in eight days and in the NHL of the 1980s, 35 was social security time. Patrick Roy, sitting quietly up ahead with a big grin on his face, the 1986 Conn Smythe Trophy winner, had been all of seven years old when I played my first NHL game. Stephane Richer was 12 the last time I had celebrated a Stanley Cup win.

Could it really have gone by that fast? To get the answer, I just had to take a quick look at the read world; my kids Jeffery and Rachelle. Jeff was going on 15 and Rachelle was well along in school. And daddy had been an absentee father for most of their days, spending long periods away from his family from September to May.

Alcatraz-on-the-St. Lawrence may have meant that a hockey team would come together in a bid to strengthen itself and win the Stanley Cup. But it also meant that quite a few fathers were away from their families for almost two months. That is a whole different kind of tension, and one which the fan never can really appreciate.

Did I still want to play?

Did I still have to play, financially?

Was I ready to hang them up, walk away with no regrets, thankful for a career with an extraordinary amount of success and very little in the way of negative reaction or debilitating physical injury? I had 14 seasons in the NHL behind me, and six Stanley Cup rings to attest to my success. I had won the Norris Trophy twice as the league's best defenceman, the Conn Smythe Trophy once as top player in the playoffs, and several First and Second All-Star team nominations.

And unlike two of the top defencemen of my generation (Brad Park and Bobby Orr), I could walk away on two strong legs.

When first Bob Gainey, and then I, clutched the Cup in the on-ice celebration at the Saddledome, I could amost hear the play-by-play guys: "Is this it for the two Canadiens veterans? Are Gainey and Robinson making their last skate with the Cup?"

It has nothing to do with ability or contribution to the team. The boys in the booth upstairs look at your birthdate on the program, note that it was some time in the 1950s, and immediately conclude that your career is over. They no longer look at you as a full contributing member of the team. Instead, you become a "retirement waiting to happen."

Or they deliver the backhanded compliment: "Jeez Larry, you sure can really play for a guy your age! Howdya do it?" They're sincere, too. After talking to you, they go off to interview the coach and the general-manager about the aging of the team.

I think a few guys upstairs should retire before I do.

Still, sitting there quietly on the charter, winging home with the Cup, even thinking such thoughts was a bit of a shock. I was one of the oldest guys in the league and had played a lot longer than 90% of the NHL players before me. But nothing prepares you for the shock of realization that 14 years have passed so quickly. Those years had become a blur, a videotape on super fast forward.

I guess one thing that made it easier for me to even entertain such thoughts was the fact that I had a business life away from hockey. I had something to do and somewhere to go after hockey. That would help cushion the shock of ending the only real career I had ever had. People reading this might silently applaud my good sense for trying to plan for the future, and at the same time wonder aloud why other players don't prepare their post-career better.

There are two answers. First, I had a lot of help and I'll get to that in a moment. Second, players don't spend much time planning in this area because they don't have the time to do it, usually. Take the average eight-month season, including playoffs, remember that we rarely have days off, add to that the travel and the tension of producing under incredible stress and then come back and ask me if players are asleep at the switch about their retirement.

It's part of the fantasy. Most people like to think that we have it made; we play half the year, get the girls, the adulation, and sign autographs; and party the other half. That is far from the truth.

Just for fun, let's compare jobs: Most people earning a wage in this country work five days a week, with weekends or two days off each week. So subtract 104 days from 365 days and you get 261. They usually get 12 to 15 statutory holidays, which get us down to 245, and then three weeks vacation, which brings us down to 230 working days.

Now for the hockey player. The 1987–88 NHL season began on Thursday, October 8, (we visited Philadelphia) and ended Sunday, April 3, (we were in Buffalo). We played two playoff series, ending our year with a loss to Boston on April 26. Our "season" started with training camp Sept. 10. Between Sept. 10, and April 26, 229 days elapsed. During that time, we might have had ten days off.

We work as long a year as you do. And how many of you spend your precious time off training for another career or planning your post-retirement days? Everything has a way of being equalized. Had any of us played in the Canada Cup (add 30 days) or gone to the Stanley Cup final (add another 30 days), our "work year" would be about 280 days. Put it like that, and you begin to realize NHL hockey is a full-time job and that the demands on our time are as strenuous as those on the average Canadian or American worker.

Our work day can be a major problem too, especially on game day. We're often at the rink at ten in the morning and still there at ten at night.

My preparation for a post-hockey career started during the 1975 Stanley Cup playoffs. I drove into a garage called Dingy's on St. Catherine Street, not far from the Forum, looking for an oil change and minor mechanical work on my four-wheel-drive Bronco. I met the co-owner, Donny Cape, a real bantam rooster of a guy and we kibitzed as the mechanics did their work. One thing I liked a lot was the fact that these guys weren't overwhelmed with a hockey player in their midst and I could be myself.

They already did a lot of work for the Forum, like maintaining the Zamboni, so they were used to so-called hockey celebrities and I found myself relaxing during what was normally a tense time.

As a kid in Marvelville, I had helped my Dad and brother a lot working on farm machinery and I had always found it realaxing to work on a car or a truck. I eventually found myself down at Dingy's most afternoons working on the Bronco or the family car.

Dingy's was an all-purpose garage, but it also specialized in Corvettes and in 1976, I asked Donny if he could find me a good car. He found me a gorgeous convertible which we bought together, fixed up, and eventually sold.

"We'll give you a special deal on painting your car," he said to me.

"If you're going to give me a special deal on painting my car,

I don't want to do business with you," was my answer. I was more concerned in making sure Dingy's got a fair deal and made their money than getting a special price. Right away you can see I was a natural, shrewd businessman. Yeah, sure.

As it turned out, I had found my downtown hangout. Instead of heading home out in the suburbs for a nap and a meal after a morning skate, I just started hanging around the garage, puttering on various cars and enjoying myself immensely. It was at least as relaxing as my nap. I would putter around on my cars, changing the oil, the plugs, cleaning and waxing, or some such thing. I was so emotionally involved in the game that I needed such a distraction.

After a while, I started noticing the business side of things as Donny and I began talking about things other than motors and tune-ups. I had not been happy with my financial advisers, or agents, but I wasn't the type of guy to say anything outright, especially since I felt I didn't know anything about the world of finance. I knew I wasn't happy with them, but I was in no position to say anything about it with any authority. I had no experience at all in business.

Donny, on the other hand, was an astute businessman and I began going to him for a second opinion. In retrospect, I can say that my agents didn't do a very good job for me. But I can also say that I was luckier than a lot of players. Some really got taken by their agents so I can consider myself lucky to some degree.

Shortly after I arrived in Montreal, I hired Dave Schatia as my first agent. He and his partner also took care of Yvon Lambert, and both of us ended up leaving them after disagreements.

My next (and last!) agent was the late Norm Caplan and two incidents led to my splitting with him and taking on Donny as an adviser.

The first was an investment opportunity, a building in a downtown Montreal industrial park, the old Murray Hill building. Donny wanted to buy it, I wanted to have a piece of it, but Norm kept saying no, it's not a good idea. Norm had a way about him when he felt strongly about something. He wouldn't shut up and would eventually wear you down. I finally threw up my hands and said "Okay, okay, you win."

There's another way of saying "you win." It's "I lose" and I certainly did on that deal; that property has appreciated very nicely since those days.

In 1980, I heard that Donny and his partner John Dingman were bidding on a building on Pare Street in suburban St. Laurent, the current site of Dingy's.

"I want a part of it," I told Donny one night while we were playing pool in his basement.

"You know that Norman Caplan told you not to buy it and not to get involved in the garage business," Donny replied.

"I don't care, I want to get involved." I wanted some business connections for my post-hockey days and I loved being around cars. I would enjoy "going to the office," during and after my hockey days.

John Dingman and Donny repeated that they didn't want me as a partner. "We don't need you, you're not a mechanic and we don't need your money." I persisted and we finally became partners, totally against Norman Caplan's will.

The second incident that decided me about Norm Caplan took place in 1981. Guy Lafleur and I were holding out together and Norm wanted to negotiate Guy Lafleur's contract. Guy didn't want him to and said, "If you want to, go ahead, but I'm not going to pay you for it." He told me he thought Norm was a ripoff.

Negotiations were not going well and it got to the point where I wasn't even going to talk with Irving Grundman anymore. Gerry Grundman and Donny arranged a telephone meeting with Irving, Donny, and myself and it was settled then and there. It wasn't "official" until three o'clock in the morning when Norm "approved it."

I was frustrated, feeling that I didn't get what I wanted but, instead, what Norman Caplan wanted. Norm had a way of leaking "impending deals" to the press, even before there was agreement, often making his hockey player client look like a jerk while Norm basked in all of the media attention.

I went home that night and I didn't know what to do. I was

practically in tears I was so frustrated. Norm and Irving had made so much noise in the papers about the agreement, and I felt so bad, I just bit my tongue and refused to do anything about it.

About eight months before Norm passed away, he finally agreed that Donny had my best interests in mind. Donny drew up a schedule of what he thought I should make and Norman got a copy. Norm was supposed to go to management with it but it turned out he never did. When he passed away, Donny went to Serge Savard with the schedule. It took about eight months to work it out because Serge didn't understand what I wanted at first. With the help of Canadiens head office personnel, we came up with a very simple agreement that made everybody happy.

The difference with Donny and Serge was that the negotiating was done quietly; it only got to the press when they announced that I had signed. I had never been comfortable with negotiating through the media and we didn't have to do it anyway.

My troubles with Norm apparently had not ended with his passing. It wasn't too long after his funeral that Donny received a telephone call from Norm's widow.

"Larry owes us $10,000," she said.

"What in the world are you talking about?" said Donny.

The upshot was that there was no documentation to support it; and no evidence of any other kind. I was mad but I wanted to get away from the ghost of Norm Caplan.

"Pay her the $10,000," I said.

"Are you nuts?" screamed Donny, and we launched into our first fight. In the end, still muttering, Donny sent off the cheque. A couple of weeks later, the books were closed on Norm Caplan's company. A little while after that, we got back all these records. Donny went through them and occasionally his head would pop out of the stacks and you'd hear something like "it doesn't show here" or "there's no record of this." Those are not what I'd call reassuring noises.

Norm Caplan was my last agent.

Donny Cape has since become my business partner. When

we have legal work to be done, he does what every business-man does, he hires a lawyer or lawyers on a fixed fee basis. When we need accounting and bookkeeping, Donny hires an accountant. I don't have an agent on salary, retainer, or com-mission and believe me, it's cheaper that way.

In other words, no more "money management" at a 10% or 15% cut of the gross. Everything we earn goes into the corpo-ration and we're both paid salaries. Donny's job is to handle investments and the day-to-day business dealings.

Seeing how Donny had operated for me, and with me, I could kick myself for paying so much to agents in my earli-er years. Hockey players are ripe fruit for "money manage-ment" experts. Agents might be more necessary in baseball or the NFL because the players earn a lot more money, and contracts might be a lot more complicated. In hockey, it seems to be pretty straightforward and I frankly don't think that the agents do much to earn their cuts, especially if they're getting a percentage.

A lot of the guys charge four or five percent of a yearly salary and that's outrageous. A young Canadien, just out of junior, came to me one day and said: "I paid my agent $10,000 to do a contract and I need to borrow some money. What do I do?"

I said: "Go and see Donny."

Donny's advice was as simple as it gets. "Call your agent."

"Well, he's got no time, he's always busy," he said. The agent was busy with his Number One client who was probably paying him a lot more than $10,000 a year. All this was unfair for the rookie and the poor guy didn't know what to do. He'd come from a small corn farm in the Ontario agricultural belt. This was all new to him.

Players often are not properly taken care of; they have to de-vote their time and energy to their sport. A business manager should be there to take care of the everyday problems. Some players have told me they're paying a guy $10,000 a year and practically don't seem him for three years, or until it comes time to negotiate again.

I once asked Donny what he thought negotiating a contract should be worth.

"I'd say it's probably worth about $250 an hour," he said How many hours?

"About ten hours and in many cases that would include the paperwork. I don't think it took more than ten hours of actual paperwork and negotiating back and forth to get your deal with Serge Savard."

Even if it takes 20 hours, we're talking $5,000 here, not $10,000, or $15,000, or $20,000. A lot of hockey players have paid the big numbers in the past, and thought they were getting a good deal.

You can't blame the young guys, they think acquiring an agent is the right thing to do. A lot of the junior clubs in the past have basically forced agents on guys who were still in junior. At the annual June entry draft, most of the top 100 or so draft choices already are represented.

When I was young, the thought of getting an agent never entered my mind. (No doubt you'll remember my description elsewhere in this book of the famous "burnt potato contract talks" with Claude Ruel.) I just wanted to play hockey and sign as quick as I could. Of course, my eyes were opened wide when John Van Boxmeer signed a year later for about eight times what I got.

As my career moved along, I became more and more conscious of my life after hockey. At first I thought the ideal would be to buy a farm in Eastern Ontario and go back to my roots after I left the game. I actually did buy the land and I still have it, but as the years went by, I had to recognize the changes in my life. I might be a good old farmboy from the Ottawa Valley, but maybe farming just wasn't what I was cut out to do anymore.

My love of polo and horses looms large in any future decisions. I currently have a small spread in St. Lazare, Quebec, west of Montreal, and I have an option on a larger property in nearby Ste. Marthe. I have six horses – polo ponies – and I have studied for my certificate in veterinary medicine. One thing I would love to do is raise and train horses, especially polo ponies. But it doesn't take a brain surgeon to understand that raising polo ponies can be expensive, especially when you're just starting out.

Some of the best professionals in the world, and I'm a long, long way away from them, will make $100,000 or so a year playing the game. The real money can come from selling polo ponies. Name players like the Gracida brothers of Miami or the Pieres of Argentina could buy a pony for $5,000 one morning and turn around and sell it for $10,000 that same afternoon just because it was once associated with them.

For the rest of us, it's an investment. A trained polo pony can sell for anything from $5,000 to $50,000 and keeping a string of them – they weren't kidding when they came up with the saying "he eats like a horse" – will take a bite out of your cash flow, no pun intended. I'm away a lot of the year so Linda Allard – Julian and Celia's daughter – looks after my horses. It's almost a full-time job.

Why so many horses? No single horse can withstand the physical pounding of a strenuous four-chukker match. Players usually change between chukkers, and some even within chukkers. We advise beginners to buy a pony for less than $1,000 and see if they like the sport first. At the beginning, we'll "twin" them with other members of the Montreal Polo Club so that they can share mounts during a match. We see that as an investment, too. The more people playing polo, the better.

That's just one aspect of my non-hockey life. There are others, some far less pleasant. Like most athletes whose names are in the limelight, I have had my share of adventures with businessmen and so-called entrepreneurs who are always seeking to align their names or products with celebrities.

In one case, I thought I had a solid opportunity to go a long way toward assuring my future in business. For many years, I was associated with a Montreal sports bar-restaurant called La Cage aux Sports, on a promotional level. For a fee, I would appear in television and/or radio spots, my picture would be included in some print ads, and I would take part in a certain number of appearances for the restaurant. Things went well, and La Cage had two, then three and four locations.

In 1987, owner George Durst, a well-known Montreal restauranteur, invited Donny and me to take part in a part-ownership deal in a new La Cage aux Sports opening up in the West Island suburbs. We had an option by a certain date to buy into the restaurant for a specific price.

At the same time, I had a standard promotional agreement with the restaurant to make a certain number of appearances and, if I could, have several teammates drop in. As it turned out, Donny and I were there almost every day when the team was in town and a lot of teammates, many of whom lived in nearby suburbs often would drop in. Things went great and the restaurant thrived.

Just before we were to sign our deal, the people at Sportscene, Durst's company, stopped returning Donny's calls. Almost three weeks went by before the word came back: The deal was off because Sportscene executives could not get along with Donny Cape.

That was a crock, of course. What had happened was that a gamble with a restaurant in a new shopping centre, facing a well-established centre, proved to be no gamble at all. The West Island, one of the better suburban areas in Greater Montreal, was in the midst of an incredible residential building boom and this time, it included the service and entertainment areas. The area was starting to rival downtown St. Catherine Street with its proliferation of clubs, restaurants, and theatres.

It had several advantages over downtown; fewer drunks and panhandlers outside the bars and clubs, cleaner and less congested streets and, most importantly for those people who like to party after the subway shuts down for the night, acres and acres of free parking, a premium in the downtown area.

What Durst and his people originally thought might take a couple of years, if not more, to turn a profit, had the cash registers ringing merrily almost from the first day. In fact, there were lineups on some nights, mid-week and weekends.

In other words, La Cage didn't need Larry Robinson or Donny Cape and would these two guys kindly get lost?

We have got lost but our leaving has taken the form of a $1.2 million lawsuit. There are too many guys out there trying to use you in this world. We are hoping this will deliver a serious message to future "entrepreneurs" who are looking to link up with "sports names."

I'm still looking for other business opportunities because I've found that I enjoy some aspects of dealing with the public. My years as a hockey player have taught me a lot of people skills; I feel very comfortable meeting new people and that is an important aspect of being a businessman today. I like the idea of being in a "problem-solving" business, too. That's one thing I like about Dingy's; people drive in with problems and drive out in the solutions.

I guess the ideal situation would be something like a combination of the garage and a restaurant as my main business interests, all the while helping me build something up involving horses. At 37, I still can dream.

There is still hockey, although my days are running out. As you no doubt know, I didn't retire after the 1986 Stanley Cup win. After long talks with Jeannette and Donny, and fully satisfied that I still could play to the standards I had set, I went back for two more seasons.

As the famous author said, "it was the best of times, and the worst of times." The Montreal Canadiens were still very competitive, finishing second in our division to Hartford in 1987 and then second overall behind Calgary last year.

Both seasons had their ups and downs and in both we were considered solid contenders for the Cup in post-season play. It didn't happen.

In 1987, we lost in six games to Philadelphia; a series we shouldn't have lost but did.

After a 21-game layoff, I returned to the regular line-up for the 1987–88 season . . . and to a season that had its ups and downs to say the least. Just after Christmas (I had been back about a month), we went into a tailspin and the shots at the coach increased. Claude Lemieux and Jean Perron had a shouting match between periods of one game; John Kordic was visibly upset with the coach on another occasion. I spoke up again, because I saw Sergio Momesso and Kjell Dahlin sitting in the press box while veterans who weren't carrying their load were being automatically pencilled into the starting line-up everyday. It was frustration talking, but frustration that had been building over a long period of time. The hockey season is a long one and incidents like these are part of the regular calendar. You almost pencil them in at the start of the year: players will bitch and carp at Game 20; coach will bench two veterans "as an example" at Game 40; the whole team gets cabin fever at Game 60, and "optimism reigns" with the playoffs approaching at Game 70.

With the extensive media coverage you get in Montreal, situations like these tend to be blown out of proportion. They are the normal responses of any large group of people forced together by circumstances over a long period of time. Especially highstrung athletes in a sport that takes such a physical and mental toll.

Late in January, after a particularly uninspired 4–1 loss to the St. Louis Blues at the Forum, it was my turn to bitch.

I was steaming. Part of the reason was a normal player's complaint: I had been getting less and less ice, while younger veterans like Petr Svoboda and Chris Chelios got more and more.

That night, the Blues had played a perfect road game; they got a lead and sat on it. We'd shoot the puck into their end, and they'd dump it out. Time and time again. It was about as exciting as curling.

A couple of writers were gathered around my cubicle in the dressingroom after the game and the frustration just welled up. As I unloaded, I wasn't paying much attention to rapidly growing scrum around me.

The "quotes" were all over TV, radio, and the newspapers the next day.

"Sure I'm frustrated. But am I upset? They played a perfect game. We'd dump it in, and they'd dump it out and they did it for 60 minutes – and we didn't do a damned thing about it.

"We didn't adjust. Who is supposed to make the adjustments?"

Jean Perron had already made one adjustment by that time. We were going to practise the next morning at 9 A.M., instead of the usual noon or 1 P.M. I wasn't thrilled about that, either.

"I suppose he's going to get tough now," I told the reporters.

"That's OK. He wants respect from the players, but in order to get respect from the players, you've got to respect them too."

The fan in the stands can see when a player is not going well and will always assume that the player is at fault. Multiply that by six or seven players, and management of the team becomes a factor.

"I suppose what will come out now is that some of the players didn't show up for the game," I continued.

"But I can think of a few players who did, and they didn't even get out on the ice. Every time Kjell Dahlin was on the ice, something happened. But he had only five or six shifts. He didn't even get out on the powerplay and he used to be one of the reasons why our powerplay was one of the best in the league."

In 1988, our powerplay was one of the worst in the NHL, a shame considering the talent on this team. No matter what we tried, it just wouldn't click and that would kill us in the playoffs.

The next morning, I was all over the headlines and kicking myself for it. But that means I regretted the furor that had resulted but not what I had said. It had to be said somehow, somewhere, and by somebody because the team was spinning its wheels. And it wasn't just the coach's fault.

Several players on the team were playing for themselves, stretching out shifts, going for the points. They knew who they were and so did their teammates, many of whom were getting frustrated by their actions. Others were defying the coach at almost every turn, and getting away with it. Bob Gainey, Rick Green, and I had taken some of these guys aside and talked with them quietly, but it didn't work.

"The rules are there for everybody, it doesn't matter if you're a rookie or if you've been in the league for 16 years like me. But some nights when a player isn't going well, maybe the coach should try somebody else," I said in a follow-up interview.

"I've been watching Sergio bust his butt in practice for the last several weeks and they won't give him a chance to prove himself. And Kjell Dahlin should be playing more too, maybe even on the powerplay."

One thing I had learned long ago in this league is that you're only as good as your next game and you can't play on your press clippings.

"It just seems like now some of the players are out there because of what they did in the past. If I'm not playing well, I should be benched. What I did a year or more before shouldn't count."

It may have cost the team a few anxious moments, especially Jean Perron and I, but my outburst seemed to wake up a few people. One of the reasons why the players took note of what I said was that they realized that I could have easily sat there quietly, cashing my cheques every two weeks, and let the situation develop as it might. They knew I was speaking for the team and not for Larry Robinson, and they also knew that we had been getting away from the things that made the Canadiens a powerhouse for years. We weren't willing to work hard every game, every period, every shift.

Management also knew, although Serge Savard kept his own counsel.

A couple of weeks later, Chris Nilan was traded to New York Rangers and a major thorn in Jean Perron's side had been removed. Chris's emotional style, 99% of the time a positive factor for the Canadiens, clashed with Jean's "coolness under fire" philosophy and the two just couldn't get along. They knew it and the team knew it and something had to give.

After those incidents, and with Kjell and Sergio in the line-up more often, we settled down to play our best hockey of the season.

Until the playoffs. Maybe we peaked too early.

In 1988, Boston finally ended their playoff jinx by beating us in five games. After finishing the season in second place overall, and with a 15-game winning streak, it all fell apart for us in the playoffs. The team had no focus; guys were trying to do it all themselves and some of the younger veterans did not appear to be as dedicated to winning as they had been two years before.

Truth be known, we began to lose it during the Hartford series and were lucky to beat the Whalers in six. At the end, they were coming on and we were fading fast.

And although we won the first game against Boston 5–2 – the game nobody saw because of the Quebec-wide power failure – we were out of it the rest of the way. It was the 1984 Montreal-Boston series all over again but switch the uniforms.

Experience teaches you that these things happen to a team. No matter how good you are, you will have major ups and downs during the year. That's what players, coaches, and management mean when they talk about mental toughness or the ability to suck it up, game after game.

Edmonton won the Stanley Cup, getting better as the playoffs went on. But they, too, had periods during the season when they couldn't buy a win and we handled them easily, three wins in as many games. The ebb and flow of a season being what it is, had we played them at different stages of the year, it might have been 0–3.

As it turned out, Calgary and Montreal, the two best teams overall during the season, couldn't get out of their divisions, getting progressively worse as the playoffs went on.

In our case, it cost Jean Perron his job.

SIXTEEN

A Young Man Goes West

FRIDAY, July 28, 1989. Another flight to Montreal from out west, but one with a difference.

For the first time in my National Hockey League career, I'm returning to Dorval Airport as a member of a team other than Montreal Canadiens.

Larry Robinson. Age 38. Defenceman. Team: Los Angeles Kings. Whew, it hasn't really sunk in yet. These last few days of July have been a whirlwind week. If the truth were known, this week really started two years ago.

Midway through the 1987–88 season, Donny Cape and Serge Savard re-opened negotiations on my contract. This sounds fancy, right? Actually, what really transpired is that they talked on the telephone. At the time I was in the last year of my then-current contract, excluding the option year. The option year is an insurance policy for NHL teams and the players under contract to them. It ensures that a player can't just get up and go at the end of the season, while providing the player with a little security in terms of his career in a certain city. A little security, I said; this device protects teams much more than it does players.

Playing out your option usually means one of two things. First, that the player and organization are so far apart in their assessments of his worth that he is playing his way out of the organization so he can go to greener pastures elsewhere. Or second, it is late in his career and the club thinks it can get one good season out of him before he hangs them up.

When Donny Cape and Serge Savard began discussing my immediate future with the Canadiens in 1988, our response was, to say the least, conditional.

"Larry feels that he and Jean Perron are on such different wavelengths that he won't feel comfortable continuing his career under these circumstances," Donny said.

I wasn't alone; if Jean Perron were to return for the 1988–89 season, Rick Green was going to retire too. Neither of us had been pleased with the 1987–88 season and all of the turmoil and recriminations that upset the dressingroom. Try as we might, along with Bob Gainey and other veterans like Bobby Smith, Ryan Walter and Guy Carbonneau, we couldn't convince the team to play for the coach, or for themselves, under those circumstances.

Reluctantly, Savard weighed all the pros and cons of Jean Perron remaining as head coach of the Canadiens, and then let him go. While the decision caused anger in the media, a sigh of relief went through the dressingroom. That very decision, however, pretty well made it certain that there wouldn't be time to negotiate a new contract for me during the off-season; Serge Savard would be otherwise occupied.

Perron had been let go and a replacement had to be found . . . Bob Gainey was rumoured to be in line for the GM's job in Minnesota . . . Rick Green was seriously considering retirement. And, of course, there was Serge's regular "summer" work–preparing for the annual entry draft, signing draft choices, setting up rookie camp and then overseeing our own training camp in early September. His plate was full and my "wait-and-see" attitude met the approval of all concerned.

When Serge and Donny could not come to immediate agreement on my numbers for the coming year (length of contract, not dollars), it was decided that I would play out my option for the first time ever. That meant: have a good year, improve my bargaining position; have a bad year and look for a hook to hang the skates on. I certainly didn't see this as a drawback; I've never looked at the downside of things and I wasn't going to start now just because I was "between contracts."

In fact, if I played the kind of year I knew I could, I would be open for bids from several clubs.

To make a long story short, I had the kind of year I knew I could; and then topped it off by having the kind of playoffs I knew I could as we went all the way. Almost. Calgary took us 4–2 in the finals but we showed everyone that the Flames and the Canadiens were in a class by themselves. The final could have gone either way; we just couldn't buy a break. I wasn't particularly happy losing the first final of my career.

Although I hate to lose, I have six Stanley Cup rings and I had to smile a little inside to see Lanny McDonald finally get his chance to lay his world-class moustache alongside Lord Stanley's silverware and give it a hairy smooch. Calgary proved to be class winners, much in the tradition of past Montreal teams, and I begrudge them nothing. Cliff Fletcher has done a masterful job with that organization and people like Terry Crisp, Tom Watt, and Doug Risebrough give that team a lot of depth behind the bench. I still think we should have beaten them, though.

My 1988–89 season could best be described as a rollercoaster.

When the Canadiens reported to training camp in September, uncertainty reigned. Jean Perron was gone, replaced by Pat Burns. Pat had done an excellent job in Hull as a junior coach, and then had done even better with the Sherbrooke Canadiens of the American League. A couple of the younger guys knew him. But that was all.

Burns came up to the plate with a couple strikes against him: The French media were all over Serge Savard for letting Perron go, and especially because of the way it had been done. Jean had been a favorite of theirs because he was adept at schmoozing with them all year long. They refused to accept the fact that he was a poor motivator and that his team was almost ready to mutiny. What upset us most was that, when the team won, he was only too happy to accept the credit, and when we lost, the players would get the blame.

The way they told the story was that Jean Perron was a great coach who was done in by a bunch of spoiled babies in the dressingroom, and second-guessing management types like Jacques Lemaire and Serge Savard upstairs. They refused to accept the possibility that the coach might be in the wrong.

To be fair, they had had a field day in 1971 supporting a dissatisfied player against a coach when Henri Richard jumped all over Al MacNeil, and then MacNeil and the Canadiens turned around and won the Stanley Cup and left some hockey writers with egg on their faces. On the human side, and I give them credit here, a situation like this leaves a bad taste in everyone's mouth because nobody likes to see one person ganged up on, and that's the image you get when a group of players goes to war with a coach or manager.

However, a year later, their tune sure has changed. Jean Perron went on to coach the Nordiques after Ron Lapointe was hospitalized with cancer. As it turned out, he had even worse problems with Quebec players than he had in Montreal, and then he had the audacity to turn around and bite the media hand that had fed him. In what can only be called supreme irony, he now is doing a radio talk show in Quebec City, a member of that very same media he accused of trying to run his Nordiques.

Several Montreal writers who had been especially tough in their criticism of Serge Savard were awfully quiet during the Quebec uprising. Nobody would readily admit that maybe, just maybe, our players had a valid complaint the year before.

That made the world at Atwater and St. Catherine especially tough for his replacement. Seen as Savard's man, Pat Burns became a target. When the season started, Jean Perron was an assistant general-manager with Quebec and a symbol of a rare Montreal uprising. Pat Burns was an ex-cop who was viewed by many as a tough warden hired to control the inmates.

All "the warden" did was take us to the best-ever record by a rookie Montreal coach, first place in the Adams, second overall behind Calgary, the conference championship and a berth in the Stanley Cup finals.

Pat Burns, the NHL Coach of the Year, a former cop who might know something about discipline, surely—but a man who knew a whole lot more about treating his players like men.

Pat Burns, who earned the respect of his players—with one or two notable exceptions among those who tend to place their own stats and needs before those of the team. Pat Burns, in my book a man who can coach right up there with Scotty Bowman and Jacques Lemaire. Pat Burns, a man whom one *La Presse* writer hinted might be tougher on French-speaking players on his team than any others. Pat Burns, a man whom another *La Presse* columnist thought might have purposely thrown a game in Boston during the playoffs so the Canadiens could get the revenue from the extra home date.

After tarring him with this brush, one of the columnists got all snotty when Mario Tremblay, now a radio and TV commentator, tore a strip off him. Several media colleagues reminded Mario that he belonged to a different team now. They can dish it out . . .

As well, another columnist and his fellow reporters were mad because he was ordered off the team charter by Serge Savard after he intimated that our coach might be anti-French in a column during the final series. The columnist and two other *La Presse* writers made a big noise of flying home on a regularly scheduled flight to protest the shabby treatment from the Canadiens. The truth was they weren't even scheduled on the charter.

Pat Burns was justifiably upset by those stories, but not as upset as his players were. We would not go as far as boycotting the media like the Nordiques did during the season, but we didn't have to like it, either.

Bob Gainey hit the nail on the head when he suggested that the writer, a known Quebec nationalist, move to the editorial or political sections of the paper, where he belonged.

A writer friend once told me great teams enjoying great seasons tend to frustrate the media. In their terms, overly successful teams make for lousy copy. Many writers are not comfortable with winning teams because success is boring to write about. Losers are great—the team's down, the players are down, management's down, and you never go begging for a quote. And when the team's doing poorly, the so-called "analysts" can offer all sorts of free advice on what's going wrong.

When the team wins, there isn't very much to say, before or after a game. And the media "analysts" are tongue-tied because they can't give anybody playing or coaching advice. Frustrates the heck out of them.

To wrap up that line of thought, the sad thing last season was that events like those playoff columns obscured what turned out to be a super year for the team, and especially for Burns.

First off, we all again witnessed how good Montreal is at renewing its resources while remaining competitive.

Flip back a few pages to the previous chapter. There I write of the trip home from Calgary with the 1986 Stanley Cup. Three young players really enjoying the ride were Gaston Gingras, Serge Boisvert and John Kordic. Just three short years later, when we hooked up with Calgary in a repeat, this trio was long gone; Gingras in his second year in St. Louis, Boisvert in Europe and Kordic in Toronto.

They had lots of company at Dorval Airport. David Maley (New Jersey), Steve Rooney (Winnipeg, New Jersey), Lucien DeBlois (Rangers), Chris Nilan (Rangers), Doug Soetaert (retired), Kjell Dahlin (Sweden), Mario Tremblay (retired), Mike Lalor (St. Louis), Sergio Momesso (St. Louis), Randy Bucyk (Calgary), Tom Kurvers (New Jersey), Steve Penney (retired), and Jean Perron (Quebec City radio).

Some 15 players and a head coach had moved on in that short period. And others like Scott Sandelin, Dominic Campedelli, and Jose Charbonneau had come and gone in the interim.

That's why the team was always near the top. Nobody but nobody restocks better than the Canadiens. After playing an excellent exhibition season–which rarely means anything–we bombed when things got serious in October. After 13 season games, we were 4-7-2 and going nowhere.

Remember my favorite saying? The fans are with you in Montreal, win or tie. But don't tie too often.

The media, on the other hand, is never with you and Pat Burns went through his first crisis at this time. We were hardly into November when the columnists were openly wondering if Burns would still be our coach at Christmas. And things did not look great when Stephane Richer, a 50-goal man for us the previous year, speared a New York Islander and was suspended for 10 games.

All we did was go 9–1 during his absence. And when stalwart Craig Ludwig was given eight games for a major-league elbow on Trent Yawney of Chicago, we didn't lose a game when he was out.

Two important things happened during this period. The first was that Burns kept his cool, treated his players like men and opened an ongoing dialogue with his veterans. The suggestions he agreed with, he put into practice. The others, he discarded. Whatever the case, you left his office feeling that he had really listened and was really interested in what you might have to say. That wasn't always true with Perron.

The second important thing was that John Kordic was traded. When he originally joined the team, he had quickly become an important cog, especially in physical series against the Bruins and Nordiques.

But as Adams Division clubs started toning down the WWF sideshow (Hartford's Torrey Robertson, Boston's Jay Miller, Quebec's Gord Donnelly were all traded out of the division last season), there was no need for a pure enforcer or policeman. The teams that would be successful were those who had big, tough forwards like Mike McPhee and Cam Neely, who played tough but cool all the time, rather than dropping their gloves every time someone looked at them cross-eyed.

So John sat and brooded. In this he was no different than any other hockey player. He wasn't playing and he wasn't happy. Trade rumours flew and all of us figured he was headed for Edmonton, his home town, when the Toronto Maple Leafs did us a great favor.

Their coach John Brophy was renowned for loving toughness and "guys who can stick their noses in," and hating small, fancy skaters who chose to sail around trouble, not through it.

So we got Russ Courtnall for John Kordic. In some countries, Serge Savard could go to jail for such robbery.

Rusty Courtnall gave us something we hadn't had in a while: exciting, breakaway speed. The fans loved his jets, just as they had adored Yvan Cournoyer and Guy Lafleur. In two or three strides, he'd be at full speed, around a flat-footed defenceman and in on the goalie. He'll be around Montreal for a long time.

Other contributions came from rookies like Brent Gilchrist, Mike Keane, Eric Desjardins, Jyrkki Lumme and Donald Dufresne. The first two had both played their junior out west and, although not big, played hard-nosed hockey. Desjardins and Dufresne came out of Quebec junior; Eric a good offensive defenceman and Donald a stay-at-home like Craig Ludwig, Rick Green and Mike Lalor.

Lumme is a terrific offensive defenceman, like fellow Finnish countrymen Reijo Ruotsalainen and Risto Siltanen. I like all three, and with Mathieu Schneider coming out of the OHL, it looks like the Canadiens will be solid behind the blue line for many years to come. Chris Chelios, Petr Svoboda and Craig Ludwig have a long way to go before they hang them up, too.

Lumme fit right in with the club when he was called up (during Ludsy's suspension) and appeared to have earned a starting role. Then came a curfew violation with Claude Lemieux in St. Louis. It wasn't the late hour as much as the company Jyrkki kept; he had the misfortune to be out with a player who was openly feuding with the coach. Lemieux got suspended for three games by Burns and Lumme got Sherbrooke. Worse still, Jyrkki suffered a knee injury in his first AHL game and his season was over.

I'm hoping he can put that behind him. I liked playing with him. I also like playing with Desjardins, one of the smartest 19-year-olds you'll ever meet. The kid never says a word, but he's strong and a very intelligent puck mover.

Overall, 1988–89 was a good season for Montreal, despite the loss to Calgary in the final. Guy Carbonneau won the Frank Selke award as best defensive forward for the second straight year. Patrick Roy won the Vezina as best goalie, and shared the Jennings with Brian Hayward for best team goaltending. Pat

Burns was Coach of the Year, and Chelly won the Norris after a terrific year.

The big transition on the Canadiens' defence took place over the last two seasons, starting with Jean Perron and continuing with Pat Burns.

The broken leg I suffered two years ago accelerated the process: more ice time was going to be given to Chelios, Svoboda and Ludwig, meaning Robinson and Green would get less. Naturally, this doesn't sit well with the player whose ice time is diminishing but that's the way it goes. You have to move over and make room for younger legs.

I certainly didn't enjoy it when I went from 30–35 minutes a game to 10–15 minutes. I maintain that a player, especially a defenceman, can't stay sharp playing only three or four minutes a period. When I expressed my misgivings to Jean Perron, he'd agree with my observations but do little to remedy the situation. I was left frustrated and so was Rick Green.

The shorter shifts continued when Pat Burns came aboard. But when I spoke to him, he had explanations and the courage of his convictions. He would look you right in the eye when he told you something and the players respect that. He could also admit that a system wasn't working.

When he realized that nobody in his six-man defensive scheme would be happy with shortened ice time, he dropped one defenceman and played a five-man rotation. Mike Lalor was the odd man out and he was upset, but the other five guys were happier. As well, we were shutting down the opposition with monotonous regularity so no one could complain about the results.

How good was our defence? Chelly, Ludsy, Petr, Rick and myself all missed parts of the season, through accident or design. And the team kept winning, at home and on the road. Away from Montreal, with less of a need to play fan-pleasing hockey, we suffocated the opposition with a relentless checking blanket, daring them to blink. When they did, we put them away. We went into Calgary twice, and won-in an arena where the Flames lost four home games all season. We never lost in Boston. We tied and won in Philadelphia. We shut down

Mario Lemieux and the Penguins twice at home and did the same thing to Wayne Gretzky and the Kings in Los Angeles.

When the team offered me a week off in Florida in February, I took it, rested up and flashed my tan when I returned to the line-up four games later. A couple of years before, the very suggestion of a mid-season vacation would have been insulting. While I was gone, the team hardly skipped a beat; not great for the ego but a solid indication of what wins hockey games.

"I want you 100 per cent mentally and physically for the real season," said Pat Burns before I went away for the mini-vacation. To ensure that I understood the message, he sat me out an extra game when I got back.

By the time the playoffs arrived, I was on top of my game, feeling good and contributing.

My personal introduction to Pat Burns had started in training camp. I've never been big on first impressions or quick judgements of people so I didn't go to camp worrying whether I was going to like or dislike the new coach. I had gone through a sticky period with Jean Perron. I did not actively dislike him, but I couldn't agree with his coaching methods.

I approached the new season with an open mind. I was asked many times during the year if the team had showed up in camp expecting to be confronted by a guy who was a cop in all senses of the word. The media played up his former career wherever we went, as if there was nothing else to write about.

As strange as it might seem to writers looking for the cute angle, Pat Burns didn't give me a "cop" feeling. What he tried to put across to us was that he wasn't there with only one thing in mind or with only one purpose, disciplining people. If we did our jobs, he said, he basically didn't care what we did off the ice as long as it wasn't detrimental to the team.

Knowing him now, after a full season, I can describe Pat Burns as a square shooter. He never says anything against you, other than to your face and in private.

Early on in the year, I think I suffered a bit because I was hanging back, reluctant to approach Burns with my concerns

because of my well-publicized comments about his predecessor, and also because I didn't want to be seen as a veteran
trying to influence a new coach.

When we finally talked and got to know each other better, I
discovered he was a guy you could go to at any time, rather
than sitting back and waiting for an invitation.

Pat and I turned out to be soul brothers of a sort because the
1988–89 season was one where we were both under the gun to
perform.

I put a lot of pressure on myself in not signing a contract, and
that was something people asked me about all year. It seemed
that every time we were on the road, there were two stories in
the paper—the Pat Burns story and the Larry Robinson-
signing-with-somebody-else story. During the season one
story persisted that I was going to play for Detroit Red Wings
because they needed a veteran to steady their young defence,
and also because my son Jeffery was going to school there at
Country Day. (Jeff has since graduated. But he was thrilled by
the big television feature that showed him visiting with me and
watching a game when we travelled to Detroit.)

It seemed that everybody but me was expecting something
big to happen.

It was early in the New Year, just after we had returned from a
West Coast trip. We had played in Los Angeles December 27,
Calgary December 29, Edmonton on New Year's Eve and
Vancouver on New Year's Day, flying home January 2. The
team was given a belated holiday; we had to return for a skate
Friday, January 6, in preparation for a Boston visit Saturday
night.

That week, the Robinsons and the Capes gathered at Don's
cottage in Ste-Agathe-Sud, in the Laurentians north of
Montreal.

"Larry, you have to consider this your last NHL contract as a
player," Don began.

"You have to approach this one differently. Now you have to
think about how many years you want to play, and are capable
of playing. And you also have to think about what happens af-

ter your career." We talked for hours, and Jeannette was included in all of the discussions. In many ways, it was like our conversations 18 years before, just prior to Claude Ruel's visit to Winchester, Ont. to negotiate my very first contract.

The consensus was I wanted to stay in Montreal because I was extremely comfortable with the surroundings, the people, and the career I had built over 18 years. In short, I was happy and so was Jeannette.

Donny Cape arranged an appointment with Serge Savard. They were going to meet at 4 p.m. on January 11, a day the New Jersey Devils were visiting, to discuss extending my contract, and after the game Donny and I would get together and see what we had. Shortly thereafter, we would sign the contract. We wanted a year with an option. We didn't even want to make an issue of more money because we were comfortable with what we had. If Serge wanted to offer a raise, he wouldn't get an argument . . . but increased salary was not an issue.

On the morning of January 11, Don called Serge's office to reconfirm the afternoon appointment.

Donna Stewart, Serge's secretary, told him: "Serge wants to talk to you."

Savard came on the line.

"How are you, Serge?"

"Fine, Donny. What's this meeting about anyway?"

That question threw Donny a bit. "You know, Larry's contract. He's ready to sign for another year."

"Oh. No, I'm not interested in signing anything."

"What do you mean, you're not interested?" Donny was genuinely surprised.

"No, you didn't want to sign when Perron was the coach before. Why should you want to sign now? Wait to the end of the year."

"Larry wants to sign because he's extremely happy with Pat Burns and he thinks he'll enjoy playing for him for a couple more years."

"I want to see what's going to be with Larry at the end of the year." Savard wasn't budging.

"Serge, you're going to end up in this double eagle business of forcing yourself to give Larry a 15 per cent raise in salary once his option is over. You're costing yourself money because he'll sign for you right now for the same salary."

"I'll worry about that when the time comes," Savard replied. "I don't want to speak to you regarding Larry's contract until the end of the season. I don't like to disturb a player during the season; I don't want to bother Larry, he's going very well right now."

"Okay," Donny agreed. Salary never came up again between Donny and Serge until after the year was over.

NHL compensation rules stipulate that the team of a player who has played out his option has first crack at him after that season. To maintain this exclusivity, they must offer him a contract before June 30. On July 1, any other team in the league may offer him a deal and his former team still has 30 days to match the offer. If they choose not to, or he decides the other offer is better, he is then free to move to the other team. The new team still might have to compensate his former team, under a formula approved by the league and the player's association.

That is what the NHL considers "free agency." Only an idiot would actually think players are free to move to the highest bidders. This system discourages player movement. The league reasoning is: "How are you gonna keep them in Winnipeg if they're all free to go to New York City?"

Anyway, the season and playoffs came and went, and then it was time for Serge Savard to resume serious bargaining. I was predisposed to staying with the Canadiens and I didn't want more money. I wanted a year and an option year. No more, no less.

On July 1, Don received a fax from Savard's office that said the Canadiens would exercise their right of refusal and to match any other offer over the next 30 days. They were offering me what they considered a 15 per cent increase on the NHL part of my contract. (My previous agreement had been a two-part deal: I was paid so much by the Montreal Canadiens and another amount by Molson's, the team owners, for publicity work and the like. The 15 per cent was only being offered on the Canadiens' part of the contract. It could be said the Canadiens were offering me a 15 per cent raise, but they weren't. The Molson money was a deferred-payment plan.)

This wasn't an offer. Montreal was saying that if anybody saw fit to offer me something, then they might show interest. That "compliment" left me very much out in the cold.

Donny and I got together right away.

"We can't leave it at this," he said. "There's no offer from Montreal and other teams are going to want to know what the ballpark is before they play. They're also going to want to know what Serge intends to do about compensation." Donny already had had preliminary talks with Detroit, Boston, and Los Angeles. Jimmy Devellano was interested, but less than before because he had just signed Borje Salming. Harry Sinden expressed serious interest, but his main worry was the compensation factor. Los Angeles had said they were interested but little else.

Donny called Serge Savard.

"Serge, there's something wrong here."

"Not at all, Donny," Savard replied. "That's just to cover my compensation."

"Are you going to do better than that?" We had to know what the ground rules were.

"Wait a week or two. I'm on vacation and we'll get together around the 20th of the month."

"Look, we can't wait. Larry wants to know what he's going to be doing this winter. Let's get this done."

"Okay, we'll get together within a week or so, when I get back."

True to this agenda, Donny called Serge back around the 10th of July. In the interim, Los Angeles had expressed some serious interest.

We had two demands. A 15 per cent increase on the full salary, which includes the Molson deferred payments, and a year and an option year for contract duration.

The answers were "No" and "No."

Donny then remembered a promise Serge had made to me in January, 1983, when the Canadiens dream team had been announced. That night, taking note of the fact that all of the members of the team voted by fans had had their sweaters retired (Doug Harvey was just about to have his famous No. 2 ceremoniously put away), Serge had turned to me and said, "Your sweater will be retired when you go."

I still wanted to stay in Montreal and Donny knew that this special reward or recognition was important to me.

"Are you still going to retire the sweater?"

Serge indicated that was unlikely.

Each active player gets two season tickets for his use. Would Savard consider transferring these to our company name and, once I had retired, allow me to purchase them?

"No."

Donny got exasperated at this point. "Serge, you don't seem to be very flexible."

Serge said he didn't feel that anybody was going to be interested in Larry Robinson, because if he stayed he was going to give him one year's salary for playing, and one year's salary for compensation, for the 18 years of service to the Canadiens. This latter item was a Canadiens' policy. Players who had played 10 years or more for Montreal would receive a full year's pay upon their retirement.

Now that "automatic" compensation seemed to have become a bargaining chip.

"I don't think anybody is going to match that," Savard said.

"Maybe not, but the point is you're not going to let Larry play the extra year," Donny declared.

"That's right."

"Nor will you let him play anywhere else." Donny wasn't happy. "I think that after 17 years with the team, he should be entitled to determine his own future. He always gave the Canadiens 110 per cent."

Serge went on to intimate that if I went to another team, compensaton would be unlikely. In Serge's mind, that bonus of a year's salary had strings attached to it.

Donny gave it one last shot. "Serge, are any of these areas negotiable?"

The reply was in the negative.

Shortly thereafter, Serge let his media friends know that I had demanded to have my sweater retired and demanded season tickets and his attitude was that I was being totally unreasonable. That upset me, especially when Jean Beliveau indignantly remarked that "nobody negotiates getting his sweater retired. It's not something that you can demand." We didn't, but it suited Serge's purposes to spread that message about. Needless to say, I was steaming.

Whether or not Serge realized it, in my mind I had ceased being a member of the Montreal Canadiens that day. Some sort of invisible line had been crossed, or invisible door had been slammed. Never in all of my years of playing for this organization had I ever thought it might end this way. Nobody is indispensable. After all, Wayne Gretzky was traded and I had always known that could happen to me.

But to leave the Canadiens through lack of interest, almost by default, was very hard to take. I thought the club and I owed each other more than that.

When that conversation ended, Don immediately called Bruce McNall, owner of the Kings. Bruce was very interested, and more importantly, he was more interested in me as an individual. The financial side of it didn't even come up in our first series of talks.

Before our conversation with Serge, Don and Bruce had arranged for the four of us—Don, his wife Heather, Jeannette and myself—to travel to Los Angeles for a familiarization tour. There were absolutely no obligations on either part; the Kings were interested in me and wanted to show me around the city and the organization in case I ever chose to move.

However, Serge's intransigence almost forced us to remain in Montreal.

When Don Cape called the Los Angeles owner and told him what had happened, McNall knew how much money I had been making and what the Canadiens had offered. Earlier he had mentioned that he was looking at a two-year deal like the one I sought from Montreal—a year plus an option. Now, however, it didn't seem to make sense to even go out there. Serge didn't feel anyone else would bite. He was pretty sure that he had *prevented* the competition from acting.

Donny reached McNall, who was vacationing in Hawaii.

"He's boxed us in, Bruce," Donny said. "We can't move unless we're going to make a substantial amount more just to break even; because of the cost-of-living factor, housing, transportation, schooling, moving." Los Angeles housing costs are scary.

McNall's response was "Come out anyway, let's get to know each other. You never know what we can work out." What I didn't know at the time was that the Kings had extensively discussed the free agent market. Players such as Guy Lafleur, Doug Wilson, Borje Salming figured prominently in their talks. Rogie Vachon and Bruce agreed that the player whom they felt would have the most positive impact on their team was Larry Robinson, and in choosing me over the others, forced Guy Lafleur to go to Quebec. The Flower had told the Kings he preferred Los Angeles over the Nordiques, especially in terms of on-ice pressure to perform, but McNall felt they needed me more and, as a result, told Guy they weren't interested.

So Donny did not need to worry that we'd be heading out west for nothing.

However, before we left, Donny put in his last words pro-Montreal.

"Larry, we have to call Serge Savard before we go out there. I think we should make every attempt to stay here; it just doesn't seem sensible to pick up at 38 years old and move."

The next day I was home in St. Lazare and Donny was at our dealership when a conference call with Savard was arranged.

"Serge, we want to clear up this situation once and for all and we want to make sure that there is absolutely no misunderstanding," Donny began.

The first several minutes of the conversation dealt with how much I wanted to stay in Monteal, and how much I didn't want to move because it could be too upsetting for my family and business ties.

Were any of the points Donny and Serge had discussed before negotiable in any way, or was Serge's offer final?

"My offer is pat and I'm not moving. I don't feel anybody is going to offer you that kind of money," Serge replied.

"Serge, how can you be so inflexible?" Donny was looking for the slightest sign of fence-mending from Serge. He was more adamant than I that staying in Montreal was the best thing.

No such sign came from my former defence partner. Again there was the intimation that should I leave Montreal, I wouldn't receive compensation.

I was hot. "Serge, you told me yourself a month ago that I would get the compensation because it was a reward for what was done in the past; for my 17 years of service with Montreal. Not just 10 years, but 17 years."

We hung up. Later, Donny called me up at home. "Larry, I think you're going to have to play here because I don't think anybody else will match or better this kind of money for one year."

We flew out to Los Angeles on Monday, July 25, arriving at lunchtime. We were greeted by Kings GM Rogatien Vachon and a couple hours after arriving we were in Bruce McNall's office.

Before we talked money, long before we talked money, this soft-spoken man drew a very clear picture of what he, and his organization, were all about.

"Number One, I want to build a class team. Number Two, I want to build a winner. If I have Number One, I'll end up with Number Two in the end. Wayne Gretzky was a very big step in that direction for us. Signing you would be another very big step." He went on to say that the Kings did not see me as a hockey player on his last legs, playing out the string. To them, I was a valuable commodity on the ice, and an even more valuable person and personality off the ice.

"You have been a leader for your entire career with the class organization of this league, and I know what you can bring with you if you join the Kings," he began. Needless to say, I felt terrific to hear these words. They were a lot more encouraging than Serge Savard's.

"We feel that on the ice and off, you will teach by example because that's what you've done for years in Montreal. We have a lot of superb, young talent, players who can only benefit from the presence of yourself and Wayne Gretzky in terms of confidence and knowledge. I see only positive things for my entire organization."

Donny's pitch for me wasn't much of one in that Bruce McNall's words had basically pre-empted any sales job on our part.

Toward the end of our meeting, Los Angeles made a very generous offer. Bruce McNall wanted me to join his "family"; if ever I needed any help with my horses—he owns an impressive stable—or any of my business ventures, he would be there for me. He was offering me two years, guaranteed, plus an option year.

If anything happened to me, and I didn't play the second year, he would pay me my full salary. And if they wanted or needed me as an assistant coach, they would pay me this coaching salary on top of that.

The Los Angeles Kings showed me and told me that they wanted Larry Robinson. This was in stark contrast with the Montreal Canadiens. I don't understand for the life of me why the Canadiens showed such a lack of interest in me. I might have understood it if I had played poorly in 1988–89, but that certainly wasn't the case. My teammates, opponents, and the media were unanimous—I had played very well, better than many of them might have expected.

We met from about 4:30 to about 8 p.m.. It was a very low-key, almost family atmosphere. We went to dinner at Spago's restaurant, one of the most famous in Hollywood, later that evening. We were joined there by Heather and Jeannette after Bruce McNall sent his private limousine for them. But before we left the office, Bruce took us around and quietly introduced us to all of his employees in the three companies he owns.

In my mind, I was already a Los Angeles King, even though I had promised myself I wouldn't decide until after I had returned to Montreal. I called my parents, Jeannette's Mom, and my kids long distance and told them I was joining Los Angeles.

The following morning, bright and early, we were back in Bruce McNall's office where we agreed to terms and a fax was sent to Serge Savard for his first right of refusal. If he had matched the offer in years and salary, I'd still be a Canadien today.

Serge Savard was on the golf course, playing in a tournament sponsored by a Montreal daily, when Bruce McNall got him on the phone. Serge had a week left in the NHL deadline to answer, but Bruce asked him to answer right away because we all knew he wasn't going to match it.

The following afternoon, I was introduced to the media as the newest member of the Los Angeles Kings. The following night, I appeared along with Bruce on *The Pat Sajak Show* on CBS and tried on my new silver "19" for a North American audience.

No more red, white, and blue. From now on, my hockey cloud would have a white, black and silver lining.

A couple of weeks have passed since I signed the new agreement and left the Montreal Canadiens. I've read a few letters to the editor in Montreal that complained about greedy hockey players and how we have loyalty only to the Big Buck and not to the team that has nurtured us and enabled us to grow over our careers. My answer to these criticisms is simple: I wanted to remain with Canadiens, but others chose another path for me.

And I feel supremely thankful for Bruce McNall's generosity and faith in me. It will be repaid many times over.

The Canadiens will be very different next year, what with Rick Green retiring and Bob Gainey playing and coaching in France. I'll miss my teammates and Pat Burns but I wish them all the best, especially Pat Burns, who will be a terrific coach for a long time, if they let him.

As for the longevity in one uniform, the 1988–89 season proved most clearly that you can come back with another team, especially when the Rangers came to town and Guy Lafleur and Chris Nilan were in Broadway Blue. I can remember all sorts of all-stars and Montreal fixtures going to other teams–Butch Bouchard with Washington, Brian Engblom and Rod Langway with Washington, Serge Savard with Winnipeg and Guy Lapointe with St. Louis and Boston, to name a few.

The all-time Canadiens team I was voted to now has only two players on it who wore the bleu-blanc-rouge for their entire NHL careers–Maurice Richard and Jean Beliveau. Jacques Plante played with Toronto, Boston, St. Louis and New York; Dickie Moore played with Toronto and St. Louis; and Doug Harvey played with Rangers, Blues and Detroit. In the final tally, they were Canadiens to the end.

One day, several years down the road, I'll come back to the Forum and the veterans' room, with the other *anciens*, and we'll have a meal, drink some Molson's and tell a few lies. The Flower, Shutty, big Yvon Lambert, the Roadrunner, Coco, Pointu, Ken Dryden, Bo, the Dougies, Murray, Bleuet, Charty, Bunny and the rest.

Bob Gainey will probably be General Manager of some NHL team by then, and Doug Risebrough will be vice-president of the Calgary Flames, if the Flames are as smart as I think they are. Serge will probably be President of the Canadiens by then, too.

But on that occasion, we'll all be Canadiens, the team that swept four Stanley Cups in a row between '76 and '79. Some time after two or three beers, we'll convince ourselves that it "shoulda been eight in a row."